YOU'RE ON!

The
THEATRE
Quiz Book

JIM BERNHARD

Skyhorse Publishing

Skyhorse Publishing books may be purchased in bulk at special discounts for sales promotion, corporate gifts, fund-raising, or educational purposes. Special editions can also be created to specifications. For details, contact the Special Sales Department, Skyhorse Publishing, 307 West 36th Street, 11th Floor, New York, NY 10018 or info@skyhorsepublishing.com.

Skyhorse® and Skyhorse Publishing® are registered trademarks of Skyhorse Publishing, Inc.®, a Delaware corporation.

Visit our website at www.skyhorsepublishing.com.

10 9 8 7 6 5 4 3 2 1

Library of Congress Cataloging-in-Publication Data is available on file.

Cover design by Jane Sheppard
Cover photo by iStock

Print ISBN: 978-1-5107-2300-9

Printed in China

For Ginger

CONTENTS

PROLOGUE

In a sketch by one of the great vaudeville comedians, a callboy rushes into the performer's dressing room in a panic, shouting, "You're on!" The comedian calmly replies, "I am? How am I doing?" That story is the inspiration for the title of this book of theatrical quizzes.

"You're on!" may also be an invitation to accept a challenge, and this book should provide plenty of that, whether you're an old theatre hand or an enthusiastic member of the audience. From Broadway to theatres throughout the United States, from ancient Greece to the contemporary avant-garde, from Shakespeare and Shaw to Shaffer and Shepard, these quizzes cover the gamut of theatrical activity. In more than 170 quizzes, 1,700 brain-teasing questions—covering some 800 shows plus 800 actors, directors, choreographers, playwrights, lyricists, composers, designers, producers, and critics—will test your knowledge of the theatre in endless hours of fun. Compete with yourself or with other theatre buffs to see who knows the most. At the same time, you'll probably learn a few facts that you didn't know before.

Any typographical errors or errors of fact that you may find in this book were put there for a purpose. I have tried to include something for everyone (and some people are always looking for mistakes).

In addition to texts of plays and musicals cited, source material was provided in part by the Internet Broadway Database (ibdb. com), a project of the Broadway League; Playbill Vault (playbill. com/vault); the Lortel Archives (lortel.org/archives), a project of the Lucille Lortel Foundation; Wikipedia (wikipedia.org); the Guide to Musical Theatre (guidetomusicaltheatre.com); All Musicals (allmusicals.com); Theatricalia (theatricalia.com), a Matthew Somerville Production; *Broadway Musicals Show by Show* by Stanley Green; *A Digest of 500 Plays*, edited by Theodore J. Shank; *American Theatre: A Chronicle of Comedy and Drama, 1869–1914, 1914–1930,* and *1930–1969,* by Gerald Bordman; and *American Musical Theatre: A Chronicle* by Gerald Bordman.

Much of the material in this book appeared previously over the past several years as weekly quizzes in GRACE NOTES (Grace-NotesStage.com), the industry standard for daily theatre news since 1999, and I am grateful to its founder and publisher, Susan Grace, for her encouragement and enthusiasm. Thanks, too, go to Nicole Mele at Skyhorse Publishing. And for the never-failing assistance of my wife and fellow writer, Virginia, I shall be eternally grateful.

I am also thankful for the years I spent as an actor, primarily at Houston's Theatre Under the Stars and Alley Theatre, and on national tours with those companies. This experience provided the opportunity to listen backstage to countless theatre stories and to soak up the lore shared by seasoned veterans of Broadway and the international stage. The colorful bits of trivia picked up in otherwise drab dressing rooms were the catalysts for many of these quizzes.

Whether you're a knowledgeable theatre buff or someone who's just dipping your toes into the excitement that live theatre brings, you're bound to find treasures in this book that will amuse and edify you. The answers appear at the end of each section. So, lower the houselights, raise the curtain, and on with the shows! Let's see how you're doing. *You're on!*

HOW TO SCORE YOUR ANSWERS

With only a few exceptions, each quiz has ten questions. In each set of ten questions, score one point for each correct answer. Add them up and cast yourself in the right role!

10—SUPERSTAR!
Your name is above the title. Caviar and chilled champagne await you in your sumptuous dressing room suite. Oh, and may we have your autograph?

9—LEADING PLAYER
Tragical, comical, historical, pastoral—you can handle any role that comes your way. There's bound to be a Tony Award in your future, if there's not already one in your past.

8—REPLACEMENT STAR
Maybe you aren't the first choice for the starring part, but you have a lot of talent, and you'll soon see your name in lights.

7—STANDBY
You're not quite ready for star billing, but you know your way around a stage and you'll do just fine in a pinch.

6—SUPPORTING PLAYER
You're on top of your craft and you're steady, reliable, and always in demand.

5—BIT PLAYER

Keep at it and you'll win bigger roles.

4—WALK-ON

Well, at least you're working.

3—UNDERSTUDY

You can always hope that someone really does break a leg.

2—APPRENTICE

You have a lot to learn.

1—AUDITIONER

Thank you very much. Next!

0—NON-PRO

There are lots of other worthwhile professions outside the theatre. Better look into them.

CURTAIN RAISERS

To get you started, here are some quizzes about plays and musicals that savvy theatre-goers should be able to breeze through. If by some chance you don't breeze through, don't worry—the next wind may blow from another direction!

By the Numbers

Supply a missing number from 1 to 10 in each of these titles of plays and musicals.

1. _____ *Degrees of Separation*

2. _____ *Men on a Horse*

3. _____ *Nights in a Barroom*

4. _____ *Touch of Venus*

5. _____ *Against Thebes*

6. _____ *to 5*

7. _____ *Guys Named Moe*

8. _____ *Trains Running*

9. _____ *Baboons Adoring the Sun*

10. *Dinner at* _____

Sidekicks

Each of these secondary characters in the first column is a foil or sidekick to a principal character in the second column. Match the sidekicks with the main characters and the plays or musicals in which they appear.

1.	Col. Hugh Pickering	Pozzo	*As You Like It*
2.	Sancho Panza	Prof. Harold Hill	*Juno and the Paycock*
3.	Marcellus Washburn	John P. Wintergreen	*Peter Pan*
4.	Alexander Throttlebottom	Faustus	*Pygmalion*
5.	Celia	Don Quixote	*The Music Man*
6.	Lucky	Captain Hook	*The Tempest*
7.	Mr. Smee	"Captain" Jack Boyle	*Of Thee I Sing*
8.	Joxer Daly	Rosalind	*Man of La Mancha*
9.	Wagner	Prospero	*Doctor Faustus*
10.	Ariel	Prof. Henry Higgins	*Waiting for Godot*

In Other Words

The following circumlocutions use synonyms to restate the titles of well-known plays and musicals. Can you translate?

1. Small Nocturnal Serenade
2. Large Watercourse
3. Humorous Young Female
4. A Drollery Occurred En Route to the Marketplace
5. The Auric Pome
6. A Method to Achieve Effortless Commercial Triumph
7. Septennial Pruritus
8. Subduing the Virago
9. Old Nick's Adherent
10. Sovereign Panthera Leo

Animal Farm

In the first column are names of animals that appear or are mentioned in plays or musicals. Identify the kind of animal, and name the shows they're in.

1. Otto	Monkeys	*Legally Blonde*
2. Shenzi, Banzai, and Ed	Duck	*The Two Gentlemen of Verona*
3. Harvey	Parrot	*Peter Pan*
4. Dover	Wire fox terrier	*Harvey*
5. Nana	Rabbit	*The Lion King*
6. The Wickersham Brothers	Spotted hyenas	*Pippin*
7. Asta	Newfoundland (or St. Bernard)	*Dr. Dolittle*
8. Polynesia	Dog (unspecified breed)	*Seussical*
9. Bruiser	Racehorse	*Nick and Nora*
10. Crab	Chihuahua	*My Fair Lady*

Love Is in the Air

Match these musicals with the songs in them that mention the word "love."

1. *Brigadoon*	"Do You Love Me?"
2. *Promises, Promises*	"I Don't Know How to Love Him"
3. *Whoopee*	"Where Is Love?"
4. *Oliver!*	"Our Language of Love"
5. *A Chorus Line*	"Almost Like Being in Love"
6. *Grease*	"Love Me or Leave Me"
7. *Jesus Christ Superstar*	"What I Did for Love"
8. *Zorba*	"Freddy, My Love"
9. *Fiddler on the Roof*	"I'll Never Fall in Love Again"
10. *Irma la Douce*	"Only Love"

Missing Links

One word is missing from each of the following phrases. When you replace it, you'll have the titles of two plays or musicals. For example: *The Music _____ of La Mancha*. Fill in the blank with the word *"Man"* and you'll have the title of two shows, *The Music Man* and *Man of La Mancha*.

1. *South _____ Overtures*

2. *A Streetcar Named _____ Under the Elms*

3. *Girl _____ for You*

4. *Strike Up the _____ Wagon*

5. *The Desert _____ of Norway*

6. *Sunday in the Park with _____ White's Scandals*

7. *Bitter _____ Charity*

8. *Call Me _____ Roberts*

9. *Love _____ with Father*

10. *All _____ Here*

Fun and Games

The title of each of these plays and musicals consists of two words joined by the conjunction "and." Match the description with the show and fill in the missing word.

1. This 1937 musical with a score by Harold Rome was presented by the International Ladies' Garment Workers' Union.

   Summer and _____

2. Two New Yorkers visit an Amish community in this 1955 musical.

   Milk and _____

3. This 1950 show was subtitled "A Musical Fable of Broadway."

   Song and _____

4. Two actors named Kerr starred on Broadway in this 1953 drama.

   Pins and _____

5. This 1935 play is about a Bronx family during the Depression.

   Me and _____

6. Tennessee Williams's 1947 play was made into an opera by Lee Hoiby and Lanford Wilson.

   Tea and _____

7. Bernadette Peters starred in the first half of the 1985 Broadway production of this musical by Andrew Lloyd Webber.

   Man And _____

8. This 1903 play by George Bernard Shaw is based on the Don Juan theme.

   Guys and _____

9. Rodgers & Hammerstein wrote this backstage romance of 1953.

   Plain and _____

10. Jerry Herman's Broadway debut was this 1961 musical set in Israel.

    Awake and _____!

Month to Month

Match the following descriptions with the plays and musicals in column two—and fill in the missing word, which is the name of a month.

1. A 1929 play by George S. Kaufman and Ring Lardner based on Lardner's short story "Some Like Them Cold"

   _____*Hares*

2. Musical comedy of 1939 by Jerome Kern and Oscar Hammerstein II that included "All the Things You Are"

   _____*: Osage County*

3. David Mamet's 2007 comedy about a US president

   Very Warm for _____

4. A play by Matthew Barber in 2003 based on a 1922 novel by Elizabeth von Arnim, and made into a movie with Joan Plowright and Miranda Richardson

   _____*Moon*

5. Ayn Rand's courtroom drama of 1934

   Fifth of _____

6. Lanford Wilson's 1978 play that is part of the Talley Trilogy

   First Monday in _____

7. A 1929 satire by Harry Wagstaff Gribble, with a title inspired by Lewis Carroll, which starred Josephine Hull and Dorothy Stickney

   30 Days Hath _____

8. A 1978 play by Jerome Lawrence and Robert E. Lee, whose setting is the US Supreme Court

   _____

9. A 1938 farce by Irving Gaumont and
Jack Sobell; made into the movie
Thieves Fall Out with Eddie Albert
and Anthony Quinn

Night of _____ 16th

10. Tracy Letts's 2008 play that won the
Pulitzer Prize

Enchanted _____

Two's Company

Match these pairs of characters with the two-person shows in which
they appear.

1. Andrew Makepeace Ladd III—
Melissa Gardner

Red

2. Peter—Jerry

A Steady Rain

3. John—Carol

A Life in the Theatre

4. Ben—Gus

'Night Mother

5. Jessie Cates—Thelma Cates

Collected Stories

6. Robert—John

The Zoo Story

7. Mark Rothko—Ken

Oleanna

8. Joey—Denny

Love Letters

9. Vanda—Thomas

The Dumbwaiter

10. Ruth Steiner—Lisa Morrison

Venus in Fur

Quick, Henry, the Flit!

Each title of these plays and musicals has a missing word, which refers to an insect or arachnid in the second column.

1. *The* _____ by Jean-Paul Sartre, based on the Greek myth of Electra and Orestes, had its American premiere at Vassar College in 1947.

   Wasp

2. _____ *Are Free* is a 1969 comedy that starred Keir Dullea and Blythe Danner in its Broadway premiere.

   Cockroaches

3. *Hunting* _____, a comedy about an immigrant Polish couple in a tenement on New York's Lower East Side, starred Diane Wiest and Ron Silver in its 1987 off-Broadway production.

   Firefly

4. *A* _____ *in Her Ear*, a 1907 farce set in Paris at the turn of the 20th century, is about a faithful husband and his double, a drunken porter.

   Bug

5. *Kiss of the* _____ *Woman* is a 1993 musical set in a Latin American prison.

   Flea

6. *The* _____ is a 1912 operetta about an Italian street singer in New York disguised as a cabin boy.

   Flies

7. *The* _____ *Comedy* (or *Play*), also known as *The World We Live In*, is a 1922 Czech satire featuring such characters as a Snail, a Beetle, a Young Butterfly, a Moth, a Cricket, an Ichneumon Fly, and a Blind Ant.

   Butterflies

8. _____, a 2004 play with a one-word title, was made into a movie starring Ashley Judd, Michael Shannon, and Harry Connick Jr.

   Insect

9. *The* _____ *and the Flame*, a drama about a   *Spider*
New York society belle, first opened in New
York in 1893.

10. *The* _____'s *Nest* is a 1927 mystery-comedy   *Moth*
previously known as *The House in the Woods*.

What's New?

Choose what it is that's new in each of these titles.

1. *The New* _____, Sigmund Romberg operetta
   ★ *Moon*
   ★ *Desert*
   ★ *Prince*
   ★ *Romance*

2. *A New* _____, musical by William Finn and James Lapine
   ★ *Life*
   ★ *Brain*
   ★ *Heart*
   ★ *Soul*

3. "Many a New _____," song from *Oklahoma!*
   ★ Beau
   ★ State
   ★ Day
   ★ Horse

4. "New _____ for Christmas," song from *Annie*
   ★ Toys
   ★ Daddy
   ★ Deal
   ★ Puppy

Continued on next page

5. *New _____ of 1934*, revue starring Imogene Coca and
   Henry Fonda
   * *Thrills*
   * *Faces*
   * *Dances*
   * *Look*

6. "Open a New _____," song from *Mame*
   * Package
   * Show
   * Letter
   * Window

7. "A New _____," song from *What Makes Sammy Run?*
   * Agent
   * Pair of Shoes
   * Book
   * Coat of Paint

8. *New _____ in Town*, musical by Bob Merrill and George
   Abbott
   * *Skyscraper*
   * *Bank*
   * *Girl*
   * *Millionaire*

9. "The New Ashmolean Marching Society and Students'
   Conservatory _____," song from *Where's Charley?*
   * Team
   * Show
   * Group
   * Band

10. *A New* _____ *to Pay Old Debts*, play by Philip Massinger
    ★ *Windfall*
    ★ *Way*
    ★ *Wife*
    ★ *Chance*

Day by Day

All seven days of the week are found in the titles of these Broadway plays and musicals. Which is which?

1. _____ *in New York*: play by Norman Krasna that starred Robert Redford, Pat Stanley, and Conrad Janis

2. *Any* _____: comedy by Muriel Resnik that starred Sandy Dennis and Gene Hackman

3. *A Memory of Two* _____*s*: 1955 one-act play by Arthur Miller set in an auto parts warehouse

4. _____*Night Fever*: musical with music by the Bee Gees

5. *Every* _____: comedy by Doty Hobart that starred Leon Janney and Sheila Trent

6. *My Girl* _____: play of 1929 by William A. Grew

7. *Eight O'Clock* _____: mystery drama by Robert Wallstein and Mignon G. Eberhart that starred Bramwell Fletcher and Celeste Holm

I See the Moon

Match these descriptions with the titles of the plays and musicals, all of which contain the word "moon"—and fill in the missing word.

1. Eugene O'Neill's play opened on Broadway in 1957 starring Wendy Hiller, Franchot Tone, and Cyril Cusack.

   The Effect of Gamma Rays on Man-in-the-Moon _____

2. James Costigan's 1960 play starred Julie Harris and Robert Redford.

   The _____ *of the August Moon*

3. This 1951 comedy by F. Hugh Herbert starred Barbara Bel Geddes and Barry Nelson.

   Moon Over _____

4. A 1945 Broadway production, it is based on the folk song "The Ballad of Barbara Allen."

   A Moon for the _____

5. This 1993 "entertainment" featured Bill Irwin, David Shiner, and the Red Clay Ramblers.

   The Moon Is _____

6. Eugene O'Neill's one-act play is set aboard the British tramp steamer *Glencairn* anchored in the West Indies.

   Little Moon of _____

7. Ken Ludwig's 1995 comedy set in the Erlanger Theatre was a vehicle for Carol Burnett.

   _____ *Round the Moon*

8. Paul Zindel's 1978 play is about a single mother and her two daughters.

   _____ *of the Moon*

9. John Patrick's long-running 1953 comedy featured John Forsythe, David Wayne, and Paul Ford.

   _____ *Moon*

10. This play by Jean Anouilh is subtitled "A Charade with Music."

    Moon of the _____

Alter Egos

Match the characters with their alter egos and name the shows they're in.

1.	Peter Parker	The Scarlet Pimpernel
2.	Pierre Birabeau	The Green Goblin
3.	Clark Kent	Balthazar
4.	Edmond Dantès	Edward Hyde
5.	Norman Osborn	St. Jimmy
6.	Portia	Spider-Man
7.	Don Diego de la Vega	Superman
8.	Sir Percy Blakeney	Zorro
9.	Johnny	The Count of Monte Cristo
10.	Henry Jekyll	The Red Shadow

Boy Meets Girl

Match these characters, who are couples (not in every case compatible), and then add the plays in which they appear.

1.	Doris	Mirabell	*Born Yesterday*
2.	Amanda Prynne	Thomas Mendip	*Much Ado About Nothing*
3.	Fonsia Dorsey	Benedick	*The Rivals*
4.	Billie Dawn	Weller Martin	*Same Time Next Year*
5.	Beatrice	George	*Private Lives*
6.	Honey	Christy Mahan	*The Playboy of the Western World*
7.	Jennet Jourdemayne	Captain Jack Absolute	*The Gin Game*
8.	Lydia Languish	Nick	*The Way of the World*
9.	Mrs. Millamant	Paul Verrall	*The Lady's Not for Burning*
10.	Pegeen Mike	Elyot Chase	*Who's Afraid of Virginia Woolf?*

CURTAIN RAISERS

ANSWERS

By the Numbers

1. *Six Degrees of Separation*
2. *Three Men on a Horse*
3. *Ten Nights in a Barroom*
4. *One Touch of Venus*
5. *Seven Against Thebes*
6. *9 to 5*
7. *Five Guys Named Moe*
8. *Two Trains Running*
9. *Four Baboons Adoring the Sun*
10. *Dinner at Eight*

Sidekicks

1. Col. Hugh Pickering is Professor Henry Higgins's fellow linguist in *Pygmalion* (and *My Fair Lady*).
2. Sancho Panza is Don Quixote's servant in *Man of La Mancha*.
3. Marcellus Washburn is Prof. Harold Hill's helper in *The Music Man*.
4. Alexander Throttlebottom is President John P. Wintergreen's vice president in *Of Thee I Sing*.
5. Celia is Rosalind's friend with whom she flees to the forest in *As You Like It*.
6. Lucky is Pozzo's servant in *Waiting for Godot*.
7. Mr. Smee is Captain Hook's bos'n in *Peter Pan*.
8. Joxer Daly is "Captain" Jack Boyle's drinking "butty" in *Juno and the Paycock*.
9. Wagner is Faustus's servant in *Doctor Faustus* (and Faust's fellow scholar in *Faust*).
10. Ariel is Prospero's spirit servant in *The Tempest*.

In Other Words

1. Small Nocturnal Serenade—*A Little Night Music*
2. Large Watercourse—*Big River*
3. Humorous Young Female—*Funny Girl*
4. A Drollery Occurred En Route to the Marketplace—*A Funny Thing Happened on the Way to the Forum*
5. The Auric Pome—*The Golden Apple*
6. A Method to Achieve Effortless Commercial Triumph—*How to Succeed in Business without Really Trying*
7. Septennial Pruritus—*The Seven-Year Itch*
8. Subduing the Virago—*The Taming of the Shrew*
9. Old Nick's Adherent—*The Devil's Disciple*
10. Sovereign Panthera Leo—*The Lion King*

Animal Farm

1. Otto is Theo's pet duck in *Pippin*.
2. Shenzi, Banzai, and Ed are spotted hyenas in *The Lion King*.
3. Harvey is an invisible rabbit over six feet tall who is Elwood P. Dowd's best friend in *Harvey*.
4. Dover is a racehorse at Ascot for whom Eliza roots in *My Fair Lady*.
5. Nana is the Darling family dog (either a Newfoundland or a St. Bernard) in *Peter Pan*.
6. The Wickersham Brothers are monkeys in *Seussical*.
7. Asta is the wire fox terrier of the Charleses in *Nick and Nora*.
8. Polynesia is a parrot who is Dr. Dolittle's sidekick in *Dr. Dolittle*.
9. Bruiser is Elle's chihuahua in *Legally Blonde*.
10. Crab is Launce's dog in *The Two Gentlemen of Verona*.

Love Is in the Air

1. *Brigadoon*—"Almost Like Being in Love"
2. *Promises, Promises*—"I'll Never Fall in Love Again"
3. *Whoopee*—"Love Me, or Leave Me"
4. *Oliver!*—"Where Is Love?"
5. *A Chorus Line*—"What I Did for Love"
6. *Grease*—"Freddy, My Love"
7. *Jesus Christ Superstar*—"I Don't Know How to Love Him"
8. *Zorba*—"Only Love"
9. *Fiddler on the Roof*—"Do You Love Me?"
10. *Irma la Douce*—"Our Language of Love"

Missing Links

1. *South Pacific Overtures*
2. *A Streetcar Named Desire Under the Elms*
3. *Girl Crazy for You*
4. *Strike Up the Band Wagon*
5. *The Desert Song of Norway*
6. *Sunday in the Park with George White's Scandals*
7. *Bitter Sweet Charity*
8. *Call Me Mister Roberts*
9. *Love Life with Father*
10. *All Over Here*

Fun and Games

1. *Pins and Needles*
2. *Plain and Fancy*
3. *Guys and Dolls*
4. *Tea and Sympathy* (Deborah Kerr and John Kerr, who were not related, starred in it on Broadway)
5. *Awake and Sing!*
6. *Summer and Smoke*
7. *Song and Dance* (Bernadette Peters starred in the first half; the second act is a ballet featuring nine dancers)
8. *Man and Superman*
9. *Me and Juliet*
10. *Milk and Honey*

Month to Month

1. *June Moon*
2. *Very Warm for May*
3. *November*
4. *Enchanted April*
5. *Night of January 16th*
6. *Fifth of July*
7. *March Hares*
8. *First Monday in October*
9. *30 Days Hath September*
10. *August: Osage County*

(Note: no titles of plays or musicals mentioning February or December were found)

Two's Company

1. Andrew Makepeace Ladd III—Melissa Gardner—*Love Letters*
2. Peter—Jerry—*The Zoo Story*
3. John—Carol—*Oleanna*
4. Ben—Gus—*The Dumbwaiter*
5. Jessie Cates—Thelma Cates—*'Night Mother*
6. Robert—John—*A Life in the Theatre*
7. Mark Rothko—Ken—*Red*
8. Joey—Denny—*A Steady Rain*
9. Vanda—Thomas—*Venus in Fur*
10. Ruth Steiner—Lisa Morrison—*Collected Stories*

Quick, Henry, the Flit!

1. *The Flies* (*Les Mouches*)
2. *Butterflies Are Free*
3. *Hunting Cockroaches*
4. *A Flea in Her Ear*
5. *Kiss of the Spider Woman*
6. *The Firefly*
7. *The Insect Comedy* (or *Play*)
8. *Bug*
9. *The Moth and the Flame*
10. *The Wasp's Nest*

What's New?

1. *The New Moon*
2. *A New Brain*
3. "Many a New Day"
4. "New Deal for Christmas"
5. *New Faces of 1934*
6. "Open a New Window"
7. "A New Pair of Shoes"
8. *New Girl in Town*
9. "The New Ashmolean Marching Society and Students' Conservatory Band"
10. *A New Way to Pay Old Debts*

Day by Day

1. *Sunday in New York*
2. *Any Wednesday*
3. *A Memory of Two Mondays*
4. *Saturday Night Fever*
5. *Every Thursday*
6. *My Girl Friday*
7. *Eight O'Clock Tuesday*

I See the Moon
1. *A Moon for the Misbegotten*
2. *Little Moon of Alban*
3. *The Moon Is Blue*
4. *Dark of the Moon*
5. *Fool Moon*
6. *Moon of the Caribbees*
7. *Moon Over Buffalo*
8. *The Effect of Gamma Rays on Man-in-the-Moon Marigolds*
9. *The Teahouse of the August Moon*
10. *Ring Round the Moon*

Alter Egos
1. Peter Parker is Spider-Man in *Spider-Man: Turn Off the Dark*.
2. Pierre Birabeau's alter ego is the Red Shadow in *The Desert Song*.
3. Clark Kent and Superman are the same in *It's a Bird . . . It's a Plane . . . It's Superman*.
4. Edmond Dantès is the Count of Monte Cristo in the play of that name.
5. Norman Osborn is the Green Goblin in *Spider-Man: Turn Off the Dark*.
6. Portia disguises herself as Balthazar in *The Merchant of Venice*.
7. Don Diego de la Vega is the secret identity of Zorro in *Zorro: The Musical*. (There are at least three stage musical versions of *Zorro*. One ran in Houston in 1998, another played on London's West End in 2008, and a third was featured at a festival in Klingenberg am Main, Bavaria, in 2013.)
8. Sir Percy Blakeney becomes the Scarlet Pimpernel in *The Scarlet Pimpernel*, which is both a musical and a play.
9. Johnny has an alter ego named St. Jimmy in *American Idiot*.
10. Henry Jekyll and Edward Hyde are the same person in the musical *Jekyll & Hyde* and the play *Dr. Jekyll and Mr. Hyde*.

Boy Meets Girl

1. Doris and George in *Same Time Next Year*
2. Amanda Prynne and Elyot Chase in *Private Lives*
3. Fonsia Dorsey and Weller Martin in *The Gin Game*
4. Billie Dawn and Paul Verrall in *Born Yesterday*
5. Beatrice and Benedick in *Much Ado About Nothing*
6. Honey and Nick in *Who's Afraid of Virginia Woolf?*
7. Jennet Jourdemayne and Thomas Mendip in *The Lady's Not for Burning*
8. Lydia Languish and Captain Jack Absolute in *The Rivals*
9. Mrs. Millamant and Mirabell in *The Way of the World*
10. Pegeen Mike and Christy Mahan in *The Playboy of the Western World*

II

ROYALS AND ARISTOCRATS

The quizzes in this section all deal with kings, queens, princes, dukes, knights, and dames. See if your blood is blue enough to make it at court!

Crowned Heads

Over what domains do these royal personages reign and in what shows?

1. Grand Duke Otto and Grand Duchess Sophie	Karlsburg	*The Lion King*
2. King Mongkut	Agrabah	*Little Me*
3. King Louis XI	Sylvania	*Call Me Madam*
4. Sultan	Rosenzweig	*Sweethearts*
5. King Mufasa	Carpathia	*The Vagabond King*
6. Grand Duke Charles	Lichtenburg	*The Student Prince*
7. Princess Sylvia and Prince Franz	France	*The King and I*
8. Prince Karl	Siam	*The Love Parade*
9. Prince Cherney	The Pride Lands	*Aladdin*
10. Queen Louise and Count Alfred	Zilania	*The Girl Who Came to Supper*

Your Majesty!

Name the English monarch who is a character in:

1.	A Shakespeare play in which England is characterized as "this other Eden, demi-paradise"	Queen Elizabeth II
2.	The musical *Rex* by Richard Rodgers, Sheldon Harnick, and Sherman Yellen	King Charles III
3.	A 2014 play by Mike Bartlett subtitled "A Future History Play"	Queen Elizabeth I
4.	A 1935 play by Laurence Housman that could not be produced in England until 1937, since the Lord Chamberlain ruled that 100 years must elapse from a monarch's accession until he or she can be portrayed on stage	King Henry II
5.	A play by Christopher Marlowe in which the monarch has a favorite courtier named Gaveston	King Richard II
6.	The revue *As Thousands Cheer* by Irving Berlin and Moss Hart	Queen Victoria
7.	Plays by Friedrich Schiller, Maxwell Anderson, and Robert Bolt	King George III
8.	A play by Peter Morgan produced in London in 2013 with a cast headed by a performer who played the same monarch in a 2006 film	King Edward II
9.	*The Lion in Winter* by James Goldman and *Becket* by Jean Anouilh	King George V
10.	A 1991 play by Alan Bennett in which the monarch struggles with mental illness	King Henry VIII

Your Highness!

Match these princesses with the plays or musicals in which they appear.

1. Princess Barbára	*The King and I*
2. Princess Fiona	*Carnival!*
3. Princess Kitty Scherbatsky	*The Mystery of Edwin Drood*
4. Princess Kosmonopolis	*On Your Toes*
5. Princess Olga	*Kismet*
6. Princess Winnifred	*Shrek the Musical*
7. Princess Ying Yaowalak	*Anna Karenina*
8. Princess Zenobia	*Sweet Bird of Youth*
9. The Princess Puffer	*The Apple Tree*
10. Princess of Ababu	*Once Upon a Mattress*

Someday My Prince Will Come

Match the prince with the play or musical in which he appears.

1. Prince Dauntless	*The Merry Widow*
2. Prince Abdullah	*My One and Only*
3. Prince Bounine	*Spamalot*
4. Prince DeLong	*Once Upon a Mattress*
5. Prince Danilo	*The King and I*
6. Prince Stubb Talmage	*Aladdin*
7. Prince Chulalongkorn	*The Little Mermaid*
8. Prince Eric	*Anastasia*
9. Prince Herbert	*Sinbad*
10. Prince Nicolai Erraclyovitch Tchatchavadze	*The Unsinkable Molly Brown*

Put Up Your Dukes

Match these dukes with the plays or musicals in which they appear.

1.	Duke of Burlingame	*King Lear*
2.	George, Duke of Clarence	*The Petrified Forest*
3.	The Duke de la Trémouille	*Happy Hunting*
4.	Duke Mahoney	*Richard III*
5.	Duke of Albany	*The Unsinkable Molly Brown*
6.	Duke of Arundel	*Sally*
7.	Duke of Czechogovinio	*Nice Work If You Can Get It*
8.	Duke of Granada	*Becket*
9.	Duke Mantee	*The Gondoliers*
10.	The Duke of Plaza-Toro	*Saint Joan*

Starry, Starry Knights

Match the description in the first column with the acting knight in the second column, and provide his last name.

1. He was the first actor ever knighted for services to the theatre.

   Sir Anthony _____

2. He played the Fool to Charles Laughton's King Lear at the Royal Shakespeare Theatre in 1959.

   Sir John _____

3. Knighted in 1945, he was the husband of Sybil Thorndike, who had been made a Dame in 1931.

   Sir Noël _____

4. His great aunt was the actress Dame Ellen Terry.

Sir Alec _____

5. Artistic director of the Shakespeare Memorial Theatre from 1948 to 1956, he has the same last name as a former US vice president.

Sir Henry _____

6. His wife, Rachel, two daughters, a son, and several grandchildren became actors.

Sir Alan _____

7. In 1946 he played the Fool to Laurence Olivier's King Lear.

Sir Ian _____

8. A college was named for him at Durham University, of which he was Chancellor.

Sir Lewis _____

9. He rose to fame in *Look Back in Anger* and was knighted in 2003, the same year he died.

Sir Michael _____

10. When he was belatedly knighted in 1970, a fellow knight said, "We have been like a row of teeth with the front tooth missing."

Sir Peter _____

There Is Nothing Like a Dame

Match the description in the first column with the theatrical Dame of the British Empire in the second column and provide her last name.

1. The mother of director Margaret Webster, she starred in Hitchcock's *The Lady Vanishes*.

   Dame Helen _____

2. Her stage and film roles included Miss Prism, Lady Bracknell, Lady Wishfort, Mrs. Candour, Mrs. Malaprop, and Miss Marple, and she won an Oscar in *The V.I.P.s*.

   Dame Judith _____

3. Most of her work was on stage, notably in plays by Shakespeare, Webster, Ibsen, Chekhov, Brecht, Pinter, and Albee—but she won an Oscar in 1985 as Best Supporting Actress in *A Passage to India*.

   Dame Edith _____

4. She has won the Triple Crown of Acting—a Tony, an Oscar, and an Emmy—two of them for playing Queen Elizabeth II.

   Dame Joan _____

5. She is remembered as a notable Medea and as Mrs. Danvers in the film *Rebecca*.

   Dame Margaret _____

6. Regarded as Britain's premier Shakespearean actress, she was Sir Henry Irving's leading lady for more than two decades, and her career lasted from the 1850s until 1922.

   Dame Peggy _____

7. She has had a long stage career, including five years with the Royal Shakespeare Company (1959–1964), but is best known as TV's Emma Peel.

Dame May _____

8. Made a Dame in 2004, she also has the title of Baroness from her late actor husband.

Dame Diana _____

9. Born Julia Elizabeth Wells, she is famous for her roles in stage and film musicals.

Dame Ellen _____

10. Though known mostly for stage work in Shakespeare, Shaw, and Restoration plays during a sixty-year career, she was nominated for three Oscars in the 1960s, for *Tom Jones*, *The Chalk Garden*, and *The Whisperers*.

Dame Julie _____

ROYALS AND ARISTOCRATS

ANSWERS

Crowned Heads
1. Grand Duke Otto and Grand Duchess Sophie reign in Lichtenburg in *Call Me Madam.*
2. King Mongkut reigns in Siam in *The King and I.*
3. King Louis XI is the king of France in *The Vagabond King.*
4. The Sultan of Agrabah is in *Aladdin.*
5. King Mufasa is the monarch of the Pride Lands in *The Lion King.*
6. Grand Duke Charles reigns in Carpathia in *The Girl Who Came to Supper.*
7. Princess Sylvia and Prince Franz are on the throne of Zilania in *Sweethearts.*
8. Prince Karl reigns in Karlsburg in *The Student Prince.*
9. Prince Cherney rules over Rosenzweig in *Little Me.*
10. Queen Louise and Count Alfred reign in Sylvania in *The Love Parade.*

Your Majesty!
1. King Richard II
2. King Henry VIII
3. Charles, the Prince of Wales, is imagined as the future king in *King Charles III.*
4. Queen Victoria, played by Helen Hayes, is the subject of the 1935 play *Victoria Regina,* which had to wait until 1937 for its first British production, one hundred years after Victoria's accession to the throne.
5. King Edward II in *The Tragedy of Edward II*
6. King George V
7. Queen Elizabeth I is a character in Schiller's *Mary Stuart,* Anderson's *Elizabeth the Queen,* and Bolt's *Vivat! Vivat! Regina!*
8. Queen Elizabeth II, portrayed by Helen Mirren in *The Audience,* was also played by Mirren in the film *The Queen.*

Continued on next page

9. King Henry II
10. King George III in *The Madness of George III* (which was made into a film called *The Madness of King George*)

Your Highness!

1. Princess Barbára—*The Apple Tree*
2. Princess Fiona—*Shrek the Musical*
3. Princess Kitty Scherbatsky—*Anna Karenina*
4. Princess Kosmonopolis—*Sweet Bird of Youth*
5. Princess Olga—*Carnival!*
6. Princess Winnifred—*Once Upon a Mattress*
7. Princess Ying Yaowalak—*The King and I*
8. Princess Zenobia—*On Your Toes*
9. The Princess Puffer—*The Mystery of Edwin Drood*
10. Princess of Ababu—*Kismet*

Someday My Prince Will Come

1. Prince Dauntless—*Once Upon a Mattress*
2. Prince Abdullah—*Aladdin*
3. Prince Bounine—*Anastasia*
4. Prince DeLong—*The Unsinkable Molly Brown*
5. Prince Danilo—*The Merry Widow*
6. Prince Stubb Talmage—*Sinbad*
7. Prince Chulalongkorn—*The King and I*
8. Prince Eric—*The Little Mermaid*
9. Prince Herbert—*Spamalot*
10. Prince Nicolai Erraclyovitch Tchatchavadze—*My One and Only*

Put Up Your Dukes

1. Duke of Burlingame—*The Unsinkable Molly Brown*
2. George, Duke of Clarence (brother of the Duke of Gloucester, later King Richard)—*Richard III*
3. The Duke de la Trémouille—*Saint Joan*
4. Duke Mahoney—*Nice Work If You Can Get It*
5. Duke of Albany—*King Lear*
6. Duke of Arundel—*Becket*
7. Duke of Czechogovinio—*Sally*
8. Duke of Granada—*Happy Hunting*

9. Duke Mantee—*The Petrified Forest*
10. The Duke of Plaza-Toro—*The Gondoliers*

Starry, Starry Knights
1. Sir Henry Irving was knighted by Queen Victoria on July 18, 1895.
2. Sir Ian Holm
3. Sir Lewis Casson
4. Sir John Gielgud
5. Sir Anthony Quayle—who has the same last name as former Vice President Dan Quayle
6. Sir Michael Redgrave's wife, Rachel Kempson, as well his daughters, Vanessa and Lynn, his son, Corin, and his granddaughters, Joely and Natasha Richardson and Jemma Redgrave, all became well-known actors.
7. Sir Alec Guinness
8. Sir Peter Ustinov, who served the university as honorary chancellor from 1992 until his death in 2004
9. Sir Alan Bates
10. Sir Noël Coward received his knighthood at the age of seventy; it was considered by others in the profession as long overdue, prompting Sir Alec Guinness to say, "We have been like a row of teeth with the front tooth missing. Now we can smile."

There Is Nothing Like a Dame
1. Dame May Whitty
2. Dame Margaret Rutherford
3. Dame Peggy Ashcroft
4. Dame Helen Mirren won an Oscar as Queen Elizabeth II in *The Queen*, a Tony as the Queen in *The Audience*, and several Emmys as Detective Jane Tennison on TV.
5. Dame Judith Anderson
6. Dame Ellen Terry
7. Dame Diana Rigg
8. Dame Joan Plowright is also Baroness Olivier of Brighton, owing to her marriage to the late Laurence Olivier.
9. Dame Julie Andrews
10. Dame Edith Evans

III

THE TITLED CLASSES

These quizzes deal with folks who have titles—political, military, and social—in front of their names. Are you familiar with these formalities?

Politics as Usual

What political office (either elective or appointive) is held by each of the following characters?

1.	George Shinn in *The Music Man*	Sheriff of Lanville County
2.	Thomas Danforth in *The Crucible*	Governor of New Amsterdam
3.	Billboard Rawkins in *Finian's Rainbow*	Former President of the US
4.	Ed Earl Dodd in *The Best Little Whorehouse in Texas*	Senator from Dogpatch
5.	Arthur Hockstader in *The Best Man*	Mayor of River City
6.	Mary Prescott in *The Prescott Proposals*	Deputy-Governor of Massachusetts
7.	Pieter Stuyvesant in *Knickerbocker Holiday*	United Nations Delegate
8.	Jack S. Phogbound in *Li'l Abner*	Governor of North and South Dakota
9.	Alexander Hamilton in *Hamilton*	Senator from Missitucky
10.	Noble Eggleston in *Little Me*	Secretary of the Treasury

Hail to the Chief

Match the presidents of the United States with the descriptions of their roles in plays and musicals:

1. He's mentioned in song lyrics in both *Annie* and *Follies*, and he is a character in *As Thousands Cheer.*

   Lyndon B. Johnson

2. He was portrayed by George M. Cohan in *I'd Rather Be Right* and by Raymond Thorne in *Annie.*

   John Adams

3. Bryan Cranston won a Tony Award for playing this president in *All the Way.*

   George Washington

4. He is the president in the Pulitzer Prize– winning *Of Thee I Sing.*

   Richard M. Nixon

5. Frank Langella played this president in a play whose characters include TV host David Frost.

   Theodore Roosevelt

6. He is one of two future presidents in *1776.*

   Franklin D. Roosevelt

7. This president appears in a musical about himself and his daughter.

   John P. Wintergreen

8. Benjamin Walker played this president in a musical whose songs include "Populism Yea Yea."

   George W. Bush

9. This president was portrayed by Will Ferrell in *Thank You America.*

   Herbert Hoover

10. This president is still a general when he appears in Rodgers and Hart's *Dearest Enemy.*

    Andrew Jackson

Pulling Rank

Which military title is held by each of the following musical characters?

1.	Big Jim Warrington in *Little Mary Sunshine*	Commodore
2.	Nellie Forbush in *South Pacific*	Sergeant
3.	Tadeusz Boleslav Stjerbinsky in *The Grand Tour*	Lieutenant Colonel
4.	Von Schreiber in *The Sound of Music*	Major
5.	Matthew Calbraith Perry in *Pacific Overtures*	General
6.	Matilda B. Cartwright in *Guys and Dolls*	Admiral
7.	Alexius Spiridoff in *The Chocolate Soldier*	Lieutenant
8.	Irving Berlin in *This Is the Army*	Colonel
9.	S. D. Grubbs in *Something for the Boys*	Ensign
10.	Richard Fay in *Rosalie*	Captain

You're in the Army Now!

Complete the titles of these plays that include names of army ranks.

1. *Privates on* _____ is a farce by Peter Nichols with music by Denis King.
   ★ *KP*
   ★ *Parade*
   ★ *Call*
   ★ *Duty*

2. *Good* _____ *Corporal* is a comedy by Milton Herbert Gropper and Joseph Shalleck set in New York during World War II.
   ★ *Grief*
   ★ *Show*
   ★ *Morning*
   ★ *Heavens*

3. *No* _____ *for Sergeants,* a comedy by Ira Levin, starred Andy Griffith in its Broadway production.
   ★ *Love*
   ★ *Time*
   ★ *Problem*
   ★ *Stripes*

4. *The Lieutenant of* _____ is a satire by Martin McDonagh set in County Galway, Ireland.
   ★ *Inishmore*
   ★ *Leenane*
   ★ *Ballyhoo*
   ★ *Galway*

5. *Captain Jinks of the* _____, a fantastic comedy by Clyde Fitch, was first produced in New York in 1901.
   ★ *Salvation Army*
   ★ *Shore Patrol*
   ★ *Royal Navy*
   ★ *Horse Marines*

6. *Major* _____ is George Bernard Shaw's play about an idealistic young woman in the Salvation Army.
   ★ *Trouble*
   ★ *Gwendolyn*
   ★ *General*
   ★ *Barbara*

7. *The* _____ *of Four Colonels* is a fantasy by Peter Ustinov set in a post–World War II German zone divided among France, Russia, Britain, and the United States.
   ★ *Argument*
   ★ *Love*
   ★ *Adventures*
   ★ *Predicament*

Continued on next page

8. *Brigadier* _____ is a 1906 comedy by Sir Arthur Conan Doyle.
   * ★ *Gerard*
   * ★ *Churchill*
   * ★ *Holmes*
   * ★ *Smith*

9. *General* _____, a drama by Ira Levin, lasted only two performances on Broadway, although it starred George C. Scott.
   * ★ *Seeger*
   * ★ *Patton*
   * ★ *Confusion*
   * ★ *Napoleon*

10. _____ *President*, a 1944 drama about Commander-in-Chief Abraham Lincoln by Nat Sherman.
    * ★ *Republican*
    * ★ *War*
    * ★ *Reluctant*
    * ★ *Union*

War Stories

Match the descriptions with the military personnel who are described and with the plays or musicals in which they appear:

1. This officer, who served in India and wrote a book called *Spoken Sanskrit,* comes to London in search of a fellow linguist.

   General Howe — *South Pacific*

2. This officer is suspected of an affair with a general's wife when her handkerchief is planted in his room.

   Sergeant Quirt — *Mother Courage*

3. In a play about the Vietnam War, this drill instructor tells a recruit, "I'm bigger than my name."

   Canteen Anna — *Billy Budd*

4. This Marine arrives on a remote island to lead a spy mission to a Japanese-held island in World War II.

   Colonel Pickering — *The Basic Training of Pavlo Hummel*

5. This commander sentences a recruit to death for striking an officer, who dies from the blow.

   Sergeant Tower — *Dearest Enemy*

6. This officer is sent to a village in Okinawa to introduce democracy.

   Lieutenant Cassio — *Irving Berlin's White Christmas*

7. This Marine vies with Capt. Flagg for the favors of a young woman amidst the carnage of World War I in France.

   Captain Fisby — *Pygmalion*

8. The commanding officer of a World War II division runs an inn in Vermont after the war.

   Lieutenant Cable — *The Teahouse of the August Moon*

9. During the Thirty Years' War, this vendor sells food and drink from a wagon.

   Captain Vere — *Othello*

10. This officer and his soldiers are detained by a socialite who plies them with refreshments during the American Revolution.

    General Waverly — *What Price Glory?*

Mrs. Who?

Fill in the blank with the missing name of a "Mrs." in these plays.

1. *The Deep Mrs. _____*   *Wiggs*

2. *Mrs. _____ and Mr. X*   *Warren*

3. *Mrs. _____ of the Cabbage Patch*   *Cheyney*

4. *The Last of Mrs. _____ (1925)*   *Dally*

5. *Mrs. _____*   *Tanqueray*

6. *The Last of Mrs._____ (1972)*   *Lincoln*

7. *Mrs. _____'s Profession*   *McThing*

8. *Mrs. _____ Has a Lover*   *January*

9. *Horowitz and Mrs. _____*   *Sykes*

10. *The Second Mrs. _____*   *Washington*

Call Me Mister

Fill in the missing name in these plays and musicals in which the title "Mister" (or "Mr.") appears.

1. *Blues for Mister* _____   *Pennypacker*

2. *Dr. Jekyll and Mr.* _____   *Wonderful*

3. *Entertaining Mr.* _____   *Pipp*

4. *Mister* _____   *Pim*

5. *Mr.* _____   *Hyde*

6. *Mr.* _____ *of Wickham*   *Charlie*

7. *Mr.* _____ *Passes By*   *Roberts*

8. *The Awakening of Mr.* _____   *Wix*

9. *The Remarkable Mr.* _____   *Hoggenheimer*

10. *The Rich Mr.* _____   *Sloane*

THE TITLED CLASSES

ANSWERS

Politics as Usual
1. George Shinn in *The Music Man* is the mayor of River City, Iowa.
2. Thomas Danforth in *The Crucible* is deputy-governor of Massachusetts.
3. Billboard Rawkins in *Finian's Rainbow* is a United States senator from Missitucky.
4. Ed Earl Dodd in *The Best Little Whorehouse in Texas* is sheriff of Lanville County.
5. Arthur Hockstader in *The Best Man* is the former president of the United States.
6. Mary Prescott in *The Prescott Proposals* is the United States delegate to the United Nations.
7. Pieter Stuyvesant in *Knickerbocker Holiday* is governor of New Amsterdam.
8. Jack S. Phogbound in *Li'l Abner* is a United States senator from the unnamed state in which Dogpatch is located.
9. Alexander Hamilton in *Hamilton* is the US secretary of the Treasury.
10. Noble Eggleston in *Little Me* is governor of North and South Dakota.

Hail to the Chief
1. Herbert Hoover
2. Franklin D. Roosevelt (named only as the president of the United States in *I'd Rather Be Right* and as FDR in *Annie*)
3. Lyndon B. Johnson
4. John P. Wintergreen (fictional)
5. Richard M. Nixon in *Frost/Nixon*
6. John Adams (as well as Thomas Jefferson)
7. Theodore Roosevelt in *Teddy & Alice*
8. Andrew Jackson in *Bloody Bloody Andrew Jackson*
9. George W. Bush
10. General George Washington

Pulling Rank
1. Captain Big Jim Warrington
2. Ensign Nellie Forbush
3. Colonel Tadeusz Boleslav Stjerbinsky
4. Admiral Von Schreiber
5. Commodore Matthew Calbraith Perry
6. General Matilda B. Cartwright
7. Major Alexius Spiridoff
8. Sergeant Irving Berlin
9. Lieutenant Colonel S. D. Grubbs
10. Lieutenant Richard Fay

You're in the Army Now!
1. *Privates on Parade*
2. *Good Morning Corporal*
3. *No Time for Sergeants*
4. *The Lieutenant of Inishmore*
5. *Captain Jinks of the Horse Marines*
6. *Major Barbara*
7. *The Love of Four Colonels*
8. *Brigadier Gerard*
9. *General Seeger*
10. *War President*

War Stories
1. Colonel Pickering in *Pygmalion*
2. Cassio is the lieutenant in *Othello* (whom Iago wrongly accuses of having an affair with Desdemona).
3. Sergeant Tower is the drill instructor in *The Basic Training of Pavlo Hummel.*
4. Lieutenant Joseph Cable in *South Pacific*
5. Captain Vere in *Billy Budd* (who sentences Billy Budd to death for striking the master-at-arms, Claggart)
6. Captain Fisby in *The Teahouse of the August Moon*
7. Sergeant Quirt and Captain Flagg are rivals in *What Price Glory?*
8. General Waverly in *Irving Berlin's White Christmas*
9. "Canteen Anna," otherwise known as Mother Courage, in *Mother Courage*
10. British General Sir William Howe in *Dearest Enemy*

Mrs. Who?

1. *The Deep Mrs. Sykes*
2. *Mrs. January and Mr. X*
3. *Mrs. Wiggs of the Cabbage Patch*
4. *The Last of Mrs. Cheyney*
5. *Mrs. McThing*
6. *The Last of Mrs. Lincoln*
7. *Mrs. Warren's Profession*
8. *Mrs. Dally Has a Lover*
9. *Horowitz and Mrs. Washington*
10. *The Second Mrs. Tanqueray*

Call Me Mister

1. *Blues for Mister Charlie*
2. *Dr. Jekyll and Mr. Hyde*
3. *Entertaining Mr. Sloane*
4. *Mister Roberts*
5. *Mr. Wonderful*
6. *Mr. Wix of Wickham*
7. *Mr. Pim Passes By*
8. *The Awakening of Mr. Pipp*
9. *The Remarkable Mr. Pennypacker*
10. *The Rich Mr. Hoggenheimer*

ALL IN THE FAMILY

Get to know your relatives in these questions, which all deal with family members—husbands, wives, mothers, fathers, children, brothers, sisters, aunts, uncles, teenagers—and one famous cousin.

Meet the Family

In which plays do the families named in the first column appear?

1.	Sycamore	*Major Barbara*
2.	Prozorov	*The Waltz of the Toreadors*
3.	Mannon	*The Taming of the Shrew*
4.	Helmer	*The Skin of Our Teeth*
5.	Hubbard	*Mourning Becomes Electra*
6.	Minola	*A Doll's House*
7.	Undershaft	*You Can't Take It with You*
8.	Absolute	*The Little Foxes*
9.	Antrobus	*The Three Sisters*
10.	St. Pé	*The Rivals*

Two for the Show

Match the Broadway productions described in the first column with the married couples who appeared in them.

1. This couple appeared together in more than two dozen Broadway productions, beginning with *Sweet Nell of Old Drury* in 1923 and ending with *The Visit* in 1958.

   Eli Wallach   Elizabeth Taylor

2. These two appeared together in nine Broadway productions, from *Yr. Obedient Husband* in 1938 to *Long Day's Journey Into Night* in 1956.

   Jason Robards Jr.   Lynn Fontanne

3. They appeared together in thirteen Broadway productions, the first of which was *King Henry VIII* in 1946 and the last was *The Flowering Peach* in 1994.

   Jason Danieley   Jessica Tandy

4. This couple appeared together on Broadway only once, in *Private Lives* in 1983—seven years after they divorced.

   Laurence Olivier   Florence Eldridge

5. He appeared in twenty-one Broadway plays, from *Long Day's Journey Into Night* in 1956 to *No Man's Land* in 1994, and she appeared in six, from *Johnny 2x4* in 1942 to *Waiting in the Wings* in 1999— but they never appeared together in the same show.

   Hume Cronyn   Anne Jackson

6. They appeared on Broadway together in three plays—*Romeo and Juliet* in 1940, and *Antony and Cleopatra* and *Caesar and Cleopatra*, both in 1951.

   Terrence Mann   Lauren Bacall

7. They were both on Broadway in *The 24-Hour Plays 2005* and *Pippin* in 2013; they were both also in *Cats* (she as a replacement) and *Jerome Robbins' Broadway* (he as a replacement).

   Alfred Lunt   Joan Plowright

8. They were together on Broadway in *Children and Art* (a Sondheim tribute) in 2005 and (as replacements) in *Next to Normal* in 2010.

   Laurence Olivier   Marin Mazzie

9. They appeared together in sixteen Broadway productions, from *The Fourposter* in 1951 to *The Petition* in 1986.

   Fredric March   Vivien Leigh

10. They appeared together on Broadway in *The Entertainer* in 1958, two years before they were married.

   Richard Burton   Charlotte d'Amboise

Mother's Day

Match the mothers named in the first column with the offspring in the second—and name the play or musical in which they appear.

1.	Mrs. Webb	Alarbus, Chiron, and Demetrius	*A Trip to Bountiful*
2.	Rose	Lewis	*Titus Andronicus*
3.	Mrs. Alving	Biff and Happy	*Pippin*
4.	Amanda Wingfield	Emily and Wally	*Gypsy*
5.	Mrs. Darling	Louise and June	*The Seagull*
6.	Linda Loman	Ludie	*The Glass Menagerie*
7.	Tamora	Oswald	*Our Town*
8.	Carrie Watts	Konstantine	*Death of a Salesman*
9.	Irina Arkadina	Laura and Tom	*Peter Pan*
10.	Fastrada	Wendy, Michael, and John	*Ghosts*

Fathers and Sons

In the first column are the first names of fathers and their sons, all of whom have appeared on Broadway. Match them with the correct surname.

1.	Robert—Alan	Huston
2.	Carl—Rob	Auberjonois
3.	Maurice—Lionel and John	Robards
4.	Ed—Keenan	Alda
5.	Walter—John	Cassidy
6.	Jason Sr.—Jason Jr.	Reiner
7.	Robert—James	Carradine
8.	René—Remy	Barrymore
9.	Jack—David, Shaun, and Patrick	Jones
10.	John—David and Keith	Wynn

Say Uncle!

Match the uncle with the play or musical in which he appears.

1.	Uncle Sid	*I Remember Mama*
2.	Uncle Desmonde	*Bring in 'Da Noise, Bring In 'Da Funk*
3.	Uncle Ernie	*The King and I*
4.	Uncle Fester	*Gypsy*
5.	Uncle Chris	*Mame*
6.	Uncle Thomas	*Orpheus Descending*
7.	Uncle Huck-A-Buck	*Ah, Wilderness!*
8.	Uncle Jocko	*The Who's Tommy*
9.	Uncle Jeff	*The Happy Time*
10.	Uncle Pleasant	*The Addams Family*

Getting Aunt-sy

Match these aunts with the Broadway plays or musicals in which they appear.

1.	Aunt Eller	*Charley's Aunt* or *Where's Charley?*
2.	Aunt Em	*Arsenic and Old Lace*
3.	Aunt Nonnie	*Gigi*
4.	Aunt Alicia	*I Remember Mama*
5.	Aunt Abby and Aunt Martha Brewster	*Oklahoma!* or *Green Grow the Lilacs*
6.	Aunt Betsey Trotwood	*All the Way Home*
7.	Aunt Ev	*Sweet Bird of Youth*
8.	Donna Lucia D'Alvadorez	*Copperfield*
9.	Aunt Hannah Lynch and Aunt Sadie Follet	*The Wiz* or *The Wizard of Oz*
10.	Aunt Jenny, Aunt Sigrid, and Aunt Trina	*The Miracle Worker*

Sibling Revelry

Can you identify these theatrical siblings?

1. These three brothers began a theatrical empire in 1900 that grew to include seventeen Broadway theatres:
   * The Mills Brothers
   * The Shubert Brothers
   * The Nederlander Brothers
   * The Jujamcyn Brothers

2. These five brothers, along with their mother, were the subject of a 1970 Broadway musical:
   * The Mills Brothers
   * The Osmond Brothers
   * The Marx Brothers
   * The Step Brothers

3. These two brothers are remembered in the name of Broadway's largest theatre:
   * George and Ira Gershwin
   * Lionel and John Barrymore
   * Dennis and Randy Quaid
   * Charles and David Koch

4. This brother and sister were a team that wrote the books for musicals by Cole Porter, Sigmund Romberg, and Irving Berlin—and a third sibling was the coauthor of books for musicals by Leonard Bernstein, Jule Styne, and Rodgers & Hammerstein:
   * Herbert and Dorothy Fields
   * Buddy and Vilma Ebsen
   * Lionel and Ethel Barrymore
   * Sam and Bella Spewack

5. These identical twins have each won a Tony Award for Best Play:
   * Anthony and Peter Shaffer
   * Julius and Philip Epstein
   * Mary-Kate and Ashley Olsen
   * Tennessee and Treat Williams

6. These two brothers made their Broadway debut in *The Ziegfeld Follies of 1936*—when the younger was only fifteen:
   * Don and Jim Ameche
   * Barry and Robin Gibb
   * Fayard and Harold Nicholas
   * Dick and Jerry Van Dyke

7. These three siblings were the children of an acting father whose real name was Blythe:
   * Edwin, Junius Brutus, and John Wilkes Booth
   * David, Keith, and Robert Carradine
   * Timothy, Joseph, and Sam Bottoms
   * Ethel, Lionel, and John Barrymore

Continued on next page

8. These three siblings are the children of an actor who was married to actress Rachel Kempson:
   ★ Vanessa, Lynn, and Corin Redgrave
   ★ Alec, Stephen, and William Baldwin
   ★ Adam, Matthew, and Anthony Arkin
   ★ Campbell, Alexander, and Devon Scott

9. This brother and sister made their Broadway debut in a revue called *Over the Top:*
   ★ Fred and Adele Astaire
   ★ Shirley MacLaine and Warren Beatty
   ★ Patti and Robert LuPone
   ★ George M. and Josie Cohan

10. These two sisters have done a cabaret act for which this quiz is named:
    ★ Phylicia Rashad and Debbie Allen
    ★ Liza Minnelli and Lorna Luft
    ★ Liz and Ann Hampton Callaway
    ★ Olivia de Haviland and Joan Fontaine

Children at Work

Match the child's role with the actor who originated it on Broadway.

1. Young Patrick Dennis in *Mame*	Eddie Hodges
2. Winthrop Paroo in *The Music Man*	Bruce Prochnik
3. Annie in *Annie*	Susan Strasberg
4. Oliver Twist in *Oliver!*	Alfonso Ribeiro
5. Anne Frank in *The Diary of Anne Frank*	Andrea McArdle
6. Helen Keller in *The Miracle Worker*	Donna Vivino

7. Rhoda Penmark in *The Bad Seed*   Zina Bethune
8. Young Cosette in *Les Misérables*   Patty Duke
9. Willie in *The Tap Dance Kid*   Frankie Michaels
10. Tessie in *The Most Happy Fella*   Patty McCormack

Brothers and Sisters

Match these sets of siblings with the plays or musicals in which they appear as characters.

1. Ruth and Eileen   *The Brothers Karamazov*
2. Adolph, Herbie, Julie, Leonard, and Milton   *Side Show*
3. Adam, Benjamin, Caleb, Daniel, Ephraim, Frank, and Gideon   *The Sound of Music*
4. Aliocha, Ivan, and Dmitri   *Arsenic and Old Lace*
5. Liesl, Friedrich, Louisa, Kurt, Brigitta, Marta, and Gretl   *The Comedy of Errors*
6. Katrin, Christine, Dagmar, and Nels   *Wonderful Town*
7. Antipholus of Ephesus and Antipholus of Syracuse   *I Remember Mama*
8. Mickey and Eddie   *Seven Brides for Seven Brothers*
9. Violet and Daisy   *Minnie's Boys*
10. Teddy, Mortimer, and Jonathan   *Blood Brothers*

Child's Play

Match these children with the plays or musicals in which they appear:

1.	Fleance	*A Tree Grows in Brooklyn*
2.	Theo	*A Little Night Music*
3.	Pepper	*Meet Me in St. Louis*
4.	Francie Nolan	*Macbeth*
5.	Lavender	*Annie*
6.	Mary Lennox	*Once*
7.	Dixie Pollitt	*Pippin*
8.	Fredrika Armfeldt	*The Secret Garden*
9.	Tootie Smith	*Matilda the Musical*
10.	Ivanka	*Cat on a Hot Tin Roof*

Hello, Thirteen . . .

In what plays and musicals will you find these teenagers?

1.	Patty Simcox	*A Little Night Music*
2.	Bibi Bonnard	*The Sound of Music*
3.	Melchior Gabor	*Ah, Wilderness!* or *Take Me Along*
4.	Kim McAfee	*Grease*
5.	Rolf Gruber	*13*
6.	Mollie Michaelson	*The Happy Time*
7.	Eva Duarte	*Bye Bye Birdie*
8.	Anne Egerman	*Spring Awakening*
9.	Evan Goldman	*Evita*
10.	Richard Miller	*Take Her, She's Mine*

Our American Cousin

1. *Our American Cousin*, the play that President Abraham Lincoln was attending the night he was shot, is a . . .
   * ★ Tragedy
   * ★ Historical pageant
   * ★ Farce
   * ★ Revue

2. The name of the theatre in which *Our American Cousin* was playing is . . .
   * ★ Ford's
   * ★ Lincoln's
   * ★ Mercury
   * ★ Colonial

3. Although he was not in the cast the night the Lincolns attended, the actor who originated the title role in the play's New York premiere was . . .
   * ★ James O'Neill
   * ★ Joseph Jefferson
   * ★ John Drew
   * ★ Maurice Barrymore

4. One of the principal characters in *Our American Cousin* is a foppish and brainless British nobleman, whose name gave rise to a term for the long, bushy sideburns that he wore. His name is . . .
   * ★ Duke Burnside
   * ★ Count Fop
   * ★ Lord Dundreary
   * ★ Viscount Muttonchop

Continued on next page

5. One scene in the play uses several supposed Americanisms to mean "get out." Which one of these words is not among them?
   * Absquatulate
   * Skedaddle
   * Taradiddle
   * Vamoose

6. The play's American hero is offered lunch by his English cousins, but he complains that he'd prefer to have all but one of the following . . .
   * Mush
   * Hot dogs
   * Clam chowder
   * Pork and beans

7. John Wilkes Booth, the noted actor who shot Lincoln, was the son of another noted actor . . .
   * Edwin Booth
   * Junius Brutus Booth
   * William Booth
   * Shirley Booth

8. After shooting Lincoln, Booth leaped onto the stage and shouted . . .
   * "Long live the Confederacy"
   * "Et tu, Brute"
   * "Sic semper tyrannis"
   * "Other than that, Mrs. Lincoln, how did you like the play?"

9. Booth planned for the anticipated laughter after one line in the play to cover the sound of his shot. The line was . . . .
   ★ "You sockdologizing old man-trap!"
   ★ "And that's why the chicken crossed the road."
   ★ "I've had a wonderful evening, but this wasn't it."
   ★ "I'll have what she's having."

10. After Lincoln was shot, his head was cradled in the lap of . . . .
    ★ Mary Todd Lincoln
    ★ Laura Keene, an actress in *Our American Cousin*
    ★ Gen. Ulysses S. Grant
    ★ A young usher whose name is not recorded

ALL IN THE FAMILY

ANSWERS

Meet the Family

1. The Sycamore family—Penelope, Paul, and their daughter, Alice—are in *You Can't Take It with You.*
2. The Prozorovs—Olga, Masha, and Irina Prozorova, and their brother, Andrei Sergeyevitch Prozorov—are in *The Three Sisters.*
3. The Mannons—Ezra, Christine, and their children, Lavinia and Orin—are in *Mourning Becomes Electra.*
4. The Helmers—Nora, Torvald, and their children, Emmy, Ivar, and Bobby—are in *A Doll's House.*
5. The Hubbards—Benjamin and Oscar, and their sister, Regina Giddens—are in *The Little Foxes* (and also in its prequel, *Another Part of the Forest,* along with their parents, Marcus and Lavinia Hubbard).
6. The Minolas—Baptista and his daughters, Katharine and Bianca—are in *The Taming of the Shrew.*
7. The Undershafts—Andrew, Lady Britomart, and their offspring, Barbara, Stephen, and Sarah—are in *Major Barbara.*
8. The Absolutes—Sir Anthony and his son, Captain Jack—are in *The Rivals.*
9. The Antrobuses—George, Maggie, and their children, Henry and Gladys—are in *The Skin of Our Teeth.*
10. The St. Pé family—Léon, Emily, and their daughters, Estelle and Sidonia—are in *The Waltz of the Toreadors.*

Two for the Show

1. Alfred Lunt and Lynn Fontanne
2. Fredric March and Florence Eldridge
3. Eli Wallach and Anne Jackson
4. Richard Burton and Elizabeth Taylor (married from 1964 to 1974 and from 1975 to 1976)

Continued on next page

5. Jason Robards Jr. and Lauren Bacall (married from 1961 to 1969)
6. Laurence Olivier and Vivien Leigh (married from 1940 to 1960)
7. Terrence Mann and Charlotte d'Amboise
8. Jason Danieley and Marin Mazzie
9. Hume Cronyn and Jessica Tandy
10. Laurence Olivier and Joan Plowright (married from 1960 until his death)

Mother's Day

1. Mrs. Webb is the mother of Emily and Wally in *Our Town*.
2. Rose is the mother of Louise and June in *Gypsy*.
3. Mrs. Alving is the mother of Oswald in *Ghosts*.
4. Amanda Wingfield is the mother of Laura and Tom in *The Glass Menagerie*.
5. Mrs. Darling is the mother of Wendy, Michael, and John in *Peter Pan*.
6. Linda Loman is the mother of Biff and Happy in *Death of a Salesman*.
7. Tamora, Queen of the Goths, is the mother of Alarbus, Chiron, and Demetrius in *Titus Andronicus*.
8. Carrie Watts is Ludie's mother in *A Trip to Bountiful*.
9. Irina Arkadina (Madame Trepleff) is Konstantine's mother in *The Seagull*.
10. Fastrada is Lewis's mother in *Pippin*.

Fathers and Sons

1. Robert Alda originated the role of Sky Masterson in *Guys and Dolls* and was in several other Broadway plays; his son, Alan Alda, appeared in *Love Letters, Glengarry Glen Ross, The Apple Tree,* and numerous other plays and musicals.
2. Carl Reiner appeared in two Broadway revues and wrote or directed several other plays; his son, Rob, now a noted Hollywood director, has appeared only once on Broadway, in *The Roast*, directed by his father, in 1980.
3. Maurice Barrymore was in *Richard II* in 1875 and last appeared on Broadway in *Becky Sharp* in 1899; his son Lionel appeared frequently on Broadway, notably as Macbeth; his son John appeared in numerous productions, notably as Hamlet. (Their sister, Ethel, was also a well-known actor.)
4. Ed Wynn was in numerous productions, including a revue called *The Perfect Fool*—which he wrote and later adopted as his nickname; Keenan

Wynn was in several Broadway shows in the 1930s and 1940s before moving to Hollywood.

5. Walter Huston appeared in numerous Broadway productions, famously as Pieter Stuyvesant in *Knickerbocker Holiday*, in which he introduced "September Song"; John Huston, better known as a movie director, acted briefly on Broadway in the 1920s and later directed there.

6. Jason Robards Sr. appeared in three Broadway productions, the first was *Lightnin'* in 1918 and the last was *The Disenchanted* in 1958; Jason Robards Jr. is credited with twenty-one Broadway productions, from *Long Day's Journey Into Night* to *No Man's Land*.

7. Robert Earl Jones appeared often on Broadway, beginning with *The Hasty Heart* in 1945 and ending with *Mule Bone* in 1991; James Earl Jones has done at least twenty Broadway productions.

8. René Auberjonois has appeared in numerous Broadway shows beginning with *King Lear*, and including *Coco*, *City of Angels* and *Sly Fox*; Remy Auberjonois has been seen in *The Country Girl*, *Irving Berlin's White Christmas*, *Death of a Salesman*, and *The Assembled Parties*.

9. Jack Cassidy appeared in many musicals, including *She Loves Me*, *Fade Out-Fade In*, and *It's a Bird . . . It's a Plane . . . It's Superman*; his sons David and Shaun appeared together in *Blood Brothers*, and son Patrick has been in several productions, including *Pirates of Penzance*, *Annie Get Your Gun*, and *42nd Street*. (Their brother Ryan is also an occasional film actor.)

10. John Carradine, though primarily known from his many movies, began his Broadway career in *The Duchess of Malfi* in 1946 and ended it in *Frankenstein* in 1981; his son David was in *The Deputy* and *The Royal Hunt of the Sun*; his son Keith began his Broadway career in *Hair* and later starred in *The Will Rogers Follies* and *Hands on a Hardbody*. (Their brothers Bruce and Robert are also film actors, but have not appeared on Broadway.)

Say Uncle!

1. Uncle Sid—*Ah, Wilderness!*
2. Uncle Desmonde—*The Happy Time*
3. Uncle Ernie—*The Who's Tommy*
4. Uncle Fester—*The Addams Family*
5. Uncle Chris—*I Remember Mama*

Continued on next page

6. Uncle Thomas—*The King and I*
7. Uncle Huck-A-Buck—*Bring in 'Da Noise, Bring In 'Da Funk*
8. Uncle Jocko—*Gypsy*
9. Uncle Jeff—*Mame*
10. Uncle Pleasant—*Orpheus Descending*

Getting Aunt-sy

1. Aunt Eller—*Oklahoma!* or *Green Grow the Lilacs*
2. Aunt Em—*The Wiz* or *The Wizard of Oz*
3. Aunt Nonnie—*Sweet Bird of Youth*
4. Aunt Alicia—*Gigi*
5. Aunt Abby and Aunt Martha Brewster—*Arsenic and Old Lace*
6. Aunt Betsey Trotwood—*Copperfield*
7. Aunt Ev—*The Miracle Worker*
8. Donna Lucia D'Alvadorez—*Charley's Aunt* or *Where's Charley?*
9. Aunt Hannah Lynch and Aunt Sadie Follet—*All the Way Home*
10. Aunt Jenny, Aunt Trina, and Aunt Sigrid—*I Remember Mama*

Sibling Revelry

1. Lee, Sam, and J. J. Shubert established the Shubert Organization.
2. The Marx Brothers—Groucho, Harpo, Chico, Gummo, and Zeppo Marx—and their mother, Minnie, were the subject of the musical *Minnie's Boys.*
3. The 1,900-seat Gershwin Theatre is named for George and Ira Gershwin. (The Barrymore Theatre is named for Ethel Barrymore, not her brothers, and it seats 1,096. The David H. Koch Theatre at Lincoln Center for the Performing Arts is not a Broadway house and is named for only one of the Koch brothers.)
4. Herbert and Dorothy Fields wrote the books for *Let's Face It!*, *Something for the Boys*, and *Mexican Hayride*, all with music by Porter; for *Up In Central Park* with Romberg's music (Dorothy also wrote the lyrics); and for *Annie Get Your Gun* with a Berlin score. Their brother, Joseph, coauthored the books for *Wonderful Town* (with Bernstein's music), *Gentlemen Prefer Blondes* (Styne), and *Flower Drum Song* (Rodgers & Hammerstein).
5. Anthony Shaffer won the 1971 Tony Award for *Sleuth*; his twin, Peter, won in 1975 for *Equus.*
6. The Nicholas Brothers made their debut when Fayard was twenty-two and Harold was fifteen.

7. Ethel, Lionel, and John Barrymore were the children of actor Maurice Barrymore, whose real name was Herbert Blythe.
8. Vanessa, Corin, and Lynn Redgrave came from an acting family that began with their grandfather, Roy Redgrave, and continued with their father, Michael, their mother, Rachel Kempson, and their various children, including Natasha Richardson, Joely Richardson, and Jemma Redgrave.
9. Fred and Adele Astaire
10. Liz and Ann Hampton Callaway starred in a cabaret act called *Sibling Revelry.*

Children at Work
1. Young Patrick Dennis in *Mame*—Frankie Michaels
2. Winthrop Paroo in *The Music Man*—Eddie Hodges
3. Annie in *Annie*—Andrea McArdle
4. Oliver Twist in *Oliver!*—Bruce Prochnik
5. Anne Frank in *The Diary of Anne Frank*—Susan Strasberg
6. Helen Keller in *The Miracle Worker*—Patty Duke
7. Rhoda Penmark in *The Bad Seed*—Patty McCormack
8. Young Cosette in *Les Misérables*—Donna Vivino
9. Willie in *The Tap Dance Kid*—Alfonso Ribeiro
10. Tessie in *The Most Happy Fella*—Zina Bethune

Brothers and Sisters
1. Ruth and Eileen—*Wonderful Town*
2. Adolph, Herbie, Julie, Leonard, and Milton (a.k.a. Harpo, Zeppo, Groucho, Chico, and Gummo)—*Minnie's Boys*
3. Adam, Benjamin, Caleb, Daniel, Ephraim, Frank, and Gideon—*Seven Brides for Seven Brothers*
4. Aliocha, Ivan, Dmitri—*The Brothers Karamazov*
5. Liesl, Friedrich, Louisa, Kurt, Brigitta, Marta, and Gretl—*The Sound of Music*
6. Katrin, Christine, Dagmar, and Nels—*I Remember Mama*
7. Antipholus of Ephesus and Antipholus of Syracuse—*The Comedy of Errors*
8. Mickey and Eddie—*Blood Brothers*
9. Violet and Daisy—*Side Show*
10. Teddy, Mortimer, and Jonathan—*Arsenic and Old Lace*

Child's Play

1. Fleance—*Macbeth*
2. Theo—*Pippin*
3. Pepper—*Annie*
4. Francie Nolan—*A Tree Grows in Brooklyn*
5. Lavender—*Matilda the Musical*
6. Mary Lennox—*The Secret Garden*
7. Dixie Pollitt—*Cat on a Hot Tin Roof*
8. Fredrika Armfeldt—*A Little Night Music*
9. Tootie Smith—*Meet Me in St. Louis*
10. Ivanka—*Once*

Hello, Thirteen . . .

1. Patty Simcox—*Grease*
2. Bibi Bonnard—*The Happy Time*
3. Melchior Gabor—*Spring Awakening*
4. Kim McAfee—*Bye Bye Birdie*
5. Rolf Gruber—*The Sound of Music*
6. Mollie Michaelson—*Take Her, She's Mine*
7. Eva Duarte—*Evita*
8. Anne Egerman—*A Little Night Music*
9. Evan Goldman—*13*
10. Richard Miller—*Ah, Wilderness!* (or *Take Me Along*)

Our American Cousin

1. A farce, as performed for the Lincolns. The script of the original play, by British playwright Tom Taylor, does not exist, but is thought to have been written as a melodrama. But one of the actors, E. A. Sothern, added so much comic business and ad libbed so many gags that it soon became a farcical comedy.
2. Ford's Theatre in Washington, DC, was named for its owner and manager, John T. Ford.
3. Joseph Jefferson (III) originated the role of Asa Trenchard, the American cousin.
4. Lord Dundreary (a role originated by E. A. Sothern, who wore bushy sideburns that became known as "dundrearies")
5. "Taradiddle" is not among the words meaning "get out." It means "pretentious nonsense."
6. Hot dogs are not mentioned.
7. Junius Brutus Booth was the father of John Wilkes Booth—and Edwin Booth.
8. "Sic semper tyrannis" (Latin for "Thus always to tyrants")
9. "You sockdologizing old man-trap"
10. Laura Keene (a star of the play, who made her way to the presidential box, where she cradled Lincoln's head on her lap. His blood stained her cuff, which can now be seen in the National Museum of American History.)

V

LITERALLY LITERARY

You don't have to be an English major, but it just might help you get the answers to these questions, which are all about literary matters.

Hitting the Books

Match these musicals with the authors of their literary sources. Extra bragging rights if you can also name the specific work by each author.

1.	*First Impressions*	T. S. Eliot
2.	*My Fair Lady*	Homer
3.	*The Boys from Syracuse*	Edna Ferber
4.	*The Fantasticks*	Jane Austen
5.	*Cats*	Ferenc Molnar
6.	*Half a Sixpence*	William Shakespeare
7.	*The Golden Apple*	Edmond Rostand
8.	*Fanny*	George Bernard Shaw
9.	*Carousel*	H. G. Wells
10.	*Show Boat*	Marcel Pagnol

Brush Up Your Shakespeare

Match these lines with the Shakespeare plays that they open.

1.	"Two households, both alike in dignity . . . "	*Richard III*
2.	"When shall we three meet again . . . "	*Henry V*
3.	"Who's there?"	*The Merchant of Venice*
4.	"Hence! Home, you idle creatures, get you home."	*Romeo and Juliet*
5.	"I thought the King had more affected the Duke of Albany than Cornwall."	*Antony and Cleopatra*
6.	"Nay, but this dotage of our general's O'erflows the measure."	*Macbeth*
7.	"Now is the winter of our discontent /Made glorious summer by this sun of York . . . "	*Hamlet*
8.	"O for a Muse of fire, that would ascend/The brightest heaven of invention . . . ."	*King Lear*
9.	"If music be the food of love, play on . . . "	*Julius Caesar*
10.	"In sooth, I know not why I am so sad."	*Twelfth Night*

O, Ho!

Identify the Shakespearean character whose name begins with "O" and the play in which he or she appears.

1.	Goneril's steward	Orsino	*A Midsummer Night's Dream*
2.	A fantastic fop	Oliver	*Othello*
3.	One of the Triumvirs	Orlando	*Twelfth Night*
4.	A general in the service of Venice	Osric	*Julius Caesar*
5.	Duke of Illyria	Oberon	*As You Like It*
6.	A rich countess	Ophelia	*King Lear*
7.	A son of Sir Rowland de Boys	Othello	*Hamlet*
8.	A son of Sir Rowland de Boys	Oswald	*Twelfth Night*
9.	Daughter to Polonius	Olivia	*As You Like It*
10.	King of the Fairies	Octavius	*Hamlet*

Pop Quiz for English Majors

Match these musicals with the literary classics on which they were based and the authors of those classics.

1.	*Her First Roman*	*Arms and the Man*	Mark Twain
2.	*She Shall Have Music*	*The Rivals*	Oscar Wilde
3.	*Ernest in Love*	*She Stoops to Conquer*	William Wycherley
4.	*All in Love*	*Buried Alive/The Great Adventure*	Eugene O'Neill
5.	*O Marry Me!*	*The Adventures of Huckleberry Finn*	George Bernard Shaw
6.	*Darling of the Day*	*The Importance of Being Earnest*	Richard Brinsley Sheridan
7.	*The Chocolate Soldier*	*Caesar and Cleopatra*	Ben Jonson
8.	*Big River*	*The Country Wife*	Oliver Goldsmith
9.	*New Girl in Town*	*Volpone*	George Bernard Shaw
10.	*Foxy*	*Anna Christie*	Arnold Bennett

Famous Last Words

Match these notable curtain lines with the plays in which they are uttered.

1. "I'm telling you . . . Joxer . . . th' whole worl's . . . in a terr . . . ible state o' . . . chassis!"

   Hedda Gabler

2. " . . . I made the last payment on the house today. Today, dear. And there'll be nobody home. We're free and clear. We're free. We're free . . . We're free . . . "

   A Streetcar Named Desire

3. "[*To the audience*] The Curtain Line Has been spoken! [*To the wings*] Bring it down!"

   Who's Afraid of Virginia Woolf?

4. "Go, bid the soldiers shoot."

   The Caretaker

5. "This game is seven-card stud."

   Pygmalion

6. "Listen . . . if I . . . got down . . . if I was to . . . get my papers . . . would you . . . would you let . . . would you . . . if I got down . . . and got my . . . . [*Long silence*]"

   Waiting for Godot

7. "Yes, let's go. [*They do not move.*]"

   Juno and the Paycock

8. "Good God! People don't do such things."

   Hamlet

9. "I am, George . . . I am."

   Death of a Salesman

10. " . . . Nonsense: She's going to marry Freddy. Ha ha! Freddy! Freddy!! Ha ha ha ha ha ha!!!!! [*He roars with laughter as the play ends.*]"

    Camino Real

It's All Greek to Me

Name these plays and musicals, all of which are based on Greek mythology.

1. About Greeks in a war with the Amazons, this 1942 Rodgers and Hart musical was the last show they wrote together:
   * *Babes in Arms*
   * *By Jupiter*
   * *The Boys from Syracuse*
   * *On Your Toes*

2. The *Iliad* and the *Odyssey*—updated to 1900–1910 in the state of Washington—are the basis of this 1954 musical by Jerome Moross and John La Touche:
   * *The Golden Apple*
   * *The Girl of the Golden West*
   * *Golden Boy*
   * *The Apple Tree*

3. Inspired by the myth of Phaedra, who fell in love with her stepson Hippolytus, this play by Eugene O'Neill was first produced in 1924:
   * *Desire Under the Elms*
   * *Strange Interlude*
   * *The Iceman Cometh*
   * *Ah, Wilderness!*

Continued on next page

4. The *Oresteia* of Aeschylus inspired this 1939 play by T. S. Eliot in which the Greek House of Atreus is symbolized by an English family, and the Furies (known as Eumenides) pursue the principal character:
   ★ *The Cocktail Party*
   ★ *The Family Reunion*
   ★ *The Elder Statesman*
   ★ *Murder in the Cathedral*

5. This play by Aristophanes was "freely adapted" into a musical by Stephen Sondheim and Burt Shevelove and was first performed in 1974 in Yale University's swimming pool:
   ★ *The Birds*
   ★ *The Wasps*
   ★ *The Frogs*
   ★ *The Clouds*

6. Originally titled *Odyssey*, this 1975 musical, based on the myth of Ulysses, starred Yul Brynner and Joan Diener, and had its closing notice posted as soon as the curtain fell on Broadway's opening night:
   ★ *It's All Greek to Me*
   ★ *Ulysses in Nighttown*
   ★ *All the Way Home*
   ★ *Home Sweet Homer*

7. In this 2007 musical, based on a 1980 film, the Greek Muses move between Mount Olympus and Venice Beach, California:
   * *Ishtar*
   * *Xanadu*
   * *Ozymandias*
   * *Olympia*

8. During the Nazi occupation of Paris in 1944, Jean Anouilh transposed this drama based on a Sophocles play about the children of Oedipus from ancient Greece to a setting "without historical or geographical implications."
   * *Antigone*
   * *Oedipus Rex*
   * *Electra*
   * *Medea*

9. This 1955 translation by Christopher Fry is of a 1935 play by Jean Giraudoux, the French title of which means "The Trojan War Will Not Take Place."
   * *The Trojan Women*
   * *Ondine*
   * *Duel of Angels*
   * *Tiger at the Gates*

10. Based on Aristophanes's *Lysistrata*, this 1961 musical starred Cyril Ritchard and Janice Rule.
   * *The Happiest Girl in the World*
   * *The Girl in Pink Tights*
   * *The Girl Who Came to Supper*
   * *There's A Girl in My Soup*

Critics Crack the Quip

What performers were the object of these critics' quips?

1. "A bad play saved by a bad performance." (George S. Kaufman)
   ★ Katharine Cornell
   ★ Gertrude Lawrence
   ★ Fredric March
   ★ Groucho Marx

2. "She is about as Latin as a New England boiled dinner."
   (Douglas Watt)
   ★ Jane Alexander
   ★ Lucille Ball
   ★ Carmen Miranda
   ★ Judi Dench

3. "[She] barged down the Nile last night as Cleopatra and sank."
   (John Mason Brown)
   ★ Claudette Colbert
   ★ Judith Anderson
   ★ Tallulah Bankhead
   ★ Viven Leigh

4. "[He] played Mr. Darcy with all the flexibility of a telephone
   pole." (Brooks Atkinson)
   ★ Montgomery Clift
   ★ Laurence Olivier
   ★ Farley Granger
   ★ George C. Scott

5. "Watch [her] run the gamut of emotion from A to B."
   (Dorothy Parker)
   ✮ Katharine Hepburn
   ✮ Eva LeGallienne
   ✮ Lynn Fontanne
   ✮ Ethel Merman

6. "[She] played the part as though she had not yet signed the
   contract with the producer." (George Jean Nathan)
   ✮ Colleen Dewhurst
   ✮ Maureen Stapleton
   ✮ Kim Stanley
   ✮ Mary Martin

7. ". . . playing Eben like a refugee from a Texas lunatic asylum."
   (Robert Brustein)
   ✮ Robert Preston
   ✮ Jason Robards Jr.
   ✮ Rip Torn
   ✮ Tommy Lee Jones

8. "That which marred his acting was that which marred his
   character—his colossal, animal selfishness." (William Winter)
   ✮ John Wilkes Booth
   ✮ Edwin Forrest
   ✮ John Barrymore
   ✮ George M. Cohan

Continued on next page

9. "Fallen archness" (Franklin Pierce Adams)
   * Elaine Stritch   * Beatrice Lillie
   * Helen Hayes   * Edith Evans

10. "He gives the impression he is a Rotarian pork butcher about to tell a dirty story." (Felix Barker)
    * Anthony Hopkins   * James Earl Jones
    * Patrick Stewart   * Al Pacino

That's Insulting!

Match these insulting remarks from plays and musicals with the speakers and the persons to whom they are addressed.

1. " . . . you starveling, you eel-skin, you dried neat's-tongue, you bull's pizzle, you stock-fish —O for breath to utter what is like thee! —you tailor's yard, you sheath, you bow-case, you vile standing tuck!"

   Linda Loman to Happy and Biff

2. "For nine years . . . I have done everything in my power to protect this boy from your idiotic, cockeyed nincompoopery!"

   Stanley Kowalski to Blanche DuBois

3. " . . . you squashed cabbage leaf, you disgrace to the noble architecture of these columns, you incarnate insult to the English language . . . "

   Prince Hal to Sir John Falstaff

4. "A knave, a rascal, an eater of broken meats; a base, proud, shallow, beggarly, three-suited, hundred-pound, filthy, worsted-stocking knave; a lily-liver'd, action-taking, whoreson, glass-gazing, superserviceable, finical rogue; one-trunk-inheriting slave; one that wouldst be a bawd in way of good service, and art nothing but the composition of a knave, beggar, coward, pander, and the son and heir of a mongrel bitch."

   Martha to George

5. "I swear . . . if you existed I'd divorce you . . .   Sir John Falstaff to
   I haven't been able to see you for years . . .   Prince Hal
   you're a blank, a cipher."

6. "Out of my door, you witch, you rag, you   Dwight Babcock to
   baggage, you polecat, you ronyon! Out, out! I'll   Mame Dennis
   conjure you, I'll fortune-tell you."   Burnside

7. " . . . You come in here and sprinkle the place   Gwendolyn Fairfax
   with powder and spray perfume and cover the   to Cecily Cardew
   light bulb with a paper lantern, and lo and
   behold the place has turned into Egypt and
   you are the Queen of the Nile! Sitting on your
   throne and swilling down my liquor! I say *Ha!*
   —Ha! Do you hear me? *Ha —ha— ha!*"

8. "Why thou clay-brained guts, thou knotty-   Kent to Oswald
   pated fool, thou whoreson, obscene, greasy
   tallow-catch."

9. "Get out of here, both of you, and don't come   Henry Higgins to
   back. I don't want you tormenting him any more   Eliza Doolittle
   . . . Pick up this stuff. I'm not your maid any
   more. Pick it up, you bum, you! You're a pair of
   animals! Not one, not another living soul would
   have had the cruelty to walk out on that man in
   a restaurant!"

10. "From the moment I saw you I distrusted   Ford to "Mother
    you. I felt that you were false and deceitful. I   Prat" (Sir John
    am never deceived in such matters. My first   Falstaff in drag)
    impressions are invariably right."

See You in the Funny Papers

In the first column are plays and musicals based on comic strips. Match them with the artists in the second column who created the source material.

1. *Annie*		Garry Trudeau
2. *Doonesbury*		Stan Lee/Steve Ditko
3. *Li'l Abner*		Richard F. Outcault
4. *You're a Good Man, Charlie Brown*		Al Capp
5. *It's a Bird . . . It's a Plane . . . It's Superman*		Harold Gray
6. *Spider-Man: Turn Off the Dark*		Lee Falk
7. *Little Nemo*		Windsor McCay
8. *Bringing Up Father*		Joe Shuster/Jerry Siegel
9. *Mandrake the Magician and the Enchantress*		Charles M. Schulz
10. *Buster Brown*		George McManus

Exit Lines

Which theatre personalities are reputed to have uttered these last words before their deaths?

1. "I knew it. I knew it. Born in a hotel room—and God, damn it—died in a hotel room."   Laurence Olivier

2. "Is everybody happy? I want everybody to be happy. I know I'm happy."   Sarah Bernhardt

3. "Sister, you are trying to keep me alive as an old curiosity. But I am done. I am finished."   John Wilkes Booth

4. "Curtain! Fast music! Lights! Ready for the last finale! Great! The show looks good, the show looks good!"   Tallulah Bankhead

5. "Dying is easy. Comedy is hard."   Eugene O'Neill

6. "This isn't *Hamlet*. It's not meant to go in the bloody ear."   Florenz Ziegfeld

7. "Codeine . . . bourbon."   Edmund Gwenn

8. "How slow my death agony is."   Humphrey Bogart

9. "I should never have switched from Scotch to Martinis."   Ethel Barrymore

10. "Useless . . . useless."   George Bernard Shaw

LITERALLY LITERARY

ANSWERS

Hitting the Books

1. *First Impressions*—Jane Austen (*Pride and Prejudice*)
2. *My Fair Lady*—George Bernard Shaw (*Pygmalion*)
3. *The Boys from Syracuse*—William Shakespeare (*The Comedy of Errors*)
4. *The Fantasticks*—Edmond Rostand (*Les Romanesques*)
5. *Cats*—T. S. Eliot (*Old Possum's Book of Practical Cats*)
6. *Half a Sixpence*—H. G. Wells (*Kipps: The Story of a Simple Soul*)
7. *The Golden Apple*—Homer (the *Iliad* and the *Odyssey*)
8. *Fanny*—Marcel Pagnol (the trilogy *Marius*, *Fanny*, and *César*)
9. *Carousel*—Ferenc Molnar (*Liliom*)
10. *Show Boat*—Edna Ferber (*Show Boat*)

Brush Up Your Shakespeare

1. "Two households . . ." —*Romeo and Juliet*
2. "When shall we three . . ." —*Macbeth*
3. "Who's there?" —*Hamlet*
4. "Hence, home . . ." —*Julius Caesar*
5. "I thought the King . . ." —*King Lear*
6. "Nay, but this dotage . . ." —*Antony and Cleopatra*
7. "Now is the winter . . ." —*Richard III*
8. "O for a Muse . . ." —*Henry V*
9. "If music be . . ." —*Twelfth Night*
10. "In sooth, I know not . . ." —*The Merchant of Venice*

O, Ho!
1. Goneril's steward is Oswald in *King Lear*.
2. A fantastic fop is Osric in *Hamlet*.
3. One of the Triumvirs is Octavius (Caesar) in *Julius Caesar*.
4. A general in the service of Venice is Othello in *Othello*.
5. The Duke of Illyria is Orsino in *Twelfth Night*.
6. A rich countess is Olivia in *Twelfth Night*.
7. A son of Sir Rowland de Boys is Orlando in *As You Like It*.
8. A son of Sir Rowland de Boys is also Oliver in *As You Like It*.
9. Daughter to Polonius is Ophelia in *Hamlet*.
10. King of the Fairies is Oberon in *A Midsummer Night's Dream*.

Pop Quiz for English Majors
1. *Her First Roman—Caesar and Cleopatra* by George Bernard Shaw
2. *She Shall Have Music—The Country Wife* by William Wycherley
3. *Ernest in Love—The Importance of Being Earnest* by Oscar Wilde
4. *All in Love—The Rivals* by Richard Brinsley Sheridan
5. *O Marry Me!—She Stoops to Conquer* by Oliver Goldsmith
6. *Darling of the Day—Buried Alive* and *The Great Adventure* by Arnold Bennett
7. *The Chocolate Soldier—Arms and the Man* by George Bernard Shaw
8. *Big River—The Adventures of Huckleberry Finn* by Mark Twain
9. *New Girl in Town—Anna Christie* by Eugene O'Neill
10. *Foxy—Volpone* by Ben Jonson

Famous Last Words
1. "I'm telling you . . ." —*Juno and the Paycock*
2. "I made the last payment . . ." —*Death of a Salesman*
3. "The Curtain Line . . ." —*Camino Real*
4. "Go bid the soldiers shoot." —*Hamlet*
5. "This game is seven card stud." —*A Streetcar Named Desire*
6. "Listen . . . if I . . ." —*The Caretaker*
7. "Yes, let's go . . ." —*Waiting for Godot*
8. "Good God! People don't do such things." —*Hedda Gabler*
9. "I am, George . . ." —*Who's Afraid of Virginia Woolf?*
10. ". . . Nonsense . . . She's going to marry . . ." —*Pygmalion*

It's All Greek to Me

1. *By Jupiter*
2. *The Golden Apple*
3. *Desire Under the Elms*
4. *The Family Reunion*
5. *The Frogs*
6. *Home Sweet Homer*
7. *Xanadu*
8. *Antigone*
9. *Tiger at the Gates* (The French title is *La guerre de Troie n'aura pas lieu*.)
10. *The Happiest Girl in the World*

Critics Crack the Quip

1. "A bad play saved by a bad performance" —Gertrude Lawrence in *Skylark*
2. "She is about as Latin as a New England boiled dinner." —Jane Alexander in *Goodbye, Fidel*
3. "[She] barged down the Nile last night as Cleopatra and sank." —Tallulah Bankhead in *Antony and Cleopatra*
4. "[He] played Mr. Darcy with all the flexibility of a telephone pole." —Farley Granger in *Pride and Prejudice*
5. "Watch [her] run the gamut of emotion from A to B." —Katharine Hepburn in *The Lake*
6. "[She] played the part as though she had not yet signed the contract with the producer." —Maureen Stapleton in *The Emperor's Clothes*
7. " . . . playing Eben like a refugee from a Texas lunatic asylum." —Rip Torn in *Desire Under the Elms*
8. "That which marred his acting was that which marred his character—his colossal, animal selfishness." —Edwin Forrest
9. "Fallen archness" —Helen Hayes as Cleopatra in *Caesar and Cleopatra*
10. "He gives the impression he is a Rotarian pork butcher about to tell a dirty story." —Anthony Hopkins in *Macbeth*

That's Insulting!
1. Sir John Falstaff to Prince Hall (*Henry IV, Part 1*)
2. Dwight Babcock to Mame Dennis Burnside (*Auntie Mame*)
3. Henry Higgins to Eliza Doolittle (*Pygmalion*)
4. Kent to Oswald (*King Lear*)
5. Martha to George (*Who's Afraid of Virginia Woolf?*)
6. Ford to "Mother Prat" (Falstaff in drag) (*The Merry Wives of Windsor*)
7. Stanley Kowalski to Blanche DuBois (*A Streetcar Named Desire*)
8. Prince Hal to Sir John Falstaff (*Henry IV, Part 1*)
9. Linda Loman to Happy and Biff (*Death of a Salesman*)
10. Gwendolen Fairfax to Cecily Cardew (*The Importance of Being Earnest*)

See You in the Funny Papers
1. *Annie*—Harold Gray ("Little Orphan Annie")
2. *Doonesbury*—Garry Trudeau ("Doonesbury")
3. *Li'l Abner*—Al Capp ("Li'l Abner")
4. *You're a Good Man, Charlie Brown*—Charles M. Schulz ("Peanuts")
5. *It's a Bird . . . It's a Plane . . . It's Superman*—Joe Shuster/Jerry Siegel ("Superman")
6. *Spider-Man: Turn Off the Dark*—Stan Lee/Steve Ditko ("Spider-Man")
7. *Little Nemo*—Windsor McCay ("Little Nemo")
8. *Bringing Up Father*—George McManus ("Bringing Up Father" also known as "Maggie and Jiggs")
9. *Mandrake the Magician and the Enchantress*—Lee Falk ("Mandrake the Magician")
10. *Buster Brown*—Richard F. Outcault ("Buster Brown")

Exit Lines

1. Eugene O'Neill
2. Ethel Barrymore
3. George Bernard Shaw
4. Florenz Ziegfeld
5. Edmund Gwenn
6. Laurence Olivier (when a nurse, trying to moisten his lips, carelessly put water in his ear)
7. Tallulah Bankhead
8. Sarah Bernhardt
9. Humphrey Bogart
10. John Wilkes Booth

WHAT'S IN A NAME?

Every Tom, Dick, and Harry—or Tess, Deb, and Harriet—should be able to answer these. Can you?

On a First Name Basis

In column one are first names, which are all titles of musicals. Match them with the proper last names. Some are real persons and others are fictional.

1. *Sophie*	Peters
2. *Fanny*	Whiteside
3. *Jimmy*	Kane
4. *Sherry!*	Tucker
5. *Sally*	Walker
6. *Fiorello!*	LaFlamme
7. *Sunny*	Cabanis
8. *Rose-Marie*	LaGuardia
9. *Irene*	Green
10. *Sugar*	O'Dare

Hello, Sally!

Sally is a popular name for characters in musicals. Can you place the following in the right show?

1. Sally Bowles   *Whoopee*
2. Sally Adams   *Hot Spot*
3. Sally Cato   *Big River*
4. Sally Durant Plummer   *Cabaret*
5. Sally Morgan   *Me and My Girl*
6. Sally Smith   *Oliver!*
7. Sally Hopwinder   *The Who's Tommy*
8. Sally Phelps   *Call Me Madam*
9. Sally Simpson   *Follies*
10. Old Sally   *Mame*

Keeping up with the Joneses

Identify these Broadway figures who are all named Jones.

1. Father of a noted pop singer, he appeared on Broadway in *Roberta* in 1933 but became better known as a singer in such movies as *The Firefly* and *Show Boat*.

   Tommy Lee Jones

2. He replaced Anthony Perkins in the leading role in *Company* during rehearsals, but withdrew from the cast shortly after opening night on Broadway in 1970.

   Tom Jones

3. Son of another actor named Jones, he made his Broadway debut in 1958 in *Sunrise at Campobello,* and is the voice of Darth Vader and of CNN.

    Dean Jones

4. This Jones has appeared on Broadway in more than 14 productions, and also played the president of the United States on TV's *24.*

    Shirley Jones

5. This movie star appeared in one Broadway play, *Portrait of a Lady,* in 1954.

    Margo Jones

6. This director staged the original Broadway productions of two plays by Tennessee Williams.

    Cherry Jones

7. He designed scenery, costumes, or lighting for 56 Broadway productions from 1915 to 1951.

    James Earl Jones

8. She appeared in the title role of the 1968 musical *Maggie Flynn,* which also featured her husband.

    Jennifer Jones

9. He is the lyricist of *110 in the Shade* and *I Do! I Do!*

    Allan Jones

10. He appeared as Stephen Dedalus with Zero Mostel as Leopold Bloom in the 1974 production of *Ulysses in Nighttown,* and later achieved fame in movies.

    Robert Edmond Jones

Has Anybody Here Seen Kelly?

Match the character named Kelly with the play or musical in which he or she appears.

1. Bill Kelly is a stunt pilot who enters a dance marathon.

   The Gang's All Here

2. Hop Kelly is a daredevil busboy who jumps off the Brooklyn Bridge (a character based on the real-life Steve Brodie).

   Harvey

3. Ragtime Kelly is the pianist in Gus Jordan's Suicide Hall.

   It's a Wise Child

4. Jack Kelly is a newsboy who enlists the help of President Theodore Roosevelt.

   Chicago

5. Ruth Kelly is a nurse at Dr. Chumley's sanitarium.

   Kelly

6. Velma Kelly is accused of murdering her husband and her sister, whom she found in bed together.

   Little Nellie Kelly

7. John Kelly is a New York City police captain with an attractive daughter.

   The Musical Comedy Murders of 1940

8. Michael Kelly is an undercover cop who is kidnapped and disappears into a mansion's secret passage.

   Steel Pier

9. Doctor Indian Ike Kelly is the dispenser of cure-alls in a medicine show.

   Diamond Lil

10. Cool Kelly is an iceman who wants the woman he marries to be "one hundred per cent pure."

    Newsies the Musical

Literal Translations

In the first column are literal translations into English from various foreign languages of the last names of Broadway notables. Match them with the correct last names—and provide first names for them. The person's first initial and the language of origin (not necessarily the ethnic origin of the person) are hints.

1. J. Cloak (Italian)	Banderas
2. R. Brown (Spanish)	Loewe
3. J. Knight (German)	Kern
4. H. Left-Handed (Italian)	Pinza
5. F. Lion (German)	Mantello
6. J. Tailor (German)	Blitzstein
7. E. Tongs (Italian)	Moreno
8. A. Flags (Spanish)	Mancini
9. J. Nucleus (German)	Schneider
10. M. Lightning Stone (German)	Ritter

Initial That!

What do the initials in the names of these theatre personalities stand for?

1. S. Epatha Merkerson
   * ✯ Samantha
   * ✯ Sharon
   * ✯ Sigourney
   * ✯ [Nothing at all]

Continued on next page

2. E. G. Marshall
   ★ Everett Grunz
   ★ Egbert Glatzmeier
   ★ Eduardo Gonzalez
   ★ Edmund Gwenn

3. George C. Scott
   ★ Cadwallader
   ★ Christopher
   ★ Campbell
   ★ Cavalier

4. George S. Kaufman
   ★ Shakespeare
   ★ Simon
   ★ Samuel
   ★ Sylvester

5. George S. Irving
   ★ Samson
   ★ Siddartha
   ★ Stephen
   ★ Shelasky

6. George M. Cohan
   ★ Michael
   ★ Murgatroyd
   ★ Montmorency
   ★ Moskowitz

7. Lee J. Cobb
   * Jehoshaphat
   * Jacoby
   * Jennifer
   * Jupiter

8. F. Murray Abraham
   * Fahrid
   * Florenz
   * Frederick
   * [Nothing at all]

9. BD Wong
   * Benedict Dumbledore
   * Bo Diddley
   * Bradley Darryl
   * Bob Dylan

10. N. Richard Nash
    * Nicholas
    * Nathan
    * Nebuchadnezzar
    * Nobody

Tony! Tony!

Name these "Tonys" who have won or have been nominated for Tony Awards.

1. Tony who won twice for Best Play, for *Angels in America: Perestroika* and *Angels in America: Millennium Approaches*, and was nominated for two others.

   Tony Roberts

2. Tony who won Best Scenic Design three times: for *Guys and Dolls*, *House of Blue Leaves*, and *Pippin* —and was nominated for thirteen other Tony Awards.

   Tony Shalhoub

3. Tony who was nominated Best Actor in *Oh, Captain!*

   Tony Straiges

4. Tony who was nominated Best Actor in *How Now, Dow Jones* and as Best Featured Actor in *Play It Again, Sam*.

   Tony Lo Bianco

5. Tony who was nominated for Best Choreography and Best Direction for *Joseph and the Amazing Technicolor Dreamcoat*.

   Antoinette Perry

6. Tony who was nominated as Best Actor in a Leading Role for *On the Town*.

   Tony Tanner

7. Tony who was nominated as Best Featured Actor in *Golden Boy* and *Conversations with My Father*, and for Best Actor in *Act One*.

   Tony Kushner

8. Tony who was nominated as Best Actor in *A View From the Bridge*.

   Tony Randall

9. Tony who won for Best Scenic Design for *Sunday in the Park with George*—and was nominated for one other Tony Award.

   Tony Walton

10. Tony for whom the Tony Awards are named.

    Tony Yazbeck

B. & B.

Identify these theatre notables, whose first and last names begin with the letter "B."

1.	B. B. who was Mrs. Florenz Ziegfeld Jr.	Betty Buckley
2.	B. B. who was Broadway's first Grizabella in *Cats*.	Barbara Bel Geddes
3.	A composer and lyricist, this B.B. wrote songs for a series of revues with his name in the title.	Busby Berkeley
4.	Daughter of a noted designer, this B.B. originated the role of Maggie in *Cat on a Hot Tin Roof*.	Brenda Braxton
5.	B. B. who famously played Lady Bracknell in *The Importance of Being Earnest*.	Billy Barnes
6.	Among this B. B.'s plays are *The Quare Fellow* and *Borstal Boy*.	Bob Balaban
7.	The original Danny Zuko in *Grease*, this B. B. later starred on Broadway in *Nick & Nora*.	Brian Bedford
8.	This B. B.'s Broadway credits include *Dreamgirls*, *Cats*, *Legs Diamond*, *Jelly's Last Jam*, *Smokey Joe's Café*, and *Chicago*.	Billie Burke
9.	B. B. who has acted on Broadway, opposite Glenn Close in *A Delicate Balance*, in films, and on TV; directed movies and TV; produced movies; and written children's books.	Barry Bostwick
10.	After choreographing almost twenty Broadway shows in the 1920s, this B. B. had an illustrious film career, then returned to Broadway one final time in 1971.	Brendan Behan

Standing Pat

Match the descriptions with the proper "Patricks."

1. A character who ages from a little boy to a young man in a play and a musical—and the author of the underlying novel on which those dramatic works are based.

2. Correspondent with George Bernard Shaw, on whose letters *Dear Liar* was based.

3. Known best as a dancing movie actor, appeared in revivals of *Grease* and in *Chicago* during their Broadway runs.

4. Title character in *The Loud Red Patrick*, a 1956 Broadway play by John Boruff, based on a collection of stories by Ruth McKenney.

5. Doogie Howser on TV, Hedwig on Broadway, and host of the Oscars, the Emmys, and four Tony Award shows.

6. Noted Shakespearean actor, and the Green Goblin in *Spider Man: Turn Off the Dark*.

7. Author of the Pulitzer Prize-winning *Teahouse of the August Moon*; also wrote *The Hasty Heart*, *The Curious Savage*, and the screenplay of *Love Is a Many-Splendored Thing*.

Patrick Henry

Patrick MacNee

Patrick Flannigan

Neil Patrick Harris

Patrick Dennis

Patrick Swayze

Mrs. Patrick Campbell

8. A character in Percy Mackaye's 1920 play   Patrick Page
   George Washington, along with Martha
   Washington, Alexander Hamilton, Betsy
   Ross, and Tom Paine.

9. Known as TV's John Steed, opposite   John Patrick
   Diana Rigg in *The Avengers*; replaced   Shanley
   Anthony Quayle in *Sleuth* on Broadway.

10. Author of *Doubt;* also known for the   John Patrick
    screenplay of *Moonstruck*.

Anyone for Anagrams?

Rearrange the letters in these anagrams to yield the names of well-known Broadway stars. As an aid in sorting them out, the initials of the stars are given in parentheses.

1. POTENTIAL UP (P.L.)
2. ENTER BESPATTERED (B.P.)
3. SANG 'LA' URBANELY (A.L.)
4. HEY, NAB DINNER (B.D.)
5. COYLY NICEST (C.T.)
6. DOMINANT HUFFS (D.H.)
7. MERITED THROWBACK (M.B.)
8. ENTANGLED WHIZ, SON (D.W.)
9. CAN-CAN GIRL, HON (C.C.)
10. CHURLISH TEMPER ROMP (C.P.)

The Name's the Same

Identify these Broadway performers who share a first name with other actors:

1. Ethel, who sang "Broadway Baby" in the original production of *Follies*:
   ★ Merman
   ★ Barrymore
   ★ Shutta
   ★ Waters

2. Alan, who was Inspector Clouseau in one film, made in 1968:
   ★ Alda
   ★ Arkin
   ★ Bates
   ★ Rickman

3. John, who won Tony Awards as Best Actor in a Musical in 1975 and 1978:
   ★ Cullum
   ★ McMartin
   ★ Lithgow
   ★ Schneider

4. Helen, who appeared with James Stewart in a 1970 Broadway revival of *Harvey*:
   ★ Hayes
   ★ Mirren
   ★ Morgan
   ★ Traubel

5. Carol, who made her Broadway debut when she was 19 as an understudy in the musical *Let's Face It*:
   - ☆ Lawrence
   - ☆ Burnett
   - ☆ Channing
   - ☆ Swarbrick

6. Martin, who played Cassius in a production of *Julius Caesar* that also featured Orson Welles, George Coulouris, and Joseph Cotten:
   - ☆ Short
   - ☆ Gabel
   - ☆ Sheen
   - ☆ Balsam

7. Alfred, who played Benedick opposite Katharine Hepburn's Beatrice in *Much Ado About Nothing* and Claudius in Richard Burton's *Hamlet*:
   - ☆ Drake
   - ☆ Molina
   - ☆ Lunt
   - ☆ Ryder

8. Katharine, who was married to director Guthrie McClintic:
   - ☆ Hepburn
   - ☆ Cornell
   - ☆ Houghton
   - ☆ McPhee

Continued on next page

9. Laurence, who portrayed Spock's half-brother in *Star Trek V: The Final Frontier*:
   * ★ Luckinbill
   * ★ Harvey
   * ★ Olivier
   * ★ Fishburne

10. Brian, who won a Tony Award for *Kiss Me, Kate*:
   * ★ Murray
   * ★ Bedford
   * ★ D'Arcy James
   * ★ Stokes Mitchell

Try Them on for Size

Match these descriptions of characters with their names, all of which include a word denoting size, and the plays or musicals in which they appear.

1.	She warns Officer Lockstock that a bad title "could kill a show pretty good."	Little Buttercup	*Dreamgirls*
2.	He says, "There ain't nothin' more powerful than the odor of mendacity."	Big Deal	*Hairspray*
3.	He sings "Takin' the Long Way Home" 'cause his "baby don't live there no more."	Li'l Abner Yokum	*Cat on a Hot Tin Roof*
4.	He tells Lieutenant Brannigan he's a scoutmaster from East Cicero, Illinois.	Fatso O'Rear	*August: Osage County*

5. With his pal Hubie Cram and two others, he starts a jukebox business and sings "It's Legitimate."   Little Charles Aiken   *Urinetown*

6. Also known as Mrs. Cripps, she is "the rosiest, roundest, and reddest beauty in all Spithead."   Little Inez Stubbs   *West Side Story*

7. He has an affair with his cousin, Ivy Weston, who turns out to be his half sister.   Big Daddy Pollitt   *L'il Abner*

8. He is pursued by Daisy Mae Scragg.   Tiny Joe Dixon   *H. M. S. Pinafore*

9. Along with Snowboy, Gee-Tar, and A-Rab, he is one of the Jets.   Big Jule   *Do Re Mi*

10. Seaweed's sister; she is turned away from the Corny Collins Show along with Tracy Turnblad.   Little Sally   *Guys and Dolls*

WHAT'S IN A NAME?

ANSWERS

On a First Name Basis
1. *Sophie* Tucker
2. *Fanny* Cabanis
3. *Jimmy* Walker
4. *Sherry* (Sheridan) Whiteside
5. *Sally* Green
6. *Fiorello* LaGuardia
7. *Sunny* Peters
8. *Rose-Marie* LaFlamme
9. *Irene* O'Dare
10. *Sugar* Kane

Hello, Sally!
1. Sally Bowles—*Cabaret*
2. Sally Adams—*Call Me Madam*
3. Sally Cato—*Mame*
4. Sally Durant Plummer—*Follies*
5. Sally Morgan—*Whoopee*
6. Sally Smith—*Me and My Girl*
7. Sally Hopwinder—*Hot Spot*
8. Sally Phelps—*Big River*
9. Sally Simpson—*The Who's Tommy*
10. Old Sally—*Oliver!*

Keeping up with the Joneses
1. Allan Jones
2. Dean Jones
3. James Earl Jones
4. Cherry Jones
5. Jennifer Jones

Continued on next page

6. Margo Jones (directed Tennessee Williams's *Summer and Smoke* in 1948 and codirected *The Glass Menagerie* in 1945)
7. Robert Edmond Jones
8. Shirley Jones (her husband was Jack Cassidy)
9. Tom Jones
10. Tommy Lee Jones (billed as Tom Lee Jones)

Has Anybody Here Seen Kelly?

1. Bill Kelly—*Steel Pier*
2. Hop Kelly—*Kelly*
3. Ragtime Kelly—*Diamond Lil*
4. Jack Kelly—*Newsies the Musical*
5. Ruth Kelly—*Harvey*
6. Velma Kelly—*Chicago*
7. John Kelly—*Little Nellie Kelly*
8. Michael Kelly—*The Musical Comedy Murders of 1940*
9. Doctor Indian Ike Kelly—*The Gang's All Here*
10. Cool Kelly—*It's a Wise Child*

Literal Translations

1. Cloak is (Joe) Mantello in Italian.
2. Brown is (Rita) Moreno in Spanish.
3. Knight is (John) Ritter in German.
4. Left-Handed is (Henry) Mancini in Italian.
5. Lion is (Frederick) Loewe in German.
6. Tailor is (John) Schneider in German.
7. Tongs is (Ezio) Pinza in Italian.
8. Flags is (Antonio) Banderas in Spanish.
9. Nucleus is (Jerome) Kern in German.
10. Lightning Stone is (Marc) Blitzstein in German.

Initial That!

1. S. Epatha Merkerson—originally Sharon, but now S. is her legal first name
2. E. G. Marshall—Everett Grunz—his real full name
3. George C. Scott—Campbell
4. George S. Kaufman—Simon
5. George S. Irving—Shelasky (His full name is George Irving Shelasky.)

6. George M. Cohan—Michael
7. Lee J. Cobb—Jacoby (His real full name is Leo Jacoby.)
8. F. Murray Abraham—Either Fahrid, Frederick, or [Nothing at all]. (Many sources maintain that Abraham's birth name was Fahrid Murray Abraham, but he has been quoted in a Los Angeles publication as saying that is not true, and that for his stage name he added the F., which does not actually stand for anything, in honor of his father, whose name was Frederick.)
9. BD Wong—Bradley Darryl
10. N. Richard Nash—Nathan (His real name is Nathan Richard Nasbaum.)

Tony! Tony!

1. Tony Kushner, who won two Tony Awards, was also nominated for Best Book and Best Score for *Caroline, or Change*, but lost to Jeff Whitty for Best Book and to Robert Lopez and Jeff Marx for Best Score, all for *Avenue Q.*
2. Tony Walton won three Tony Awards and was nominated for thirteen others for shows including *The Apple Tree, Anything Goes, Chicago, Grand Hotel, She Loves Me, Steel Pier,* and *The Will Rogers Follies.*
3. Tony Randall was nominated as Best Actor in *Oh, Captain!* but lost to Robert Preston in *The Music Man.*
4. Tony Roberts was nominated for Best Actor in *How Now, Dow Jones,* but lost to Robert Goulet in *The Happy Time,* and for Best Featured Actor in *Play It Again, Sam,* but lost to Al Pacino in *Does a Tiger Wear a Necktie?*
5. Tony Tanner was nominated for two Tony Awards for *Joseph and the Amazing Technicolor Dreamcoat,* but lost Best Direction to Tommy Tune for *Nine* and Best Choreography to Michael Bennett and Michael Peters for *Dreamgirls.*
6. Tony Yazbeck was nominated as Best Actor for *On the Town,* but the Tony Award was won by Michael Cerveris in *Fun Home.*
7. Tony Shalhoub was nominated for Best Featured Actor in *Conversations with My Father,* but lost to Larry Fishburne in *Two Trains Running;* and in *Golden Boy,* but lost to Courtney B. Vance in *Lucky Guy;* and for Best Actor in *Act One,* but lost to Bryan Cranston in *All the Way.*
8. Tony Lo Bianco was nominated as Best Actor in *A View from the Bridge,* but lost to Harvey Fierstein in *Torch Song Trilogy.*
9. Tony Straiges won the Tony Award for *Sunday in the Park with George* and was nominated for *Into the Woods,* but lost to Maria Björnson for *The Phantom of the Opera.*
10. Antoinette Perry was an actress, director, cofounder of the American Theatre Wing, and the namesake of the Tony Awards.

B. & B.
1. Billie Burke
2. Betty Buckley
3. Billy Barnes
4. Barbara Bel Geddes (daughter of designer Norman Bel Geddes)
5. Brian Bedford
6. Brendan Behan
7. Barry Bostwick
8. Brenda Braxton
9. Bob Balaban
10. Busby Berkeley

Standing Pat
1. Patrick Dennis (a character in both *Auntie Mame* and *Mame*, both based on the novel *Auntie Mame* by Patrick Dennis, pen name of Edward Everett Tanner III)
2. Mrs. Patrick Campbell
3. Patrick Swayze
4. Patrick Flannigan
5. Neil Patrick Harris
6. Patrick Page
7. John Patrick
8. Patrick Henry
9. Patrick MacNee
10. John Patrick Shanley

Anyone for Anagrams?
1. Patti LuPone
2. Bernadette Peters
3. Angela Lansbury
4. Brian Dennehy
5. Cicely Tyson
6. Dustin Hoffman
7. Matthew Broderick
8. Denzel Washington
9. Carol Channing
10. Christopher Plummer

The Name's the Same

1. Ethel Shutta (*Follies*, in 1971, was at the Winter Garden Theatre, the same venue at which Shutta had made her Broadway debut in *The Passing Show* in 1922.)
2. Alan Arkin (Peter Sellers declined the part following his success in *A Shot in the Dark*. Sellers resumed the role in 1975 with *The Return of the Pink Panther*.)
3. John Cullum (in 1975 for *Shenandoah* and in 1978 for *On the Twentieth Century*)
4. Helen Hayes
5. Carol Channing (as Eve Arden's understudy. Twenty-five years later, Arden stepped into Channing's role in a road company of *Hello, Dolly!*)
6. Martin Gabel
7. Alfred Drake
8. Katharine Cornell
9. Laurence Luckinbill
10. Brian Stokes Mitchell

Try Them on for Size

1. Little Sally in *Urinetown*
2. Big Daddy Pollitt in *Cat on a Hot Tin Roof*
3. Tiny Joe Dixon in *Dreamgirls*
4. Big Jule in *Guys and Dolls*
5. Fatso O'Rear in *Do Re Mi*
6. Little Buttercup in *H. M. S. Pinafore*
7. Little Charles Aiken in *August: Osage County*
8. Li'l Abner Yokum in *Li'l Abner*
9. Big Deal in *West Side Story*
10. Little Inez Stubbs in *Hairspray*

VII

WINING AND DINING

If you're a fan of fine food and beverages, then you'll dig in with gusto to these questions, which have to do with eating and drinking. Come and get it!

Bon Appétit!

Match the descriptions with the titles of these plays and musicals, each of which includes the name of a meal—which you must supply.

1. George S. Kaufman and Moss Hart's comedy has a character modeled on critic Alexander Woollcott.

   _____*At Eight*

2. Lee Kalcheim's play features two characters similar to the husband-wife radio team of Tex and Jinx.

   Before _____

3. A musical by Noël Coward and Harry Kurnitz based on Terrence Rattigan's *The Sleeping Prince.*

   _____*at Tiffany's*

4. Eugene O'Neill's gloomy one-act play has two characters—one of whom has no lines and is seen only when his hand reaches onstage.

   _____*with Les and Bess*

Continued on next page

5. This drama by George S. Kaufman and Edna Ferber was made into a movie with a cast that included both Lionel and John Barrymore.

The Long Christmas _____

6. Thornton Wilder's one-act play takes place over ninety years in a family dining room.

_____ Hour

7. This musical by Edward Albee and Bob Merrill was closed by its producer, David Merrick, after four previews rather than subject the public "to an excruciatingly boring evening."

Sing for Your _____

8. Gilda Radner and Sam Waterston starred in this comedy by Jean Kerr.

The Man Who Came to _____

9. This play by William Inge was Paul Newman's Broadway debut.

The Girl Who Came to _____

10. This 1939 W.P.A. Federal Theatre musical revue—not by Rodgers and Hart—had the same title as a Rodgers and Hart song written the previous year.

_____

Soup's On!

Choose the right food to fill in the blanks in these dialogue excerpts from plays and musicals.

1. Grumio: "What say you to a piece of _____ and mustard?"

Cake

2. Madame Desmermortes: "Oh, Mr. Messerschmann, my butler tells me you only eat _____?"

Duck

3. Galileo: "Somebody who knows me sent me a
   _____. I still enjoy eating."   Bacon

4. Grand Duchess: ". . . If they have got sour   Cornflakes
   cream and pot cheese, I will make you some
   _____!"

5. Higgins: "It's awfully good _____. I wonder   Noodles
   where Mrs. Pearce gets it?"

6. Mrs. Gibbs: "_____'ll be ready in a minute.   Chicken
   Sit down and drink your coffee."

7. Mrs. Miller: "He's been eating bluefish for   Beef
   years—only I tell him each time it's _____."

8. Mrs. Levi: ". . . I think it would be nice just   Blintzes
   this once if you order a real nice dinner. I
   guess you can afford it . . . A _____ wouldn't
   hurt."

9. Johnny: ". . . The way I feel about you I feel   Weakfish
   a _____ à l'Orange Flambée with a purée of
   water chestnuts coming on!"

10. Meg: ". . . Too tired to eat your breakfast, I   Goose
    suppose? Now you eat up those _____ like a
    good boy. Go on."

A Night on the Town

Which musicals feature these night spots?

1.	Kit Kat Klub	*Goldilocks*
2.	Hot Box Club	*Paint Your Wagon*
3.	Bal du Paradis	*The Pajama Game*
4.	Trocadero Night Club	*Cabaret*
5.	Fat Cat Roof Garden	*Show Boat*
6.	Seminole-Ritz Hotel Night Club	*Sweet Charity*
7.	Hernando's Hideaway	*Sugar*
8.	Mme. Delphine's Night Club	*Guys and Dolls*
9.	Fandango Ballroom	*Can-Can*
10.	Jake's Palace	*Maytime*

Grocery List

The missing word in each of the following titles of Broadway plays and musicals is an item that might appear on a grocery shopping list. The items are listed in random order in the second column. Note: one food item is used twice.

1. *The _____ Soldier*
2. *_____ Babies*
3. *The _____ Is Green*
4. *Time Out for _____*
5. *Big _____, Little _____*
6. *Animal _____*
7. *_____ and Sympathy*
8. *There's a Girl in My _____*
9. *The _____ and _____ Man*
10. *A Taste of _____*

Tea, Chocolate, Sugar, Butter, Fish, Corn, Honey, Egg, Crackers, Soup, Ginger

High Spirits

Match these dialogue excerpts about alcoholic beverages with the plays or musicals from which they come.

1. "Gin was mother's milk to her."   *Juno and the Paycock*

2. "If I had a thousand sons, the first humane principle I would teach them should be to forswear thin potations and to addict themselves to sack."   *The Cocktail Party*

3. "Stir, never shake. Bruises the gin."   *Guys and Dolls*

4. "Women drink more often than you think. Not many drink openly like me. Most of them hide it—and it's almost always vodka or cognac."   *Pygmalion*

5. "As I was drinkin' gin and water, And me bein' the One-Eyed Riley . . . "   *Henry IV, Part 2*

6. " . . . this one evening this boy went with us, and we ordered our drinks, and when it came his turn, he said . . . I'll have bergin . . . . give me some bergin, please . . . bergin and water."   *Mister Roberts*

7. " . . . What am I looking around here for? Oh, yes—liquor! We've had so much excitement around here this evening that I *am* boxed out of my mind! Here's something. Southern Comfort! What is that, I wonder?"   *Auntie Mame*

Continued on next page

8. " . . . I said 'Ain't there anything in the world that'll make you come out to the ship with me?' And she said, 'Yes, there is, one thing and one thing only—a good stiff drink of Scotch.'"   *Who's Afraid of Virginia Woolf?*

9. "Dulce de Leche. What's in it besides milk?"   *The Sea Gull*
— "Oh, sugar, and—sort of native flavoring."
— "What's the name of the flavoring?"
— "Bacardi."

10. "Well, what about a bottle o' stout or a dhrop o' whisky?"   *A Streetcar Named Desire*
— "A bottle o' stout ud be a little too heavy for me stummock afther me tay . . . A-a-ah, I'll thry the ball o' malt."

Fruit Salad

Complete and match these titles of these plays and musicals that contain the name of a fruit.

1. The author of this Russian play considered it a comedy, but the director of the initial production treated it as a tragedy.   _____*Blossoms*

2. This political satire about the fictional English King Magnus and Prime Minister Proteus, although originally written in English, was premiered in Polish in Warsaw.   *The* _____ *Tree*

3. This operetta introduced "A Kiss in the Dark."

   Top _____

4. This play's title is from a poem by Langston Hughes.

   The _____ *Cart*

5. Critic Brooks Atkinson described this play about Noah and the ark as "the story of mankind living out its destiny under the benevolent eye of God."

   The _____ *Orchard*

6. A British play about a dissatisfied insurance salesman, it was said by many critics to be too much like *Death of a Salesman*.

   The _____

7. This musical consists of three unrelated one-act musicals that can be presented in any order.

   A _____ *in the Sun*

8. The star of this musical won a Tony for his performance in a role that he based on TV star Milton Berle.

   The _____ *of Wrath*

9. Tony Award winner as Best Play, it is based on a Pulitzer Prize–winning novel by an author who also won the Nobel Prize for literature.

   Flowering _____

10. By Irving Berlin and George S. Kaufman, this musical was the second Broadway show for the Marx Brothers.

    The Flowering _____

WINING AND DINING

ANSWERS

Bon Appetit!
1. *The Man Who Came to Dinner*
2. *Breakfast with Les and Bess* (Tex McCrary and Jinx Falkenberg had a morning interview show called "Hi, Jinx" on NBC's New York radio station.)
3. *The Girl Who Came to Supper*
4. *Before Breakfast* (It has only two characters—Mrs. Rowland and her husband Alfred, whose hand is seen briefly when he reaches onstage for a bowl of hot water.)
5. *Dinner at Eight*
6. *The Long Christmas Dinner*
7. *Breakfast at Tiffany's*
8. *Lunch Hour*
9. *Picnic*
10. *Sing for Your Supper* (It was the title of a 1939 musical revue—as well as a Rodgers and Hart song written for *The Boys from Syracuse* in 1938; it was also the title of a 1941 romantic film comedy.)

Soup's On!
1. "What say you to a piece of beef and mustard?" (*The Taming of the Shrew*)
2. "Oh, Mr. Messerschmann, my butler tells me you only eat noodles?" (*Ring Round the Moon*)
3. "Somebody who knows me sent me a goose. I still enjoy eating." (*Galileo*)
4. ". . . If they have got sour cream and pot cheese, I will make you some blintzes!" (*You Can't Take It with You*)
5. "It's awfully good cake. I wonder where Mrs. Pearce gets it?" (*My Fair Lady*)
6. "Bacon'll be ready in a minute. Sit down and drink your coffee." (*Our Town*)

Continued on next page

7. "He's been eating bluefish for years—only I tell him each time it's weakfish." (*Ah, Wilderness!*)
8. ". . . I think it would be nice just this once if you order a real nice dinner. I guess you can afford it . . . A chicken wouldn't hurt." (*The Matchmaker*)
9. ". . . The way I feel about you I feel a Duck à l'Orange Flambée with a purée of water chestnuts coming on!" (*Frankie and Johnny in the Clair de Lune*)
10. ". . . Too tired to eat your breakfast, I suppose? Now you eat up those cornflakes like a good boy. Go on." (*The Birthday Party*)

A Night on the Town
1. Kit Kat Klub—*Cabaret*
2. Hot Box Club—*Guys and Dolls*
3. Bal du Paradis—*Can-Can*
4. Trocadero Night Club—*Show Boat*
5. Fat Cat Roof Garden—*Goldilocks*
6. Seminole-Ritz Hotel Night Club—*Sugar* (a.k.a. *Some Like It Hot*)
7. Hernando's Hideaway—*The Pajama Game*
8. Mme. Delphine's Night Club—*Maytime*
9. Fandango Ballroom—*Sweet Charity*
10. Jake's Palace—*Paint Your Wagon*

Grocery List
1. *The Chocolate Soldier*
2. *Sugar Babies*
3. *The Corn Is Green*
4. *Time Out for Ginger*
5. *Big Fish, Little Fish*
6. *Animal Crackers*
7. *Tea and Sympathy*
8. *There's a Girl in My Soup*
9. *The Butter and Egg Man*
10. *A Taste of Honey*

High Spirits

1. "Gin was mother's milk . . ." —Eliza in *Pygmalion*
2. "If I had a thousand sons . . ." —Falstaff in *Henry IV, Part 2*
3. "Stir, never shake . . ." —Young Patrick in *Auntie Mame* (and *Mame*)
4. "Women drink more often . . ." —Masha in *The Sea Gull*
5. "As I was drinkin' gin and water . . ." —Unidentified Guest (Sir Henry Harcourt Reilly) in *The Cocktail Party*
6. ". . . this one evening . . ." —George in *Who's Afraid of Virginia Woolf?*
7. "What am I looking around here for?" —Blanche in *A Streetcar Named Desire*
8. "I said 'Ain't there anything . . .'"—Ensign Pulver in *Mister Roberts*
9. "Dulce de Leche . . ." —Sarah and Sky in *Guys and Dolls*
10. "Well, what about a bottle 'o stout . . ." —Jack Boyle and Mrs. Madigan in *Juno and the Paycock*

Fruit Salad

1. *The Cherry Orchard* (by Anton Chekhov who disagreed with director Konstantin Stanislavsky)
2. *The Apple Cart* (by George Bernard Shaw)
3. *Orange Blossoms* (by Victor Herbert, Buddy DeSylva, and Fred De Gresac)
4. *A Raisin in the Sun* (by Lorraine Hansberry, with title from Langston Hughes's poem "Harlem")
5. *The Flowering Peach* (by Clifford Odets)
6. *Flowering Cherry* (by Robert Bolt)
7. *The Apple Tree* (Jerry Bock and Sheldon Harnick's adaptation of three stories: Mark Twain's *The Diary of Adam and Eve,* Frank R. Stockton's *The Lady or the Tiger?* and Jules Feiffer's *Passionella*)
8. *Top Banana* (Phil Silvers based his character on Milton Berle)
9. *The Grapes of Wrath* (by Frank Galati, based on John Steinbeck's novel of the same name)
10. *The Cocoanuts* (in 1925)

VIII

HEAVEN HELP US!

Bow your head and get down on your knees. These quizzes all have to do with the deity, clergy, churches, and matters of religion. Amen!

In God, We Trust

Characters in musicals sometimes find it helpful to communicate in song with the Deity. Match these songs, all of which are addressed to God, with the musicals in which they appear.

1. "If I Were a Rich Man"	*Miss Saigon*
2. "Why Me?"	*The Civil War*
3. "Gethsemane"	*Sister Act*
4. "Save the People"	*Fiddler on the Roof*
5. "Miracle Song"	*Two by Two*
6. "How Come?"	*Jesus Christ Superstar*
7. "Father, How Long?"	*The Roar of the Greasepaint —The Smell of the Crowd*
8. "Bless Our Show"	*Children's Letters to God*
9. "Why God Why?"	*Godspell*
10. "Who Can I Turn To?"	*Altar Boyz*

Men of the Cloth (I)

In the left column are clergymen who are characters in the plays or musicals in the right column. Match the shows and the reverends.

1. Bishop of Bathingstoke	*Romeo and Juliet*
2. Rev. John Witherspoon	*The Importance of Being Earnest*
3. Reverend Mr. Crisparkle	*A Man for All Seasons*
4. Cardinal Wolsey	*Ghosts*
5. Pastor Manders	*Richard III*
6. Rev. Tooker	*Shadowlands*
7. Reverend Canon Chasuble, D.D.	*1776*
8. Rev. Harry Harrington	*Cat on a Hot Tin Roof*
9. Cardinal Bourchier	*The Mystery of Edwin Drood*
10. Friar Laurence	*Jekyll & Hyde*

And Then There Were Nuns

Match the nuns with the musicals or plays in which they appear.

1. The Mother Abbess, Sister Berthe, Sister Margaretta, Sister Sophia	*Execution of Justice*
2. Mother Superior, Mary Patrick, Mary Robert, Mary Lazarus	*Agnes of God*
3. Sister Mary Regina, Sister Robert Anne, Sister Mary Hubert, Sister Mary Amnesia, Sister Mary Leo	*The Devils*
4. Sister Boom Boom	*The Sound of Music*
5. Sister Aloysius, Sister James	*The Runner Stumbles*
6. Mother Miriam Ruth	*Sister Act*

7. Sister Jean of the Angels, Sister Claire, Sister Gabrielle, Sister Louise *Nunsense*

8. Sister Lee, Sister Melanie, Sister Monica Marie, Sister Helen *Doubt*

9. Sister Mary Ignatius *Do Black Patent Leather Shoes Really Reflect Up?*

10. Sister Rita *Sister Mary Ignatius Explains It All For You*

Men of the Cloth (II)

Match the clergy with the plays or musicals in which they appear.

1. Reverend Winemiller *Anything Goes*
2. Rev. Dr. Harper *The Night of the Iguana*
3. Rabbi Chemelwitz *Leap of Faith*
4. Reverend Dr. Moon *Rain* or *Sadie Thompson*
5. Rev. Alfred Davidson *Arsenic and Old Lace*
6. High Lama *Angels in America*
7. "Reverend" Jonas Nightingale *Summer and Smoke*
8. Monsignor O'Hara *Kismet*
9. Imam of the Mosque *Shangri-La*
10. Reverend T. Lawrence Shannon *Sister Act*

Starring God

God is a character in each of these plays and musicals. Can you identify them?

1. In the opening scene of this fifteenth-century play, God laments how "all creatures be to me unkind" and sends Death to summon the hero to give a reckoning of his life.

   The Happiest Girl in the World

2. In this comedy, purportedly written "by God with David Javerbaum," God says, "Even I consider it bizarre that the last words on children's lips before they go to sleep would address the prospect of their own premature death."

   J. B.

3. John Cleese was the recorded voice of God in the Broadway production of this musical.

   Children of Eden

4. Although based on the Greek comedy *Lysistrata* by Aristophanes, most of the deities in this musical, including Jupiter, have Roman names.

   An Act of God

5. The deity in this play by Marc Connelly was known as "The Lord" in the first Broadway production, "De Lawd" in the movie version, and simply as "God" in a Broadway revival.

   The Creation of the World and Other Business

6. In the Broadway production of this play, Raymond Massey played a character called "Mr. Zuss," who represents God.

   Everyman

7. This musical, in which Zeus appears, *Amphytrion 38*
   was nominated for a Tony for Best
   Musical but lost to *In the Heights.*

8. In this musical by Stephen Schwartz *Spamalot*
   and John Caird, God is known simply
   as "Father."

9. The 1937 Broadway production *Xanadu*
   of this comedy by Jean Giraudoux
   starred Alfred Lunt as Jupiter.

10. Critic Clive Barnes's mixed review of *The Green Pastures*
    this play by Arthur Miller said God
    was portrayed "as a benevolent and
    avuncular paranoiac madly hungry for
    praise."

Men of the Cloth (III)

Match the clergy with the plays or musicals in which they appear.

1.	Reverend John Hale	*Candida*
2.	Rev. Jeremiah Brown	*The Marriage of Bette and Boo*
3.	Father De Leo	*Doubt*
4.	Reverend Samuel Gardner	*Inherit the Wind*
5.	Cardinal Barberini	*The Crucible*
6.	Father Ambrose	*The Rose Tattoo*
7.	Father Flynn	*Late Nite Catechism*
8.	Father Martinez	*The Waltz of the Toreadors*
9.	Reverend Alexander Mill	*Galileo*
10.	Father Donnally	*Mrs. Warren's Profession*

Get Me to the Church on Time
Match the places of worship with the plays or musicals in which they are featured.

1.	Nonnberg Abbey	*Pygmalion* and *My Fair Lady*
2.	Canterbury Cathedral	*Sister Act*
3.	Save-A-Soul Mission	*Doubt*
4.	Chapel at Arles	*Elmer Gantry*
5.	St. Katherine's, San Francisco	*Purlie Victorious*
6.	St. George's, Hanover Square	*The Sound of Music*
7.	Big Bethel Church	*Candida*
8.	St. Nicholas Church, the Bronx	*Guys and Dolls*
9.	Atlantic Ocean Tabernacle	*Pippin*
10.	St. Dominic's, Victoria Park	*Murder in the Cathedral*

Things That You're Liable to Read in the Bible
Identify these plays and musicals, which are all based on material in the Bible. One extra point if you can identify which Biblical books are the sources.

1.	This play by Archibald MacLeish, about a millionaire businessman whose children are all killed and whose property is destroyed, won the Pulitzer Prize and the Tony Award.	*The Diary of Adam and Eve*
2.	This play by Clifford Odets has characters representing a Lion, a Fawn, and a Goat.	*Salome*
3.	This musical by Tim Rice and Alan Menken has had only nine performances on Broadway, in a concert version.	*The Flowering Peach*

4. A one-act musical adapted from a Mark Twain story, it was part of a full-length work by Sheldon Harnick and Jerry Bock.

Godspell

5. This show is a musical adaptation of No. 2 above by Peter Stone, Richard Rodgers, and Martin Charnin.

J.B.

6. Originally conceived as a vehicle for Sarah Bernhardt, this play by Oscar Wilde was banned as blasphemous by the Lord Chamberlain.

King David

7. A musical by Andrew Lloyd Webber and Tim Rice, it was first presented as a fifteen-minute school show.

Two by Two

8. A 1980 revival of this musical by Vinnette Carroll, Micki Grant, and Alex Bradford was Jennifer Holliday's Broadway debut.

Jesus Christ Superstar

9. By Stephen Schwartz and John-Michael Tebelak, this musical is structured as a series of parables.

Joseph and the Amazing Technicolor Dreamcoat

10. Norman Jewison directed a 1973 film version of this musical by Andrew Lloyd Webber and Tim Rice.

Your Arms Too Short to Box with God

HEAVEN HELP US!

ANSWERS

In God, We Trust
1. "If I Were a Rich Man"—*Fiddler on the Roof*
2. "Why Me?"—*Two by Two*
3. "Gethsemane"—*Jesus Christ Superstar*
4. "Save the People"—*Godspell*
5. "Miracle Song"—*Altar Boyz*
6. "How Come?"—*Children's Letters to God*
7. "Father, How Long?"—*The Civil War*
8. "Bless Our Show"—*Sister Act*
9. "Why God Why?"—*Miss Saigon*
10. "Who Can I Turn To?"—*The Roar of the Greasepaint—The Smell of the Crowd*

Men of the Cloth (I)
1. Bishop of Bathingstoke—*Jekyll & Hyde*
2. Rev. John Witherspoon—*1776*
3. Reverend Mr. Crisparkle—*The Mystery of Edwin Drood*
4. Cardinal Wolsey—*A Man for All Seasons*
5. Pastor Manders—*Ghosts*
6. Rev. Tooker—*Cat on a Hot Tin Roof*
7. Reverend Canon Chasuble, D.D.—*The Importance of Being Earnest*
8. Rev. Harry Harrington—*Shadowlands*
9. Cardinal Bourchier—*Richard III*
10. Friar Laurence—*Romeo and Juliet*

And Then There Were Nuns
1. The Mother Abbess, Sister Berthe, Sister Margaretta, and Sister Sophia—*The Sound of Music*
2. Mother Superior, Mary Patrick, Mary Robert, and Mary Lazarus—*Sister Act*

Continued on next page

3. Sister Mary Regina, Sister Robert Anne, Sister Mary Hubert, Sister Mary Amnesia, and Sister Mary Leo—*Nunsense*
4. Sister Boom Boom (a man who dresses in a nun's habit)—*Execution of Justice*
5. Sister Aloysius and Sister James—*Doubt*
6. Mother Miriam Ruth—*Agnes of God*
7. Sister Jean of the Angels, Sister Claire, Sister Gabrielle, and Sister Louise—*The Devils*
8. Sister Lee, Sister Melanie, Sister Monica Marie, and Sister Helen—*Do Black Patent Leather Shoes Really Reflect Up?*
9. Sister Mary Ignatius—*Sister Mary Ignatius Explains It All for You*
10. Sister Rita—*The Runner Stumbles*

Men of the Cloth (II)
1. Reverend Winemiller—*Summer and Smoke*
2. Rev. Dr. Harper—*Arsenic and Old Lace*
3. Rabbi Chemelwitz—*Angels in America: Millennium Approaches* & *Angels in America: Perestroika*
4. Rev. Dr. Moon (a.k.a. Moonface Martin)—*Anything Goes*
5. Rev. Alfred Davidson—*Rain* or *Sadie Thompson*
6. High Lama—*Shangri-La*
7. "Reverend" Jonas Nightingale—*Leap of Faith*
8. Monsignor O'Hara—*Sister Act*
9. Imam of the Mosque—*Kismet*
10. Reverend T. Lawrence Shannon—*The Night of the Iguana*

Starring God
1. *Everyman*
2. *An Act of God*
3. *Spamalot*
4. *The Happiest Girl in the World*
5. *The Green Pastures*
6. *J.B.*
7. *Xanadu*
8. *Children of Eden*
9. *Amphytrion 38*
10. *The Creation of the World and Other Business*

Men of the Cloth (III)

1. Reverend John Hale—*The Crucible*
2. Rev. Jeremiah Brown—*Inherit the Wind*
3. Father De Leo—*The Rose Tattoo*
4. Reverend Samuel Gardner—*Mrs. Warren's Profession*
5. Cardinal Barberini—*Galileo*
6. Father Ambrose—*The Waltz of the Toreadors*
7. Father Flynn—*Doubt*
8. Father Martinez—*Late Nite Catechism*
9. Reverend Alexander Mill—*Candida*
10. Father Donnally—*The Marriage of Bette and Boo*

Get Me to the Church on Time

1. Nonnberg Abbey—*The Sound of Music*
2. Canterbury Cathedral—*Murder in the Cathedral*
3. Save-A-Soul Mission—*Guys and Dolls*
4. Chapel at Arles—*Pippin*
5. St. Katherine's, San Francisco—*Sister Act*
6. St. George's, Hanover Square—*Pygmalion* (and *My Fair Lady*)
7. Big Bethel Church—*Purlie Victorious* (and *Purlie*)
8. St. Nicholas Church, the Bronx—*Doubt*
9. Atlantic Ocean Tabernacle—*Elmer Gantry*
10. St. Dominic's, Victoria Park—*Candida*

Things That You're Liable to Read in the Bible

1. *J.B.*—based on the book of *Job*
2. *The Flowering Peach*—story of Noah and the ark in *Genesis*
3. *King David*—material in the books of *Samuel, 1st Chronicles*, and *Psalms*
4. *The Diary of Adam and Eve*—a fantasy based on events in *Genesis*, which was one act of *The Apple Tree*
5. *Two by Two*—a musical adaptation of *The Flowering Peach*, based on *Genesis*
6. *Salome*—accounts in *Matthew* and *Mark*
7. *Joseph and the Amazing Technicolor Dreamcoat*—from *Genesis*
8. *Your Arms Too Short to Box with God*—*Matthew*
9. *Godspell*—parables from the Gospels of *Matthew* and *Luke*
10. *Jesus Christ Superstar*—material from the four Gospels of *Matthew, Mark, Luke*, and *John*

IX

MIND YOUR OWN BUSINESS

And we do mean business! Whatever your occupation or profession, you'll probably find a quiz about it here—from business and finance to medicine, law, education, and, of course, theatre.

Business as Usual

Match the following business establishments with the plays or musicals in which they appear.

1.	Sincere Trust Insurance Company	*Wish You Were Here*
2.	Mushnik's Skid Row Florists	*What Makes Sammy Run?*
3.	Moon Lake Casino	*The Boy Friend*
4.	Susanswerphone Answering Service	*Kinky Boots*
5.	Marks & Co. Booksellers	*Thoroughly Modern Millie*
6.	World Wide Pictures	*Redhead*
7.	Simpson Sisters' Waxworks	*84 Charing Cross Road*
8.	Mme. Dubonnet's Finishing School	*Bells Are Ringing*
9.	Camp Karefree	*Summer and Smoke*
10.	Price and Son Shoe Factory	*Little Shop of Horrors*

High Finance

How much cash is involved in the following situations—and in which Broadway musicals do they occur?

1. At the fair in Kansas City, Will Parker wins what sum in order to marry Ado Annie—but then spends it all on presents for her?
   ★ One thousand dollars
   ★ Fifty dollars
   ★ Ten dollars in quarters
   ★ One dollar

2. Eliza wants how much from Col. Pickering for a flower—and how much does he give her?
   ★ She wants one pound and he gives one shilling.
   ★ She wants half a crown and he gives nothing.
   ★ She wants a shilling and he gives a pound.
   ★ She wants tuppence and he gives three ha'pence.

3. What is the amount of the hourly raise asked by workers at the Sleep-Tite Pajama Factory?
   ★ Fifteen dollars
   ★ One dollar
   ★ Seven and a half cents
   ★ One cent

4. The Biltmore Garage wants to be paid how much to host Nathan Detroit's crap game?
   ★ Ten percent of the pot
   ★ A grand
   ★ Repair charges due on Nathan's car
   ★ Nothing

5. What is Bloody Mary's asking price for the grass skirts she hawks?
   * Fifty dollars
   * Fo' dolla'
   * Three dollars and ninety-five cents
   * Eight sand dollars

6. The fictitious Ralph and Shirley Mudge claim to be an orphan's parents in order to win a reward of what amount?
   * Five million dollars
   * Fifty thousand dollars
   * Fifty dollars
   * Fifty cents

7. How much is charged for the girls' services in the early days of the establishment later called the Chicken Ranch?
   * Three dollars
   * Fifty cents
   * Whatever the client can pay
   * A dozen eggs

8. Rose asks Papa for how much money in order to get June's act ready for the Orpheum Circuit?
   * One hundred and ten bucks
   * Eighty-eight bucks
   * Forty bucks
   * Twelve dollars and fifty-three cents

Continued on next page

9. What does Artie Kipps give his fiancée, Ann, as a lover's token?
    * One ruble
    * A Kennedy half-dollar
    * Half a sixpence
    * A wooden nickel

10. Bill Calhoun signs an IOU in the name of Fred Graham for what amount?
    * One million dollars
    * One hundred thousand dollars
    * Ten thousand dollars
    * Ten dollars

More Business as Usual

The following business firms are in what plays or musicals?

1.	Hotel Flamingo	*Sweeney Todd*
2.	Maraczek's Parfumerie	*Hello, Dolly!*
3.	World Wide Wicket Company	*Carousel*
4.	Consolidated Life	*A Streetcar Named Desire*
5.	Mrs. Lovett's Meat Pie Shop	*Lady in the Dark*
6.	Harmonia Gardens Restaurant	*She Loves Me*
7.	Last Chance Saloon	*Mame*
8.	Bascombe's Cotton Mill	*Destry Rides Again*
9.	Allure Magazine	*How to Succeed in Business without Really Trying*
10.	Knickerbocker Bank	*Promises, Promises*

Career Choices

Match the characters with their occupations and the plays or musicals in which they appear.

1.	Andrew Makepeace Ladd III	Cruise director	*Redhead*
2.	Ella Peterson	Hardware salesman	*Glengarry Glen Ross*
3.	Hjalmar Ekdal	Draper's apprentice	*Love Letters*
4.	Mr. De Pinna	Waxworks artist	*Half A Sixpence*
5.	Theodore Hickman (Hickey)	Answering service operator	*Sail Away!*
6.	Sam Craig	United States senator	*The Wild Duck*
7.	Mimi Paragon	Real estate salesman	*You Can't Take It with You*
8.	Richard Roma	Cartoonist	*The Iceman Cometh*
9.	Arthur Kipps	Iceman (retired)	*Bells Are Ringing*
10.	Essie Whimple	Photograph retoucher	*Woman of the Year*

Medicine: What's Up Doc?

What is the actual occupation of the following "doctors"?

1. Dr. Kitchell in *Bells Are Ringing*
   - ★ Surgeon
   - ★ Dentist
   - ★ Psychiatrist
   - ★ Orthopedist

2. Doc in *Pipe Dream*
   - ★ Psychologist
   - ★ Oncologist
   - ★ Marine biologist
   - ★ College president

3. Doc in *West Side Story*
   - ★ Coroner
   - ★ Illegal meth lab operator
   - ★ Hospital administrator
   - ★ Druggist

Continued on next page

4. Doc Delaney in *Come Back, Little Sheba*
    * Chiropractor
    * Rocket scientist
    * Veterinarian
    * Quiz show host

5. Dr. Pangloss in *Candide*
    * Alchemist
    * Tailor
    * Magician
    * Philosophy professor

6. Doctor Dillamond in *Wicked*
    * Professor of witchcraft
    * Metallurgist
    * Sorcerer
    * Professor of history

7. Dr. Chasuble in *The Importance of Being Earnest*
    * Clergyman
    * Oxford don
    * Patent medicine salesman
    * Lexicographer

8. Dr. Billeaux in *Urinetown*
    * Urologist
    * Lawyer
    * Head of research and development
    * Proctologist

9. Doc Pierce in *Calamity Jane* is a physician and
    * Grocer
    * Barber
    * Undertaker
    * Jail chaplain

10. Dr. Frank N. Furter in *The Rocky Horror Show*
    * Pediatrician
    * Gastroenterologist
    * Mad scientist
    * Witch doctor

Law: Trial Run

Criminal trials figure prominently in a number of plays and musicals. Match these defense attorneys with their clients and the shows in which they appear.

Defense Attorney:	Defendant:	Show:
1. Otis H. Baker	Karen Andre	*Compulsion*
2. Henry Drummond	Tom Robinson	*The Caine Mutiny Court-Martial*
3. Atticus Finch	Lt. Stephen Maryk	*The Andersonville Trial*
4. Lt. j.g. Daniel A. Kaffee, Lt. Cdr. Joanne Galloway, and Lt. j.g. Sam Weinberg	Leonard Vole	*Inherit the Wind*
5. Defense Attorney Stevens	Bertram Cates	*Execution of Justice*
6. Billy Flynn	Artie Strauss/Judd Steiner	*A Few Good Men*
7. Sir Wilfrid Robarts, Q.C.	Dan White	*To Kill a Mockingbird*
8. Jonathan Wilk	Roxie Hart	*The Night of January 16th*
9. Lt. Barney Greenwald	Henry Wirz	*Witness for the Prosecution*
10. Douglas Schmidt	LCpl. Harold W. Dawson / Pfc. Louden Downey	*Chicago*

Education: It's Academic

What subject is taught by each of the following?

1. Henry Higgins in *Pygmalion* (and *My Fair Lady)*
   * Elocution
   * Phonetics
   * Grammar
   * Calisthenics

2. Junior Dolan in *On Your Toes*
   * Dance
   * Physical education
   * Music
   * Russian

3. Dr. Vivian Bearing in *Wit*
   * Philosophy
   * English
   * Art history
   * Comedy technique

4. Robert in *Proof*
   * Mathematics
   * Nuclear physics
   * Nutrition
   * Law

5. Marian Paroo in *The Music Man*
   * Library science
   * Flower arranging
   * Piano
   * Origami

6. Miss Greta Bell in *Fame: The Musical*
   * Dance
   * Political science
   * Home economics
   * Civics

7. George and Nick in *Who's Afraid of Virginia Woolf?*
   * Chemistry and economics
   * Engineering and military science
   * History and biology
   * Education and accounting

8. Mr. Karp in *A Chorus Line*
   * Metal shop
   * Math
   * Art
   * Drama

9. Charles Kenyon in *Good News*
   * Astronomy
   * Anthropology
   * Architecture
   * Archeology

10. Tommy Turner in *The Male Animal*
    * Anatomy
    * Sex education
    * English
    * Veterinary medicine

Journalism: Press Conference

Match the journalists in column one with the newspapers in column two and the plays or musicals in which they appear in column three.

1.	Mary Sunshine	*Waterbury Standard*	*Nelly Bly*
2.	E. K. Hornbeck	*New York World*	*The Man Who Came to Dinner*
3.	Hildy Parks	*Grover's Corners Sentinel*	*An Enemy of the People*
4.	Charles Webb	*Mesalia Journal*	*Chicago*
5.	Benjamin Kidd	*Baltimore Herald*	*The Front Page*
6.	Bert Jefferson	*Chicago Herald-Examiner*	*Our Town*
7.	Joseph Pulitzer	*People's Messenger*	*Inherit the Wind*
8.	Sid Davis	*New York Herald*	*The Desert Song*
9.	Phineas T. Fogarty	*Paris Daily Mail*	*Newsies the Musical*
10.	Hovstad	*Evening Star*	*Ah, Wilderness!*

Law Enforcement: Open Up—It's the Police!

Match these descriptions with the names of the police officers and with the plays or musicals in which they appear.

1. A detective sergeant arrives in a snowstorm to protect the guests at Monkswell Manor from a murderer.

   Doppler

   An Inspector Calls

2. A lieutenant aims to shut down an illegal gambling operation.

   Krupke

   70, Girls, 70

3. An officer is writing a play about his experiences on the police force.

   Dogberry

   The Threepenny Opera

4. An officer and his partner, Officer Barrel, sing the "Cop Song."

   Callahan

   The Mousetrap

5. An inspector questions the Birling family about a young woman's suicide.

   O'Hara

   West Side Story

6. A constable says he's "comprehended two aspicious persons."

   Tiger Brown

   Urinetown

7. A detective and his partner investigate a gang of fur thieves at the Sussex Arms.

   Lockstock

   Sleuth

8. An officer is inept at controlling street violence.

   Brannigan

   Much Ado About Nothing

9. The chief of police is an old army pal of an archvillain.

   Goole

   Arsenic and Old Lace

10. An inspector is not who he seems to be.

    Trotter

    Guys and Dolls

Theatre: Leading Ladies

Match the characters, all of whom are leading ladies of the theatre, with the plays or musicals in which they appear.

1. Lilli Vanessi	*The Seagull*
2. Magnolia Hawks	*Applause*
3. Dorothy Brock	*The Royal Family*
4. Julie Cavendish	*Face the Music*
5. Margo Channing	*Dames at Sea*
6. Desirée Armfeldt	*Kiss Me, Kate*
7. Irina Arkadina	*Show Boat*
8. Mona Kent	*A Little Night Music*
9. Frieda Hatzfeld	*42nd Street*
10. Kit Baker	*Music in the Air*

Theatre: An Actor's Life for Me

Match the characters in the first column—all of whom are actors— with the plays or musicals in which they appear.

1. Bobby Pepper	*Enter Laughing*
2. Frank Elgin	*The Dresser*
3. Don Lockwood	*42nd Street*
4. Sir	*The Country Girl*
5. George (or Stanley)	*Dinner at Eight*
6. David Kolowitz	*Moon Over Buffalo*
7. Scottie Templeton	*Curtains*
8. Billy Lawlor	*The Actor's Nightmare*
9. George Hay	*Singin' in the Rain*
10. Larry Renault	*Tribute*

Jurisprudence: Here Comes the Judge!
Name the musicals or plays that feature these judges.

1. Judge Turpin exiles Benjamin Barker to Australia.
   Seussical

2. Judge Aristide Forestier threatens to close a dance hall.
   Harvey

3. Judge Brack threatens an academic's wife with scandal.
   Here's Love

4. Justice Louis Brandeis presides over adoption proceedings for an orphan.
   The Grass Harp

5. Judge Charlie Cool joins his friends in a tree house and helps two sisters resolve their differences.
   First Monday in October

6. Judge John Hathorne tries to wring a false confession from a defendant.
   Sweeney Todd

7. Judge Omar Gaffney is the Dowd family lawyer.
   Can-Can

8. Judge Yertle remands an elephant to an asylum for the criminally insane.
   The Crucible

9. Judge Ruth Loomis is an appointee to the US Supreme Court.
   Annie

10. Judge Martin Group presides over a sanity hearing.
    Hedda Gabler

MIND YOUR OWN BUSINESS

ANSWERS

Business as Usual
1. Sincere Trust Insurance Company—*Thoroughly Modern Millie*
2. Mushnik's Skid Row Florists—*Little Shop of Horrors*
3. Moon Lake Casino—*Summer and Smoke* (It's also mentioned in *A Streetcar Named Desire* and *The Glass Menagerie*, all by Tennessee Williams.)
4. Susanswerphone Answering Service—*Bells Are Ringing*
5. Marks & Co. Booksellers—*84 Charing Cross Road*
6. World Wide Pictures—*What Makes Sammy Run?*
7. Simpson Sisters' Waxworks—*Redhead*
8. Mme. Dubonnet's Finishing School—*The Boy Friend*
9. Camp Karefree—*Wish You Were Here*
10. Price and Son Shoe Factory—*Kinky Boots*

High Finance
1. Fifty dollars—*Oklahoma!*
2. She wants tuppence, but he has only three ha'pence (halfpence)—*My Fair Lady*
3. Seven and a half cents—*The Pajama Game*
4. A grand (one thousand dollars)—*Guys and Dolls*
5. Fo' dolla' (four dollars)—*South Pacific* ("Fo' Dolla'" is the name of one of the stories in James Michener's *Tales of the South Pacific*, on which the musical is based.)
6. Fifty thousand dollars—*Annie*
7. Three dollars—*The Best Little Whorehouse in Texas* (When the Depression hits, poultry is accepted as payment, resulting in the name Chicken Ranch.)
8. Eighty-eight bucks—*Gypsy*
9. Half a sixpence—*Half a Sixpence*
10. Ten thousand dollars—*Kiss Me, Kate*

More Business as Usual
1. Hotel Flamingo—*A Streetcar Named Desire*
2. Maraczek's Parfumerie—*She Loves Me*
3. World Wide Wicket Company—*How to Succeed in Business without Really Trying*
4. Consolidated Life—*Promises, Promises*
5. Mrs. Lovett's Meat Pie Shop—*Sweeney Todd*
6. Harmonia Gardens Restaurant—*Hello, Dolly!*
7. Last Chance Saloon—*Destry Rides Again*
8. Bascombe's Cotton Mill—*Carousel*
9. Allure Magazine—*Lady in the Dark*
10. Knickerbocker Bank—*Mame*

Career Choices
1. Andrew Makepeace Ladd III, United States Senator—*Love Letters*
2. Ella Peterson, answering service operator—*Bells Are Ringing*
3. Hjalmar Ekdal, photograph retoucher—*The Wild Duck*
4. Mr. De Pinna, iceman (retired)—*You Can't Take It with You*
5. Thedore Hickman (Hickey), hardware salesman—*The Iceman Cometh*
6. Sam Craig, cartoonist—*Woman of the Year*
7. Mimi Paragon, cruise director—*Sail Away!*
8. Richard Roma, real estate salesman—*Glengarry Glen Ross*
9. Arthur Kipps, draper's apprentice—*Half a Sixpence*
10. Essie Whimple, waxworks artist—*Redhead*

Medicine: What's Up, Doc?
1. Dr. Kitchell—dentist
2. Doc in *Pipe Dream*—marine biologist
3. Doc in *West Side Story*—druggist
4. Doc Delaney—chiropractor
5. Dr. Pangloss—philosophy professor
6. Doctor Dillamond—professor of history (and talking goat)
7. Dr. Chasuble—clergyman
8. Dr. Billeaux—head of research and development at Urine Good Company
9. Doc Pierce—physician and undertaker
10. Dr. Frank N. Furter—mad scientist

Law: Trial Run

1. Otis H. Baker defends Henry Wirz on charges of conspiracy and murder in *The Andersonville Trial*.
2. Henry Drummond defends Bertram Cates, charged with teaching evolution, in *Inherit the Wind*.
3. Atticus Finch defends Tom Robinson on a charge of rape in *To Kill a Mockingbird*.
4. Lt. j.g. Daniel A. Kaffee, Lt. Cmdr. Joanne Galloway, and Lt. j.g. Sam Weinberg defend Lance Corporal Harold Dawson and Private Louden Downey on a murder charge in a *A Few Good Men*.
5. Defense Attorney Stevens defends Karen Andre, accused of murder, in *The Night of January 16th*.
6. Billy Flynn defends Roxie Hart on a murder charge in *Chicago*.
7. Sir Wilfrid Robarts, Q. C. defends Leonard Vole on murder charges in *Witness for the Prosecution*.
8. Jonathan Wilk defends Artie Strauss and Judd Steiner on charges of kidnap and murder in *Compulsion*.
9. Lt. Barney Greenwald defends Lt. Stephen Maryk on mutiny charges in *The Caine Mutiny Court-Martial*.
10. Douglas Schmidt defends Dan White for murder in *Execution of Justice*.

Education: It's Academic

1. Henry Higgins—phonetics
2. Junior Dolan—music
3. Dr. Vivian Bearing—English
4. Robert—mathematics
5. Marian Paroo—piano
6. Miss Greta Bell—dance
7. George—history, Nick—biology
8. Mr. Karp—drama
9. Charles Kenyon—astronomy
10. Tommy Turner—English

Journalism: Press Conference
1. Mary Sunshine, *Evening Star—Chicago*
2. E. K. Hornbeck, *Baltimore Herald—Inherit the Wind*
3. Hildy Parks, *Chicago Herald-Examiner—The Front Page*
4. Charles Webb, *Grover's Corners Sentinel—Our Town*
5. Benjamin Kidd, *Paris Daily Mail—The Desert Song*
6. Bert Jefferson, *Mesalia Journal—The Man Who Came to Dinner*
7. Joseph Pulitzer, *New York World—Newsies the Musical*
8. Sid Davis, *Waterbury Standard—Ah, Wilderness!*
9. Phineas T. Fogarty, *New York Herald—Nelly Bly*
10. Hovstad, *People's Messenger—An Enemy of the People*

Law Enforcement: Open Up—It's the Police!
1. Detective Sergeant Trotter—*The Mousetrap*
2. Lieutenant Brannigan—*Guys and Dolls*
3. Officer O'Hara—*Arsenic and Old Lace*
4. Officer Lockstock—*Urinetown*
5. Inspector Goole—*An Inspector Calls*
6. Constable Dogberry—*Much Ado About Nothing*
7. Detective Callahan (and Officer Kowalski)—*70, Girls, 70*
8. Officer Krupke—*West Side Story*
9. Chief of Police Tiger Brown—*The Threepenny Opera*
10. Inspector Doppler—*Sleuth*

Theatre: Leading Ladies
1. Lilli Vanessi—*Kiss Me, Kate*
2. Magnolia Hawks—*Show Boat*
3. Dorothy Brock—*42nd Street*
4. Julie Cavendish—*The Royal Family*
5. Margo Channing—*Applause*
6. Desirée Armfeldt—*A Little Night Music*
7. Irina Arkadina—*The Seagull*
8. Mona Kent—*Dames at Sea*
9. Frieda Hatzfeld—*Music in the Air*
10. Kit Baker—*Face the Music*

Theatre: An Actor's Life for Me

1. Bobby Pepper—*Curtains*
2. Frank Elgin—*The Country Girl*
3. Don Lockwood—*Singin' in the Rain*
4. Sir—*The Dresser*
5. George (or Stanley)—*The Actor's Nightmare*
6. David Kolowitz—*Enter Laughing*
7. Scottie Templeton—*Tribute*
8. Billy Lawlor—*42nd Street*
9. George Hay—*Moon Over Buffalo*
10. Larry Renault—*Dinner at Eight*

Jurisprudence: Here Comes the Judge!

1. Judge Turpin—*Sweeney Todd*
2. Judge Aristide Forestier—*Can-Can*
3. Judge Brack—*Hedda Gabler*
4. Justice Louis Brandeis—*Annie*
5. Judge Charlie Cool—*The Grass Harp*
6. Judge John Hathorne—*The Crucible*
7. Judge Omar Gaffney—*Harvey*
8. Judge Yertle (the Turtle)—*Seussical*
9. Judge Ruth Loomis—*First Monday in October*
10. Judge Martin Group—*Here's Love*

X

STAR QUALITY

These questions are all about actors who have that indefinable *je ne sais quoi* called "star quality." You've seen their names up in lights. After you answer the questions, you can line up at the stage door for an autograph.

Casting Call

Match these sets of actors with the roles they all played (either during the original Broadway run or in subsequent productions) and the names of the shows.

1.	Jack Klugman Rex Robbins Jonathan Hadary John Dossett Boyd Gaines	Elwood P. Dowd	*How to Succeed in Business without Really Trying*
2.	David Burns Paul Ford Iggie Wolfington Paul Benedict	King Arthur	*Peter Pan*
3.	Celeste Holm Shelley Winters Jacqueline Sundt Barbara Cook Christine Ebersole Jessica Boevers	Miss Adelaide	*The Music Man*

Continued on next page

4. Richard Burton   Herbie   *Hello, Dolly!*
    Richard Harris
    Robert Goulet
    Jeremy Irons
5. Vivian Blaine   Ado Annie Carnes   *Annie Get Your Gun*
    Helen Gallagher
    Sheila MacRae
    Norma Donaldson
    Faith Prince
    Lauren Graham
6. Cyril Ritchard   Mayor Shinn   *Harvey*
    George Rose
    Christopher Hewett
    Stephen Hanan
    J. K. Simmons
    Paul Schoeffler
7. Frank Fay   Horace   *Gypsy*
    Joe E. Brown   Vandergelder
    Jack Buchanan
    Bert Wheeler
    James Stewart
    Jim Parsons
8. Ethel Merman   J. Pierrepont   *Guys and Dolls*
    Bernadette Peters   Finch
    Crystal Bernard
    Cheryl Ladd
    Susan Lucci
    Reba McEntire

9.	David Burns	Captain Hook	*Oklahoma!*
	Cab Calloway		
	Billy Daniels		
	Max Showalter		
	Eddie Bracken		
	Jay Garner		
10.	Robert Morse	Annie Oakley	*Camelot*
	Darryl Hickman		
	Matthew Broderick		
	Daniel Radcliffe		

Original Casting

Which actors created these roles in the original Broadway productions?

1. Linda Loman in *Death of a Salesman* (1949)
   * ☆ Mildred Natwick
   * ☆ Mildred Dunnock
   * ☆ Marian Seldes
   * ☆ Teresa Wright

2. Mitch in *A Streetcar Named Desire* (1947)
   * ☆ Victor Jory
   * ☆ Lee J. Cobb
   * ☆ Karl Malden
   * ☆ Ed Begley

3. Sabina in *The Skin of Our Teeth* (1942)
   * ☆ Beatrice Lillie
   * ☆ Elaine Stritch
   * ☆ Katharine Hepburn
   * ☆ Tallulah Bankhead

Continued on next page

4. Nick in *Who's Afraid of Virginia Woolf?* (1962)
   * ☆ George Grizzard
   * ☆ George Peppard
   * ☆ Alan Alda
   * ☆ Larry Blyden

5. Big Mama in *Cat on a Hot Tin Roof* (1955)
   * ☆ Mildred Natwick
   * ☆ Mildred Dunnock
   * ☆ Marian Seldes
   * ☆ Teresa Wright

6. James Tyrone Jr. in *Long Day's Journey Into Night* (1956)
   * ☆ George C. Scott
   * ☆ Jason Robards Jr.
   * ☆ Christopher Plummer
   * ☆ Burgess Meredith

7. Berenice Sadie Brown in *The Member of the Wedding* (1950)
   * ☆ Claudia McNeill
   * ☆ Hattie McDaniel
   * ☆ Ethel Waters
   * ☆ Dorothy Dandridge

8. Alan Seymour in *Picnic* (1953)
   * ☆ Paul Newman
   * ☆ Kirk Douglas
   * ☆ Harvey Keitel
   * ☆ Franchot Tone

9. Lavinia Hubbard in *Another Part of the Forest* (1946)
   * ★ Mildred Natwick
   * ★ Mildred Dunnock
   * ★ Marian Seldes
   * ★ Teresa Wright

10. Madame Arcati in *Blithe Spirit* (1941)
    * ★ Mildred Natwick
    * ★ Mildred Dunnock
    * ★ Marian Seldes
    * ★ Teresa Wright

Also Starring Robert Preston

Robert Preston starred on Broadway opposite a bevy of leading ladies. Can you match the actress and the show?

1. Rosemary Harris	*I Do! I Do!*
2. Bernadette Peters	*Nobody Loves an Albatross*
3. Mary Martin	*Janus*
4. Barbara Cook	*Mack & Mabel*
5. Uta Hagen	*His and Hers*
6. Celeste Holm	*Ben Franklin in Paris*
7. Kim Hunter	*The Lion in Winter*
8. Ulla Sallert	*The Tender Trap*
9. Margaret Sullavan	*The Magic and the Loss*
10. Carol Rossen	*The Music Man*

Replacement Parts

The actresses in the first list were all replacements for the star of an original Broadway production. Match the replacements with the original stars, roles, and shows.

Replacement	Original star	Role	Show
1. Pearl Bailey	Gwen Verdon	Anna	*Camelot*
Thelma Carpenter		Leonowens	
Phyllis Diller			
Betty Grable			
Ethel Merman			
Bibi Osterwald			
Martha Raye			
Ginger Rogers			
2. Cloris Leachman	Julie Andrews	Miss Hannigan	*Evita*
Martha Wright			
3. Liza Minnelli	Carol Channing	Eva Peron	*The Sound of*
Lenora Nemetz			*Music*
Ann Reinking			
4. Pamela Charles	Mary Martin	Dolly Levi	*Chicago*
Lola Fisher			
Sally Ann Howes			
Margot Moser			
Rosemary Rainer			
5. Constance Carpenter	Rosalind	Roxie Hart	*My Fair Lady*
Annamary Dickey	Russell		
Celeste Holm			
Patricia Morison			
6. Greer Garson	Gertrude	Mame Dennis	*Annie*
Beatrice Lillie	Lawrence		

7. Alice Ghostley	Patti LuPone	Nellie Forbush	*The King and I*
June Havoc			
Betty Hutton			
Ruth Kobart			
Marcia Lewis			
Dolores Wilson			
8. Jeannie Carson	Dorothy	Guenevere	*South Pacific*
Nancy Dussault	Loudon		
Martha Wright			
9. Loni Ackerman	Julie Andrews	Maria Rainer	*Hello, Dolly!*
Derin Altay			
Pamela Blake			
Florence Lacey			
Nancy Opel			
10. Patricia Bredin	Mary Martin	Eliza Doolittle	*Auntie Mame*
Kathryn Grayson			
Janet Pavek			

Did You Know Them When?

Many movie stars began their careers on the Broadway stage, and some (but not all) returned to it years later. Match the roles in which they made their first and their last (or later) Broadway appearances with the movie stars.

1. Charles Widgin Rochambeau in *Children*   Gene Wilder
   from Their Games (1963) and Roberto
   Miranda in *Death and the Maiden* (1992)

2. Performer in *New Faces of 1936* and Georges   Clark Gable
   in *La Cage aux Folles* (1985)

Continued on next page

3. Performer in a 1922 musical spectacle called *Better Times* and Cary Lockwood in *Nikki*, a 1931 musical comedy — Joan Crawford

4. Regina Giddens in *The Little Foxes* (1981) and Amanda Prynne in *Private Lives* (1983) — Cary Grant

5. Hotel Valet in *The Complaisant Lover* (1961) and Harry Berlin in *Luv* (1966) — Gene Hackman

6. A Man (Dick Roe, the lover) in *Machinal* (1928) and The Lover in *Love, Honor and Betray* (1930) — June Allyson

7. Floy Jennings in *The Earth Between* (1929) and Maxine Faulk in *The Night of the Iguana* (1961) — Van Johnson

8. Performer in a revue called *Innocent Eyes* (1924) and performer in *The Passing Show of 1924* — Humphrey Bogart

9. Performer in a musical revue called *Sing Out the News* (1938) and Ann Stanley in *Forty Carats* (1970) — Elizabeth Taylor

10. Ernie Crockett in *Drifting* (1922) and Duke Mantee in *The Petrified Forest* (1935) — Bette Davis

Life Begins at Eighty

Each of these actors was over the age of eighty when he or she . . .

1. . . . replaced Angela Lansbury in *A Little Night Music.*
   - ★ Cicely Tyson
   - ★ Elaine Stritch
   - ★ Glynis Johns
   - ★ Diana Rigg

2. . . . appeared in a one-man show called *A Word or Two* at the Stratford Shakespeare Festival and in Los Angeles.
   - ★ Jason Robards Jr.
   - ★ George C. Scott
   - ★ Henry Fonda
   - ★ Christopher Plummer

3. . . . co-starred with Rex Harrison in *Aren't We All?*
   - ★ Claudette Colbert
   - ★ Debbie Reynolds
   - ★ Gertrude Lawrence
   - ★ Bette Davis

4. . . . was a transvestite in Harvey Fierstein's *Casa Valentina.*
   - ★ John Cullum
   - ★ Frank Langella
   - ★ Eli Wallach
   - ★ Joel Grey

5. . . . played Grandpa Vanderhof on Broadway in *You Can't Take It with You.*
   - ★ Fredric March
   - ★ John Gielgud
   - ★ James Earl Jones
   - ★ Sid Caesar

Continued on next page

6. . . . was in Gore Vidal's *The Best Man* on Broadway and in Noël Coward's *Blithe Spirit* on Broadway and on tour.
   * ★ Elizabeth Taylor
   * ★ Margaret Truman
   * ★ Julie Andrews
   * ★ Angela Lansbury

7. . . . appeared on Broadway in Craig Wright's comedy, *Grace*, and toured in the one-man show, *FDR*.
   * ★ Kirk Douglas
   * ★ Edward Asner
   * ★ James Whitmore
   * ★ Tab Hunter

8. . . . played the nurse in *Medea* opposite Zoe Caldwell.
   * ★ Judith Anderson
   * ★ Katharine Hepburn
   * ★ Maggie Smith
   * ★ Martha Raye

9. . . . appeared opposite Stephen Spinella in *The Velocity of Autumn*.
   * ★ Rita Moreno
   * ★ Estelle Parsons
   * ★ Frances Sternhagen
   * ★ Marian Seldes

10. . . . starred in a reworked version of a musical, *The Visit*, by Terrence McNally, John Kander and Fred Ebb.
    * ★ Beatrice Arthur
    * ★ Ethel Merman
    * ★ Chita Rivera
    * ★ Gwen Verdon

Broadway Debuts

Who made their Broadway debuts in the following roles?

1. Marcelle in the Feydeau farce *Hotel Paradiso* (1957):
   * ★ Angela Lansbury
   * ★ Elaine Stritch
   * ★ Katharine Hepburn
   * ★ Lana Turner

2. Roland Maule in Noël Coward's *Present Laughter* (1982):
   * ★ Ian McKellen
   * ★ John Cullum
   * ★ Nathan Lane
   * ★ Matthew Broderick

3. Wildcat Jackson in *Wildcat* (1960):
   * ★ Carol Channing
   * ★ Nancy Walker
   * ★ Lucille Ball
   * ★ Clare Boothe Luce

4. Tessie in Frank Loesser's *The Most Happy Fella* (1959):
   * ★ Patti LuPone
   * ★ Bernadette Peters
   * ★ Lena Horne
   * ★ Tessie O'Shea

5. Snout in *A Midsummer Night's Dream* (1971):
   * ★ Richard Burton
   * ★ Anthony Hopkins
   * ★ Patrick Stewart
   * ★ Mickey Rooney

Continued on next page

6. Edward in Dore Schary's *Sunrise at Campobello* (1958):
   * James Earl Jones
   * Christopher Plummer
   * Brian Dennehy
   * Steve Martin

7. Miss Imogen Parrott in Arthur Wing Pinero's *Trelawny of the "Wells"* (1975):
   * Glenn Close
   * Meryl Streep
   * Tyne Daly
   * Stockard Channing

8. Mr. Arthur Gower in Arthur Wing Pinero's *Trelawny of the "Wells"* (1975):
   * Mandy Patinkin
   * Frank Langella
   * Alan Cumming
   * Mel Brooks

9. Multiple roles in Leonard Sillman's revue *New Faces of 1956*:
   * Imogene Coca
   * Eartha Kitt
   * Ann Miller
   * Maggie Smith

10. Maria in *Twelfth Night* (1958):
    * Judi Dench
    * Judy Holliday
    * Judy Garland
    * Judith Anderson

Broadway to Hollywood

Match the actors in the first column, who played leading roles in the movie version of a Broadway musical, with the actors in the second column, who originated those roles on Broadway, and with the correct shows in the third column.

Movie actors	Original Broadway actors	Show
1. Rosalind Russell, Karl Malden, Natalie Wood	Pat Suzuki, Larry Blyden, Juanita Hall	*West Side Story*
2. Jean Simmons, Frank Sinatra, Marlon Brando	Andrea McArdle, Dorothy Loudon, Reid Shelton	*Chicago*
3. Shirley Jones, Gordon MacRae, Gloria Grahame	Carol Lawrence, Larry Kert, Chita Rivera	*The Wiz*
4. Natalie Wood, Richard Beymer, Rita Moreno	Mary Martin, Ezio Pinza, Myron McCormick	*Mame*
5. Renée Zellweger, Catherine Zeta-Jones, Richard Gere	Stephanie Mills, Hinton Battle, Dee Dee Bridgewater	*Gypsy*
6. Nancy Kwan, Jack Soo, Juanita Hall	Angela Lansbury, Charles Braswell, Willard Waterman	*South Pacific*
7. Aileen Quinn, Carol Burnett, Albert Finney	Gwen Verdon, Chita Rivera, Jerry Orbach	*Flower Drum Song*
8. Mitzi Gaynor, Rossano Brazzi, Ray Walston	Joan Roberts, Alfred Drake, Celeste Holm	*Guys and Dolls*
9. Diana Ross, Michael Jackson, Lena Horne	Isabel Bigley, Sam Levene, Robert Alda	*Oklahoma!*
10. Lucille Ball, Robert Preston John McGiver	Ethel Merman, Jack Klugman, Sandra Church	*Annie*

STAR QUALITY

ANSWERS

Casting Call

1. Jack Klugman, Rex Robbins, Jonathan Hadary, John Dossett, Boyd Gaines—Herbie in *Gypsy*
2. David Burns, Paul Ford, Iggie Wolfington, Paul Benedict—Mayor Shinn in *The Music Man*
3. Celeste Holm, Shelley Winters, Jacqueline Sundt, Barbara Cook, Christine Ebersole, Jessica Boevers—Ado Annie Carnes in *Oklahoma!*
4. Richard Burton, Richard Harris, Robert Goulet, Jeremy Irons—King Arthur in *Camelot*
5. Vivian Blaine, Helen Gallagher, Sheila MacRae, Norma Donaldson, Faith Prince, Lauren Graham—Miss Adelaide in *Guys and Dolls*
6. Cyril Ritchard, George Rose, Christopher Hewett, Stephen Hanan, J. K. Simmons, Paul Schoeffler—Captain Hook in *Peter Pan*
7. Frank Fay, Joe E. Brown, Jack Buchanan, Bert Wheeler, James Stewart, Jim Parsons—Elwood P. Dowd in *Harvey*
8. Ethel Merman, Bernadette Peters, Crystal Bernard, Cheryl Ladd, Susan Lucci, Reba McEntire—Annie Oakley in *Annie Get Your Gun*
9. David Burns, Cab Calloway, Billy Daniels, Max Showalter, Eddie Bracken, Jay Garner—Horace Vandergelder in *Hello, Dolly!*
10. Robert Morse, Darryl Hickman, Matthew Broderick, Daniel Radcliffe—J. Pierrepont Finch in *How to Succeed in Business without Really Trying*

Original Casting

1. Mildred Dunnock
2. Karl Malden
3. Tallulah Bankhead
4. George Grizzard
5. Mildred Dunnock

Continued on next page

6. Jason Robards Jr.
7. Ethel Waters
8. Paul Newman
9. Mildred Dunnock
10. Mildred Natwick

Also Starring Robert Preston

1. Rosemary Harris appeared as Queen Eleanor in *The Lion in Winter* opposite Robert Preston as King Henry II.
2. Bernadette Peters was Mabel Normand and Preston was Mack Sennett in *Mack and Mabel*.
3. Mary Martin was Agnes and Preston was Michael, her husband, in the two-character musical *I Do! I Do!*
4. Barbara Cook was Marian Paroo and Preston was her suitor, Harold Hill, in *The Music Man*.
5. Uta Hagen played Grace Wilson and Preston was George Wilson, her ex-husband, in *The Magic and the Loss*.
6. Celeste Holm was Maggie Palmer and Preston was Clem Scott, husband-and-wife playwrights, in *His and Hers*.
7. Kim Hunter was Sylvia Crewes and Preston was Joe McCall, who woos her but finally returns to his wife, in *The Tender Trap*.
8. Ulla Sallert played Madame La Comtesse Diane de Vobrillac and Preston was her old friend, Benjamin Franklin, in *Ben Franklin in Paris*.
9. Margaret Sullavan played Jessica and Preston was her husband, Gil, in *Janus*.
10. Carol Rossen was Jean Hart, secretary to Nat Bentley, played by Preston in *Nobody Loves an Albatross*.

Replacement Parts

1. Pearl Bailey, Thelma Carpenter, Phyllis Diller, Betty Grable, Ethel Merman, Bibi Osterwald, Martha Raye, and Ginger Rogers were all replacements for Carol Channing as Mrs. Dolly Gallagher Levi in *Hello, Dolly!*
2. Cloris Leachman and Martha Wright replaced Mary Martin as Ensign Nellie Forbush in *South Pacific*.
3. Liza Minnelli, Lenora Nemetz, and Ann Reinking were replacements for Gwen Verdon as Roxie Hart in *Chicago*.

4. Pamela Charles, Lola Fisher, Sally Ann Howes, Margot Moser, and Rosemary Rainer were all replacements for Julie Andrews as Eliza Doolittle in *My Fair Lady*.

5. Constance Carpenter, Annamary Dickey, Celeste Holm, and Patricia Morison replaced Gertrude Lawrence as Anna Leonowens in *The King and I*.

6. Greer Garson and Beatrice Lillie were replacements for Rosalind Russell as Mame Dennis in *Auntie Mame*.

7. Alice Ghostley, June Havoc, Betty Hutton, Ruth Kobart, Marcia Lewis, and Dolores Wilson all replaced Dorothy Loudon as Miss Hannigan in *Annie*.

8. Jeannie Carson, Nancy Dussault, and Martha Wright were replacements for Mary Martin as Maria Rainer in *The Sound of Music*.

9. Loni Ackerman, Derin Altay, Pamela Blake, Florence Lacey, and Nancy Opel replaced Patti LuPone as Eva Peron in *Evita*.

10. Patricia Bredin, Kathryn Grayson, and Janet Pavek replaced Julie Andrews as Guenevere in *Camelot*.

Did You Know Them When?

1. Gene Hackman
2. Van Johnson (replacement for Gene Barry as Georges in *La Cage aux Folles*)
3. Cary Grant (as Archie Leach—he used the first name of his character Cary Lockwood as his movie name)
4. Elizabeth Taylor
5. Gene Wilder (replacement for Alan Arkin as Harry Berlin in *Luv*)
6. Clark Gable
7. Bette Davis
8. Joan Crawford (as Lucille LeSueur)
9. June Allyson (replacement for Julie Harris as Ann Stanley in *Forty Carats*)
10. Humphrey Bogart (as H. D. Bogart)

Life Begins at Eighty

1. Elaine Stritch, eighty-five, replaced Angela Lansbury, then eighty-four, in *A Little Night Music*.
2. Christopher Plummer appeared in *A Word or Two* when he was eighty-four.
3. Claudette Colbert costarred in *Aren't We All?* when she was eighty-one.
4. John Cullum was in *Casa Valentina* at age eighty-four.
5. James Earl Jones was in *You Can't Take It with You* at age eighty-four.
6. Angela Lansbury was in *The Best Man* at eighty-six, and she embarked on a *Blithe Spirit* North American tour at eighty-nine.
7. Edward Asner turned eighty-three while appearing in *Grace* and toured in *FDR* at eighty-five.
8. Judith Anderson played the nurse in *Medea* at age eighty-five.
9. Estelle Parsons appeared in *The Velocity of Autumn* at eighty-six.
10. Chita Rivera at eighty-one starred in a revised version of *The Visit*.

Broadway Debuts

1. Angela Lansbury
2. Nathan Lane
3. Lucille Ball
4. Bernadette Peters
5. Patrick Stewart
6. James Earl Jones
7. Meryl Streep
8. Mandy Patinkin
9. Maggie Smith
10. Judi Dench

Broadway to Hollywood

1. Rosalind Russell, Karl Malden, and Natalie Wood played movie roles originally played on Broadway by Ethel Merman, Jack Klugman, and Sandra Church in *Gypsy*.

2. Jean Simmons, Frank Sinatra, and Marlon Brando played roles originated by Isabel Bigley, Sam Levene, and Robert Alda in *Guys and Dolls*.

3. Shirley Jones, Gordon MacRae, and Gloria Grahame played roles originated by Joan Roberts, Alfred Drake, and Celeste Holm in *Oklahoma!*

4. Natalie Wood, Richard Beymer, and Rita Moreno played roles originated by Carol Lawrence, Larry Kert, and Chita Rivera in *West Side Story*.

5. Renée Zellweger, Catherine Zeta-Jones, and Richard Gere played roles originated by Gwen Verdon, Chita Rivera, and Jerry Orbach in *Chicago*.

6. Nancy Kwan, Jack Soo, and Juanita Hall played roles in the film that were originated on stage by Pat Suzuki, Larry Blyden, and Juanita Hall in *Flower Drum Song*.

7. Aileen Quinn, Carol Burnett, and Albert Finney played roles originated by Andrea McArdle, Dorothy Loudon, and Reid Shelton in *Annie*.

8. Mitzi Gaynor, Rossano Brazzi, and Ray Walston played roles originated by Mary Martin, Ezio Pinza, and Myron McCormick in *South Pacific*.

9. Diana Ross, Michael Jackson, and Lena Horne played roles originated by Stephanie Mills, Hinton Battle, and Dee Dee Bridgewater in *The Wiz*.

10. Lucille Ball, Robert Preston, and John McGiver played roles originated by Angela Lansbury, Charles Braswell, and Willard Waterman in *Mame*.

FUN WITH SHOW TITLES

As Little Sally says in *Urinetown*, a bad title "could kill a show pretty good." Conversely, a good title can herald the way to a boffo smash. These quizzes will ask you to identify the titles of plays and musicals from the clues given.

Four-Letter Words

Perhaps one way to economize in producing a Broadway show is to keep the title short and save on signage! Can you match these descriptions with the musicals whose titles have only four letters?

1.	Musical of 2000 with music by Elton John	*Hair*
2.	Richard Maltby Jr. and David Shire show of 1983	*Nine*
3.	Musical that opened in 1982 and ran until 2000	*Rent*
4.	1966 musical based on a novel by Patrick Dennis	*Baby*
5.	1996 musical whose author was awarded a posthumous Pulitzer Prize	*Aida*
6.	Alan Jay Lerner and André Previn 1969 collaboration about Gabrielle Chanel	*Once*
7.	1968 musical that included Diane Keaton in the cast	*Coco*
8.	2012 musical with songs by the two stars of the film on which it was based	*Fela!*
9.	Based on the life of a Nigerian musician, a musical that opened in 2009 and returned to Broadway in 2012 after a national tour	*Mame*
10.	Arthur Kopit and Maury Yeston work that won the Tony Award for Best Musical of 1982	*Cats*

Triple Plays

These plays and musicals have even shorter titles—with only three letters.

1. Musical by Walt Smith and Leon Uris based on the novel *Exodus* *Rex*
2. Comedy by Murray Schisgal that was originally directed by Mike Nichols *FOB*
3. Drama by Margaret Edson set in a hospital room *Fen*
4. Comedic drama starring Mae West and written by her under the name Jane Mast *Tru*
5. Musical about Henry VIII by Richard Rodgers, Sherman Yellen, and Sheldon Harnick *Big*
6. Obie-winning play by David Henry Hwang about conflicts among Asian-Americans *Ari*
7. Play by Caryl Churchill set in East Anglia *Box*
8. Play by Edward Albee with an onstage cube and a recorded voice *Luv*
9. One-man play by Jay Presson Allen that won a Tony for Robert Morse *Wit*
10. Musical by John Weidman, David Shire, and Richard Maltby Jr., based on a movie of the same name. *Sex*

Mixed Colors

Each of these titles of plays and musicals contains a missing color. First, complete the titles, and then mix one color in the first column with another color in the second column to produce a different color in the third column. For example, a title with the color *yellow* in it plus a title with the color *blue* would result in a title with the color *green*. (There will be more than one correct combination of titles that will produce the desired color.)

1. *The Moon is _____* + *The Last Meeting of the Knights of the _____ Magnolia* = *_____ Gardens*

2. *The Woman in _____* + *_____ Face* = *The _____ Pastures*

3. *The _____ Crook* + *Men in _____* = *_____ Time*

4. *_____ Jack* + *Flora the _____ Menace* = *The Girl in _____ Tights*

5. *The _____ Mill* + *Last of the _____ Hot Lovers* = *The Color _____*

6. *The Deep _____* + *_____ Denim* = *_____ Blossoms*

7. *The House of _____ Leaves* + *The _____ Jacket* = *Bubbling _____ Sugar*

8. *The Loud _____ Patrick* + *_____ Roses for Me* = *The _____ Pimpernel*

9. *_____ Peppers* + *When You Comin Back, _____ Ryder?* = *The _____ Alibi*

10. *The _____ Room* + *_____ Comedy / The _____ Ticket* = *The _____ Hour*

Body Language

The title of each of these Broadway shows contains a word that names a part of the human anatomy. Match the descriptions with the titles and fill in the right body parts.

1. This 1937 Rodgers and Hart musical had a score including "Where or When," "My Funny Valentine," and "The Lady Is a Tramp."

   On Your _____ *Ankles*

2. The story and music of Gloria and Emilio Estefan; this musical opened on Broadway in 2015.

   Chu _____ Chow *Arms*

3. This musical, loosely based on "Ali Baba and the Forty Thieves," first opened in 1916 in London, where it ran for five years—a record that stood for four decades.

   Best _____ Forward *Chin*

4. This 1941 Broadway musical featured June Allyson and Nancy Walker in their first major roles— and also had "Buckle Down, Winsocki" in its score.

   Babes in _____ *Ear*

5. First performed on Broadway in 1936, this Rodgers and Hart musical was revived in 1983 featuring ballerina Natalia Makarova.

   _____ on a Hardbody *Feet*

6. This 1948 revue marked the Broadway debut of Carol Channing—and was the first show directed and choreographed by Gower Champion.

   _____ Aweigh *Toes*

7. Featuring the Kean sisters, Jane and Betty, this 1955 musical, about an American movie company on location in the Mediterranean, had music by Sammy Fain and a book by Guy Bolton and Eddie Davis.

Five _____ Exercise   *Foot*

8. A 1959 play by Peter Shaffer, it starred Jessica Tandy and was directed by Sir John Gielgud.

Daddy Long _____   *Hands*

9. A 1916 play by Jean Webster, it was the basis of a 1955 movie musical with Fred Astaire and Leslie Caron.

On Your _____!   *Finger*

10. Prominently featuring a pickup truck, this new musical opened on Broadway in 2013.

Lend An _____   *Legs*

Testing Your Metal

Match these descriptions with the right Broadway plays and musicals, and fill in the missing titles with the correct metals from the third column.

1. 1886 musical play by Charles H. Hoyt about a man who goes to a costume ball dressed in kitchen utensils to look like a knight	_____ *Magnolias*	*Gold*
2. 1957 musical by Ellen Violett, David Craig, and David Baker in which Nancy Walker played a jinxed policewoman	*The Woman of* _____	*Brass*
3. 1936 drama by Francis Gallagher about construction workers on a skyscraper	_____: *The Musical with a Flip Side*	*Silver*
4. 1987 play by Robert Harling set in a beauty shop	*A* _____ *Soldier*	*Arsenic*
5. 1920 play by Paul Kester set in a sculptor's studio	*The* _____ *Cord*	*Iron*
6. 1978 musical by Gary William Friedman, Will Holt, and Bruce Vilanch about a fading actress making a comeback	_____ *and Brass*	*Tin*
7. 1952 play by Irving Elman about a businessman stuck in a rut	_____ *Eagle Guy*	*Steel*
8. 1926 play by Sidney Howard about a dangerously domineering mother	_____ *and Old Lace*	*Copper*
9. 1934 play by Melvin Levy about a ruthless sailor who jumps ship in San Francisco	_____ *Men*	*Platinum*
10. 1941 play by Joseph Kesselring about two sisters in Brooklyn who take pity on lonely old men	*The* _____ *Ring*	*Bronze*

Retitled

These titles of plays and musicals have been shortened by using only initial capital letters for some words in the titles. Your job is to figure out what those missing words are. For example, *The Merry WOW* would be *The Merry Wives of Windsor.*

1. *Sweet BOY*—1959 drama
2. *The Dark LOTS*—1910 comedy
3. *COAL God*—1980 drama
4. *The SOOT*—1942 fantastic comedy
5. *The POP*—1879 comic opera
6. *A POT Forest*—1946 play
7. *Lend MAT*—1986 comedy
8. *The TOY Life*—1939 drama
9. *RAGA Dead*—1966 tragicomedy
10. *LIT Stars*—1949 musical

Let's "C" A Show!

These musicals all have one-word titles that begin with the letter "C":

1. It's based on John van Druten's *I Am a Camera* and stories by Christopher Isherwood.

   Candide

2. T. S. Eliot won two Tony Awards for it.

   Carnival!

3. A short story by Paul Gallico was the basis of this musical—and for an earlier movie called *Lili.*

   Chicago

4. T. H. White's *The Once and Future King* provided the story line for it.

   Cabaret

Continued on next page

5. The author of the play on which this musical was based turned down offers from Giacomo Puccini and Kurt Weill to adapt it before allowing Rodgers and Hammerstein to turn it into a musical.

Company

6. It had an earlier Broadway production in 1975 before being revived in 1996 and becoming the second longest-running musical in Broadway history.

Carmelina

7. Based on an idea by Tim Rice, it has music by two members of ABBA.

Carousel

8. Created by Alan Jay Lerner, Joseph Stein, and Burton Lane, and directed by José Ferrer, this show had only seventeen Broadway performances.

Chess

9. Its book and lyrics boast a literary pedigree of Voltaire, Lillian Hellman, Hugh Wheeler, Richard Wilbur, John La Touche, Stephen Sondheim, and Dorothy Parker.

Cats

10. Based on eleven one-act plays by George Furth, this show was originally called *Threes*.

Camelot

Revues in Review

Match the names in the first column with the correct words in the second column to complete the titles of these revues.

1. George White's _____   *Follies*

2. Ziegfeld _____   *Carnival*

3. Ken Murray's _____   *Gaieties*

4. John Murray Anderson's _____   *Vanities*

5. Charlot's _____   *Frolic*

6. Earl Carroll's _____   *Blackouts*

7. Ed Wynn's _____   *Brevities*

8. Garrick _____   *Scandals*

9. Ziegfeld Midnight _____   *Almanac*

10. Broadway _____   *Revue*

Long Day's Journey

These lengthy titles of plays and musicals all consist of at least ten words (hyphenates are counted as multiple words). Can you complete them?

1. *The Roar* . . . (+8 words)
2. *A Funny* . . . (+8)
3. *The Curious* . . . (+8)
4. *I'm Getting* . . . (+9)
5. *Alexander* . . . (+9)
6. *Jacques* . . . (+9)
7. *The Effect* . . . (+9)
8. *for colored* . . . (+10)
9. *Oh Dad* . . . (+13)
10. *The Persecution* . . . (+24)

Originally Known As . . .

Match the original titles in the first column with the musicals in the second column, as they finally came to be known.

1. *Away We Go!*	*My One and Only*
2. *I Picked a Daisy*	*La Cage aux Folles*
3. *The Silver Triangle*	*Oklahoma!*
4. *Bon Voyage*	*The Fantasticks*
5. *All's Fair*	*Mame*
6. *Funny Face*	*On a Clear Day You Can See Forever*
7. *The Queen of Basin Street*	*The Music Man*
8. *My Best Girl*	*Anything Goes*
9. *Faster Than Sound*	*By Jupiter*
10. *Joy Comes to Dead Horse*	*High Spirits*

Something Sort of Grandish

Match these descriptions and fill in the missing words in these shows—all of which have the word "grand" (or slight variant) in their titles.

1.	1989 musical set in 1928 Berlin	*A Grand Night for* _____	*Coca Cola*
2.	1979 musical based on S. N. Behrman's *Jacobowsky and the Colonel*	*La Grande Duchesse de* _____	*Broadway*
3.	1993 musical about Mike Todd	*Grand* _____	*Life*
4.	1993 revue with songs by Rodgers and Hammerstein	*Le Théâtre du Grand* _____	*Gérolstein*
5.	Naturalistic horror plays	*The Grand* _____	*Singing*
6.	1955 comedy by Ronald Alexander with June Lockhart, Tom Poston, and Betsy Palmer	*El Grande de* _____	*Follies*
7.	Series of revues between 1922 and 1929, in two of which James Cagney appeared	*The Grand* _____	*Hotel*
8.	1930 comedy by Harrison Grey Fiske with Minnie Maddern Fiske	*Grand Street* _____	*Tour*
9.	Operetta of 1867 by Offenbach, Meilhac, and Halévy	*Ain't* _____ *Grand?*	*Guignol*
10.	1973 off-Broadway revue that ran almost 1,200 performances	*It's A Grand* _____	*Prize*

FUN WITH SHOW TITLES

ANSWERS

Four-Letter Words

1. *Aida*
2. *Baby*
3. *Cats*
4. *Mame*
5. *Rent*

6. *Coco*
7. *Hair*
8. *Once*
9. *Fela!*
10. *Nine*

Triple Plays

1. *Ari*
2. *Luv*
3. *Wit*
4. *Sex*
5. *Rex*

6. *FOB*
7. *Fen*
8. *Box*
9. *Tru*
10. *Big*

Mixed Colors

1. *The Moon Is Blue* + *Flora the Red Menace* = *The Color Purple*

2. *The Woman in White* + *Last of the Red Hot Lovers* = *The Girl in Pink Tights*

3. *The Black Crook* + *Men in White* = *Grey Gardens*

4. *Yellow Jack* + *Blue Denim* = *The Green Pastures*

5. *The Red Mill* + *Yellow Face* = *Orange Blossoms*

6. *The Deep Purple* + *The Last Meeting of the Knights of the White Magnolia* = *Lilac Time*

Continued on next page

7. *The House of Blue Leaves* + *Red Roses for Me* = *The Violet Hour*

8. *The Loud Red Patrick* + *The Yellow Jacket* = *The Scarlet Pimpernel*

9. *Red Peppers* + *Black Comedy/The Yellow Ticket* = *Bubbling Brown Sugar*

10. *The Blue Room* + *When You Comin' Back, Red Ryder?* = *The Crimson Alibi*

(Note: You may have other equally correct combinations—as long as you correctly named all the shows.)

Body Language

1. *Babes in Arms*
2. *On Your Feet!*
3. *Chu Chin Chow*
4. *Best Foot Forward*
5. *On Your Toes*
6. *Lend an Ear*
7. *Ankles Aweigh!*
8. *Five Finger Exercise*
9. *Daddy Long Legs*
10. *Hands on a Hardbody*

Testing Your Metal

1. *A Tin Soldier*
2. *Copper and Brass*
3. *Iron Men*
4. *Steel Magnolias*
5. *The Woman of Bronze*
6. *Platinum: The Musical with a Flip Side*
7. *The Brass Ring*
8. *The Silver Cord*
9. *Gold Eagle Guy*
10. *Arsenic and Old Lace*

Retitled

1. *Sweet BOY—Sweet Bird of Youth*
2. *The Dark LOTS—The Dark Lady of the Sonnets*
3. *COAL God—Children of a Lesser God*
4. *The SOOT—The Skin of Our Teeth*
5. *The POP—The Pirates of Penzance*
6. *A POT Forest—Another Part of the Forest*
7. *Lend MAT—Lend Me a Tenor*

8. *The TOY Life—The Time of Your Life*
9. *RAGA Dead—Rosencrantz and Guildenstern Are Dead*
10. *LIT Stars—Lost in the Stars*

Let's "C" A Show

1. *Cabaret.* Van Druten based his play on Isherwood's *Goodbye to Berlin,* part of *The Berlin Stories.*
2. *Cats.* Eliot, who died in 1965, wrote "Old Possum's Book of Practical Cats," whimsical poems on which the book and lyrics for *Cats* were based. Eliot won these two Tonys in 1983.
3. *Carnival!* The book by Michael Stewart was based on the screenplay by Helen Deutsch from Paul Gallico's "The Seven Souls of Clement O'Reilly."
4. *Camelot.* T. H. White's novel is a retelling of the King Arthur legend, which Alan Jay Lerner adapted into the musical's book.
5. *Carousel.* Ferenc Molnár decided to let Rodgers & Hammerstein adapt his play, *Liliom,* after seeing a production of *Oklahoma!*
6. *Chicago.* It has run longer than any other Broadway show except *The Phantom of the Opera.*
7. *Chess.* Tim Rice's idea was turned into a musical by Richard Nelson's book, and the music was by ABBA's Benny Andersson and Björn Ulvaeus, with lyrics by Rice.
8. *Carmelina.* Joseph Stein's book is based on the 1968 movie *Buona Sera, Mrs. Campbell. Mamma Mia,* another musical based on the same movie, had better luck at the box office.
9. *Candide.* The original book in 1956 was by Lillian Hellman with lyrics by Richard Wilbur. Additional book and lyric material were added in later productions.
10. *Company.* Furth's short plays were conceived as a vehicle for Kim Stanley, but the proposed director Anthony Perkins took the material to Stephen Sondheim and Harold Prince, who decided it would make a good musical and enlisted Furth to rewrite it.

Revues in Review

1. George White's *Scandals*
2. Ziegfeld *Follies*
3. Ken Murray's *Blackouts*
4. John Murray Anderson's *Almanac*
5. Charlot's *Revue*
6. Earl Carroll's *Vanities*
7. Ed Wynn's *Carnival*
8. Garrick *Gaieties*
9. Ziegfeld Midnight *Frolic*
10. Broadway *Brevities*

Long Day's Journey

1. *The Roar of the Greasepaint—The Smell of the Crowd*
2. *A Funny Thing Happened on the Way to the Forum*
3. *The Curious Incident of the Dog in the Night-Time*
4. *I'm Getting My Act Together and Taking It on the Road*
5. *Alexander and the Terrible, Horrible, No Good, Very Bad Day*
6. *Jacques Brel is Alive and Well and Living in Paris*
7. *The Effect of Gamma Rays on Man-in-the-Moon Marigolds*
8. *for colored girls who have considered suicide / when the rainbow is enuf*
9. *Oh Dad, Poor Dad, Mamma's Hung You in the Closet and I'm Feelin' So Sad*
10. *The Persecution and Assassination of Jean-Paul Marat as Performed by the Inmates of the Asylum of Charenton Under the Direction of the Marquis de Sade*

Originally Known As . . .

1. *Away We Go—Oklahoma!* It tried out in New Haven as *Away We Go!*, eliciting from Mike Todd the harsh criticism: "No legs, no jokes, no chance." The show-stopping final number, *Oklahoma!*, was then added, and Rodgers & Hammerstein thought that would be a better title.

2. *I Picked a Daisy—On A Clear Day You Can See Forever.* Named for principal character Daisy Gamble, the show first had Richard Rodgers as composer and Alan Jay Lerner as librettist. Rodgers bowed out and was replaced by Burton Lane. The new title is taken from one of the songs in the score.

3. *The Silver Triangle—The Music Man.* Meredith Willson's first title for his musical based on childhood reminiscences apparently alluded to the percussion instrument. The producers who first optioned it, Cy Feuer and Ernest Martin, told Willson that *The Silver Triangle* sounded like "something Ibsen had written," and they suggested *The Music Man.* As it turned out, Feuer and Martin dropped their option, and Kermit Bloomgarden produced it on Broadway—but the new title stuck.

4. *Bon Voyage—Anything Goes.* In 1934 Guy Bolton, P. G. Wodehouse, and Cole Porter wrote a musical about a shipwreck, which they called *Bon Voyage*, a title they later changed to *Hard to Get.* After the show was in rehearsal, the US steamer *Morro Castle* burned off the New Jersey coast, killing a hundred people. The shipwreck theme had to be changed quickly, and Howard Lindsay and Russel Crouse were hired to rewrite the book. In a desperate last-minute brainstorming session to come up with a new title, someone said, "Well, I guess anything goes."

5. *All's Fair—By Jupiter.* Called *All's Fair* in its Boston tryout, the show about a war between Amazon women and Greek male warriors was retitled for its Broadway opening. It is the longest-running of all Rodgers and Hart shows, 427 performances in 1942, and the last one the two of them wrote together.

6. *Funny Face—My One and Only.* This 1983 Gershwin show was first planned as a reconceived revival of the 1925 *Funny Face,* but during rehearsals book writer Timothy Meyer was replaced by Peter Stone; director Peter Sellars was replaced by Mike Nichols, and then by Tommy Tune and Thommie Walsh; a completely new book was written; six of the twelve original songs were replaced by other Gershwin tunes; and a title change was therefore deemed necessary.

Continued on next page

7. *The Queen of Basin Street—La Cage aux Folles.* The first creative team was Jay Presson Allen for the book, Maury Yeston for the score, Mike Nichols as director, and Tommy Tune as choreographer, with the locale changed from the original play's St. Tropez to New Orleans. New producers replaced this team with Harvey Fierstein, Jerry Herman, Arthur Laurents, and Scott Salmon, and restored the original title and locale.

8. *My Best Girl—Mame.* The original title is from one of the songs in the show. Perhaps inspired by the huge success of Jerry Herman's previous show, *Hello, Dolly!*, the producers decided that the main character's name should be the title.

9. *Faster Than Sound—High Spirits.* Hugh Martin and Timothy Gray adapted this musical from Noël Coward's *Blithe Spirit. Faster Than Sound* was the title of a song in the score. When Coward himself signed on as director the title changed to one more reminiscent of its source.

10. *Joy Comes to Dead Horse—The Fantasticks.* Based on Edmond Rostand's 1894 French play *Les Romanesques,* this musical was originally conceived by librettist Tom Jones and composer J. Donald Robb as a tale of Mexican and Anglo families on adjoining ranches in the Southwest. Harvey Schmidt replaced Robb as composer, and the show was rewritten as a one-act and retitled, using the whimsically spelled title of George Fleming's translation of *Les Romanesques.* It was rewritten again into two acts for its 1960 off-Broadway production, which ran for forty-two years in more than 17,000 performances, making it the world's longest-running musical. A new production opened in 2006.

Something Sort of Grandish

1. *Grand Hotel*
2. *The Grand Tour*
3. *Ain't Broadway Grand*
4. *A Grand Night for Singing*
5. *Le Théâtre du Grand-Guignol*
6. *The Grand Prize*
7. *Grand Street Follies*
8. *It's a Grand Life*
9. *La Grande Duchesse de Gérolstein*
10. *El Grande de Coca Cola*

XII

MUSIC IN THE AIR

Music, music, music! These quizzes deal with the musical side of theatre—composers, lyricists, song titles, recording artists, musical instruments—and even a little opera to add a touch of high culture! If there's something you don't know, just hum a few bars and you'll pick it up.

Playing the Classics

Match these Broadway musicals with the composers on whose music their scores are based.

1. *Kismet*	Sergei Rachmaninov
2. *Song of Norway*	Jacques Offenbach
3. *The Great Waltz*	Franz von Suppé, Gioachino Rossini, Richard Wagner, Johann Strauss, Gaetano Donizetti, and Franz Liszt
4. *Anya*	Alexander Borodin
5. *Blossom Time*	Johann Strauss Sr. and Jr.
6. *Bugs Bunny on Broadway*	Frédéric Chopin
7. *The Happiest Girl in the World*	Edvard Grieg
8. *White Lilacs*	John Philip Sousa
9. *Music in My Heart*	Franz Schubert
10. *Teddy & Alice*	Peter Ilyich Tchaikovsky

I've Heard That Song Before!

Match these Broadway musical theatre composers with the pop songs they composed apart from their theatre work.

1. Cole Porter   "I've Got My Love to Keep Me Warm"

2. Jule Styne   "Praise the Lord and Pass the Ammunition"

3. Meredith Willson   "Don't Fence Me In"

4. Frank Loesser   "Lazy Day"

5. Lee Pockriss   "I See the Moon"

6. George Fischoff   "Itsy Bitsy Teenie Weenie Yellow Polkadot Bikini"

7. Bob Merrill   "Let It Snow! Let It Snow! Let It Snow!"

8. Harold Arlen   "(What Do They Do On) A Rainy Night in Rio?"

9. Irving Berlin   "It's Only a Paper Moon"

10. Arthur Schwartz   "(How Much Is That) Doggie in the Window?"

A Night at the Opera

Name these notable opera singers who also starred in Broadway shows.

1. This basso retired from the Metropolitan Opera in 1948, then appeared on Broadway as Emile de Becque in *South Pacific* and as Cesar in *Fanny*.
   - ★ Jerome Hines
   - ★ Paul Robeson
   - ★ Ezio Pinza
   - ★ William Warfield

2. A soprano, this opera diva played an opera diva in the short-lived 2015 comedy *Living on Love.*
   * ✶ Anna Netrebko
   * ✶ Renée Fleming
   * ✶ Jessye Norman
   * ✶ Kathleen Battle

3. A Canadian soprano of Greek descent, she had a brief Broadway run in the musical *Rags.*
   * ✶ Maria Callas
   * ✶ Teresa Stratas
   * ✶ Kiri Te Kanawa
   * ✶ Tatiana Troyanos

4. This operatic baritone scored a huge success on Broadway as Tony in *The Most Happy Fella* and later appeared in *Milk and Honey.*
   * ✶ Robert Weede
   * ✶ Robert Merrill
   * ✶ Josh Groban
   * ✶ Nelson Eddy

5. A Metropolitan Opera tenor starting in 1941, noted for his hit recording of "Bluebird of Happiness," he was a replacement in the role of Tevye in *Fiddler on the Roof.*
   * ✶ Placido Domingo
   * ✶ Lauritz Melchior
   * ✶ Jan Peerce
   * ✶ Mario Lanza

Continued on next page

6. This operatic basso starred in two ill-fated Broadway musicals, *Bravo Giovanni* and *Carmelina.*
   * ★ Cesare Siepi
   * ★ Feodor Chaliapin
   * ★ Ruggero Raimondi
   * ★ Bryn Terfel

7. A dramatic soprano noted for Wagnerian roles, she was also the author of two murder mysteries, a part owner of the St. Louis Browns, a night club performer with Jimmy Durante, and the madam of a bordello in *Pipe Dream.*
   * ★ Kirsten Flagstad
   * ★ Birgit Nilsson
   * ★ Beverly Sills
   * ★ Helen Traubel

8. A Metropolitan Opera baritone, he made many TV appearances on *Mr. Rogers' Neighborhood* and starred opposite Phil Silvers in *Do Re Mi,* in which he introduced the song "Make Someone Happy."
   * ★ Leonard Warren
   * ★ John Reardon
   * ★ George London
   * ★ Dietrich Fischer-Dieskau

9. This Metropolitan Opera baritone had an extensive career
   in films and theatre, where he was a replacement as Cesar in
   Fanny and starred as Captain Hook opposite Veronica Lake in
   a touring production of *Peter Pan*.
   * Lawrence Tibbett
   * Sherrill Milnes
   * Thomas Hampson
   * Samuel Ramey

10. This mezzo-soprano began her career in theatre as the original
    Hodel in Broadway's *Fiddler on the Roof*, and later became
    known for operatic performances.
    * Joyce DiDonato
    * Marilyn Horne
    * Susan Graham
    * Julia Migenes

Play On!
What musical instrument . . .

1. . . . does Patrick Dennis pawn to buy Auntie Mame a
   Christmas bracelet in *Mame*?
   * Harmonica
   * Ukulele
   * Piccolo
   * Bugle

Continued on next page

2. . . . do the lyrics of "Seventy-Six Trombones" describe as "double-bell" in *The Music Man?*
   - ✯ Sousaphones
   - ✯ Euphoniums
   - ✯ Glockenspiels
   - ✯ Cornets

3. . . . is played by Jerry and which by Joe, the two musicians who join an all-girl band in *Sugar?*
   - ✯ Bass and saxophone
   - ✯ Trumpet and clarinet
   - ✯ Piano and drums
   - ✯ Harp and viola

4. . . . does Arvide Abernathy play in the mission band in *Guys and Dolls?*
   - ✯ Tambourine
   - ✯ Bass drum
   - ✯ Accordion
   - ✯ Fife

5. . . . was played by Patti LuPone in the 2005 revival of *Sweeney Todd?*
   - ✯ Tuba
   - ✯ Piano
   - ✯ Xylophone
   - ✯ French horn

6. . . . does Arthur Kipps play in the "Money to Burn" number in *Half a Sixpence*?
   * Kazoo
   * Marimba
   * Bagpipes
   * Banjo

7. . . . does Jacquot play for "Love Makes the World Go 'Round" in the opening of *Carnival!*?
   * Violin
   * Flute
   * Snare drum
   * Concertina

8. . . . is played by Captain von Trapp to accompany "Edelweiss" in *The Sound of Music*?
   * Harpsichord
   * Guitar
   * Zither
   * Mandolin

9. . . . is the stripper Mazeppa's "gimmick" in "You Gotta Have A Gimmick" in *Gypsy*?
   * Tin whistle
   * English horn
   * Trumpet
   * Cymbal

Continued on next page

10. . . . does Henrik Egerman play in *A Little Night Music*?
   ✶ Cello
   ✶ Organ
   ✶ Oboe
   ✶ Bassoon

Put Another Nickel In

The music of which songwriters or recording artists provides the scores for the following "jukebox musicals"?

1. *After Midnight*	Peter Allen	
2. *Holler If Ya Hear Me*	Rod Stewart	
3. *Good Vibrations*	Ellie Greenwich	
4. *The Night That Made America Famous*	Green Day	
5. *Leader of the Pack*	Brian Wilson and the Beach Boys	
6. *Smokey Joe's Café*	Harry Chapin	
7. *The Boy from Oz*	Tupac Shakur	
8. *We Will Rock You*	Duke Ellington	
9. *Tonight's the Night*	Jerry Leiber and Mike Stoller	
10. *American Idiot*	Queen	

I Feel a Song Comin' On

Match these descriptions with these Broadway plays and musicals, each of which contains the word *song* or a variant in its title, and fill in the missing words.

1. This 1958 Rodgers & Hammerstein musical is set in San Francisco's Chinatown.

   _____ *I Sing*

2. An operetta first produced in 1944, it has a score based on the music of Edvard Grieg.

   _____ *and Sing!*

3. Neil Simon, Marvin Hamlisch, and Carole Bayer Sager collaborated on this 1979 musical based on the real-life relationship of two of its creators.

   Next _____ *I'll Sing to You*

4. This 1962 play by James Saunders is based on the life an English hermit.

   _____ *Song*

5. By George S. Kaufman, Morrie Ryskind, and George and Ira Gershwin, this was the first musical to win a Pulitzer Prize for drama.

   Song of _____

6. Mary Martin and an unknown Yul Brynner starred in this 1946 musical based on a 14th-century Chinese play.

   They're _____ *Our Song*

7. Robert Anderson's 1968 play was made into a movie with Gene Hackman, Melvyn Douglas, and Dorothy Stickney in roles created onstage by Hal Holbrook, Alan Webb, and Lillian Gish.

   _____ *Song Trilogy*

Continued on next page

8. This 1926 operetta was inspired by the uprising of a group of Moroccan rebels against French colonial rule.

   Flower _____ Song

9. Harvey Fierstein wrote and starred in this 1981 collection of three plays about a New York drag queen.

   I Never Sang for My _____

10. This 1935 play by Clifford Odets is set in the Bronx and concerns the Berger family.

    The _____ Song

The Song Is Ended

From what musical was each of these songs dropped before the Broadway opening night?

1. "When Messiah Comes" *Oklahoma!*
2. "Can That Boy Fox-Trot!" *My Fair Lady*
3. "Easy to Love" *South Pacific*
4. "The Lady's Got Potential" *Anything Goes*
5. "Say a Prayer for Me Tonight" *Fiddler on the Roof*
6. "My Girl Back Home" *Gypsy*
7. "Momma's Talking Soft" *Follies*
8. "I Found a Horseshoe" *Oh, Lady! Lady!*
9. "A Real Nice Hayride" *The Music Man*
10. "Bill" *Evita*

Facing the Music

These song titles all contain the word "face." In what musicals do they appear?

1.	"My Fortune Is My Face"	*Let's Face It*
2.	"Take That Look Off Your Face"	*The Roar of the Greasepaint—The Smell of the Crowd*
3.	"I've Grown Accustomed to Her Face"	*Song and Dance*
4.	"Put on a Happy Face"	*Fade Out-Fade In*
5.	"Funny Face"	*Bye Bye Birdie*
6.	"How Can You Describe a Face?"	*My One and Only*
7.	"Sun on My Face"	*Subways Are for Sleeping*
8.	"Let's Face It"	*The Producers*
9.	"Look at That Face"	*My Fair Lady*
10.	"That Face"	*Sugar*

MUSIC IN THE AIR

ANSWERS

Playing the Classics
1. *Kismet*—Alexander Borodin (musical adaptation and lyrics by Robert Wright and George Forrest)
2. *Song of Norway*—Edvard Grieg (musical adaptation and lyrics by Robert Wright and George Forrest)
3. *The Great Waltz*—Johann Strauss Sr. and Johann Strauss Jr. (music arranged by E. W. Korngold, Julius Bittner, G. H. Clutsam, Herbert Griffiths, Frank Tours, and Russell Bennett; lyrics by Desmond Carter)
4. *Anya*—Sergei Rachmaninov (music and lyrics by Robert Wright and George Forrest)
5. *Blossom Time*—Franz Schubert (music by Sigmund Romberg, lyrics by Dorothy Donnelly)
6. *Bugs Bunny on Broadway*—Franz von Suppé, Gioachino Rossini, Richard Wagner, Johann Strauss, Gaetano Donizetti, and Franz Liszt (music by Carl Stalling and Milt Franklyn)
7. *The Happiest Girl in the World*—Jacques Offenbach (lyrics by E. Y. Harburg)
8. *White Lilacs*—Frédéric Chopin (Music by Karl Hajos, lyrics by Harry B. Smith)
9. *Music in My Heart*—Peter Ilyich Tchaikovsky (lyrics by Forman Brown)
10. *Teddy & Alice*—John Philip Sousa (original music by Richard Kapp, lyrics by Hal Hackady)

I've Heard That Song Before!
1. Cole Porter—"Don't Fence Me In"
2. Jule Styne—"Let It Snow! Let It Snow! Let It Snow!"
3. Meredith Willson—"I See the Moon"
4. Frank Loesser—"Praise the Lord and Pass the Ammunition"
5. Lee Pockriss—"Itsy Bitsy Teenie Weenie Yellow Polkadot Bikini"
6. George Fischoff—"Lazy Day"

Continued on next page

7. Bob Merrill—"(How Much Is) That Doggie in the Window?"
8. Harold Arlen—"It's Only a Paper Moon"
9. Irving Berlin—"I've Got My Love to Keep Me Warm"
10. Arthur Schwartz—"(What Do They Do On) A Rainy Night in Rio?"

A Night at the Opera

1. Ezio Pinza
2. Renée Fleming
3. Teresa Stratas
4. Robert Weede
5. Jan Peerce
6. Cesare Siepi
7. Helen Traubel
8. John Reardon
9. Lawrence Tibbett
10. Julia Migenes

Play On!

1. Bugle
2. Euphoniums
3. Bass (Jerry) and saxophone (Joe)
4. Bass drum (and cymbal)
5. Tuba
6. Banjo
7. Concertina
8. Guitar
9. Trumpet (Mazeppa says her gimmick is to "bump it with a trumpet.")
10. Cello

Put Another Nickel In

1. *After Midnight*—Duke Ellington
2. *Holler If Ya Hear Me*—Tupac Shakur
3. *Good Vibrations*—Brian Wilson and the Beach Boys
4. *The Night That Made America Famous*—Harry Chapin
5. *Leader of the Pack*—Ellie Greenwich
6. *Smokey Joe's Café*—Jerry Leiber and Mike Stoller
7. *The Boy from Oz*—Peter Allen
8. *We Will Rock You*—Queen
9. *Tonight's the Night*—Rod Stewart
10. *American Idiot*—Green Day

I Feel a Song Comin' On

1. *Flower Drum Song*
2. *Song of Norway*
3. *They're Playing Our Song*
4. *Next Time I'll Sing to You*
5. *Of Thee I Sing*
6. *Lute Song*
7. *I Never Sang for My Father*
8. *The Desert Song*
9. *Torch Song Trilogy*
10. *Awake and Sing!*

The Song Is Ended

1. "When Messiah Comes" was dropped from *Fiddler on the Roof* during Boston tryouts because producer Harold Prince thought it was "too lugubrious" and "too long."
2. "Can That Boy Fox-Trot!" was replaced with "I'm Still Here" during the Boston tryout of *Follies*.
3. "Easy to Love" was cut from Cole Porter's *Anything Goes* because the star William Gaxton had difficulty singing it.
4. "The Lady's Got Potential" was in the concept album and the movie of *Evita*, but was not in the stage version.
5. "Say a Prayer for Me Tonight" was cut from *My Fair Lady* in New Haven, but wound up in Lerner and Loewe's film *Gigi*—and was dropped yet again from the stage version of *Gigi*.
6. "My Girl Back Home" was cut from Rodgers & Hammerstein's *South Pacific* before the Broadway opening, but was reinstated for the movie and a later London revival.
7. "Momma's Talking Soft" was dropped from *Gypsy*, although fragments of it are heard in "Rose's Turn."
8. "I Found a Horseshoe" was replaced by "Sincere" in *The Music Man*.
9. "A Real Nice Hayride" was cut from *Oklahoma!* but showed up in Rodgers & Hammerstein's next show, *Carousel*, with new lyrics and a new title: "This Was a Real Nice Clambake."
10. "Bill" was deemed "too melancholy" for Jerome Kern and P. G. Wodehouse's *Oh, Lady! Lady!*, but with lyrics slightly modified by Oscar Hammerstein II it was found to be just right for *Show Boat*.

Facing the Music

1. "My Fortune Is My Face" — *Fade Out-Fade In*
2. "Take That Look Off Your Face" — *Song and Dance*
3. "I've Grown Accustomed to Her Face" — *My Fair Lady*
4. "Put on a Happy Face" — *Bye Bye Birdie*
5. "Funny Face" — *My One and Only* (and *Funny Face*, on which *My One and Only* is based)
6. "How Can You Describe a Face?" — *Subways Are for Sleeping*
7. "Sun on My Face" — *Sugar*
8. "Let's Face It" — *Let's Face It*
9. "Look at That Face" — *The Roar of the Greasepaint—The Smell of the Crowd*
10. "That Face" — *The Producers*

XIII

WELCOME TO THE THEATRE!

If you want to see a show, you have to know where it's playing! These quizzes will ask you to identify the names of theatres on Broadway and around the United States—and then see how well you know the lingo used in them.

Name That Theatre!

Match these names of Broadway theatres in the first column with their former names in the second column.

1.	Richard Rodgers	Virginia
2.	Bernard B. Jacobs	Uris
3.	Gerald Schoenfeld	Royale
4.	Neil Simon	Ritz
5.	August Wilson	46th St.
6.	Al Hirschfeld	Alvin
7.	Stephen Sondheim	Plymouth
8.	Walter Kerr	Biltmore
9.	Samuel J. Friedman	Henry Miller's
10.	Gershwin	Martin Beck

At a Theatre Near You

These theatres (both real and fictional) are settings for scenes in which musicals?

1.	Colonial Theatre, Boston, 1959	*Dreamgirls*
2.	Ford's Theatre, Baltimore, June 1948	*The Girl in Pink Tights*
3.	Zangler Theatre, New York, 1930s	*Follies*
4.	Arch Street Theatre, Philadelphia, 1933	*Crazy for You*
5.	Minsky's Burlesque, New York, 1930s	*Mame*
6.	Niblo's Garden, New York, 1866	*Kiss Me, Kate*
7.	Apollo Theatre, Harlem, early 1960s	*George M!*
8.	Weismann Theatre, New York, "Tonight"	*Curtains*
9.	Columbia Theatre, Cedar Rapids, 1890s	*Gypsy*
10.	Shubert Theatre, New Haven, 1929–30	*42nd Street*

In Residence

Identify these member companies of the League of Resident Theatres.

1.	Founded in 1963 by Oliver Rea and Peter Zeisler, this Minnesota theatre was named for its Irish-born first artistic director.	Asolo
2.	Bob and Vivian Altfeld and Nina Vance founded this theatre in Texas in 1947, named for its first location in a dance studio in a cul-de-sac between two buildings.	Old Globe
3.	Named in memory of a playwright, this Illinois company was originally founded as a theatre and school by his parents in 1922.	Barter

214

4. This Florida theatre, founded in 1958, was named for the building in which it was first housed, an historic theatre moved from an Italian town.   Trinity

5. Robert Porterfield founded this Virginia company in 1933 and named it from the fact that it accepted payment for tickets in farm produce in lieu of cash.   Goodman

6. Founded in 1979, under the leadership of Blanka and Jiri Zizka, this theatre in Pennsylvania took its name from a project dedicated to an imaginary sister of William Shakespeare's.   Clarence Brown

7. Originally founded in 1951 by Paul Soper, this Tennessee theatre company was renamed in 1970 for the legendary director of such films as *The Yearling* and *National Velvet*.   Wilma

8. Founded in 1965 by Jon Jory and Harlan Kleiman, this Connecticut theatre is named for its location in a warehouse on a dock in a harbor.   Guthrie

9. A company originally established in 1937, it got its name because it was first housed in a building designed for Shakespearean plays at an international exposition in California.   Alley

10. Founded in 1963, this Rhode Island theatre was named for the Methodist church that housed the first production, and the square on which it was located.   Long Wharf

Who Was That Theatre I Saw You With?

Identify each of these historic legitimate theatres:

1. Dozens of cities once had theatres of this name; the three that survived are in St. Louis, Detroit, and Atlanta. Their namesake was a pioneer movie producer known as "The Lone Eagle." Roxy

2. The flagship theatre founded by these brothers, who were druggists in Shreveport, Louisiana, is in New Orleans, but there were once more than sixty theatres of this name. Fisher

3. This Detroit theatre bears the name of the family who owned a company that built bodies for General Motors cars. Shubert

4. The first theatre of this name opened in Seattle in 1904, but the flagship now operated by the Nederlander Organization is in Los Angeles. Mechanic

5. This San Francisco theatre is named for a theatrical producer who wrote the play on which the musical *The Song of Norway* was based. Forrest

6. This former New York theatre bore the nickname of a producer who later established Radio City Music Hall. Pantages

7. This Baltimore theatre, which opened in 1965 and ceased operations in 2004, was founded by and named for an entrepreneur whose name is reminiscent of automobile repair. Curran

8. Philadelphia's pre-Broadway road house, this theatre was named for a nineteenth-century American Shakespearean actor. Saenger

9. This New Haven theatre, once a popular   Ford's
   pre-Broadway tryout venue, was named for
   one of three brothers who founded a theatrical
   empire.

10. This theatre in Washington, DC, closed in 1865   Fox
    and did not reopen until 1968.

You Gotta Know the Lingo

What is the meaning of each of these theatrical terms?

1. French scene
   * ★ A scene involving nudity
   * ★ Section of a play between the entrance or exit of any character
   * ★ Unintelligible dialogue, in need of translation
   * ★ Dialogue that is explicitly erotic

2. Tormentor
   * ★ A prompter who is notoriously slow in giving cues
   * ★ A malicious actor who delights in practical jokes onstage
   * ★ A hard, vertical piece of stage rigging attached to a horizontal piece known as a teaser
   * ★ An audience member who coughs loudly

3. The gods (chiefly British)
   * ★ Critics for major newspapers
   * ★ Living playwrights whose permission must be secured in order to change dialogue
   * ★ Star performers who demand "worship" from other cast members
   * ★ The highest balcony of a theatre

Continued on next page

4. Ghost light
   * Green-colored illumination used to indicate the presence of a spirit onstage
   * A light bulb that is left burning onstage during periods when the stage is not in use, for safety reasons
   * An imaginary light that the electrician claims has been focused on an actor, when in reality it has not
   * A brand name of theatrical lighting equipment

5. Italian (noun)
   * A rehearsal at which the lines are said rapidly
   * A production by Franco Zeffirelli
   * Stylish dance shoe
   * The theatrical equivalent of a "spaghetti western"

6. Sitzprobe
   * A medical procedure to relieve stress in dancers
   * A rehearsal technique in which the actors touch each other while speaking dialogue
   * In musical theatre, a rehearsal with singers and orchestra, at which all the actors are usually seated
   * An official inquiry into stagehands accused of sitting down on the job

7. Swing (noun)
   * A role whose gender is ambiguous
   * A chorus member who covers many, or sometimes all, of the chorus parts and who performs only when the primary performer of that part is unable to go on
   * A performer who can do acrobatics while singing
   * A rolling piece of scenery that moves from one side of the stage to the other

8. Vomitorium
   * An offstage area provided for actors who become nauseated during a performance
   * A backstage receptacle in which to deposit unfavorable reviews
   * A section of the auditorium reserved for small children who are likely to throw up
   * A passage from the stage that goes below a tier of seats

9. Gobo
   * A ghost or goblin who inhabits a theatre
   * A stencil or template placed in front of a lighting source to control the shape of the light emitted
   * A stock character in commedia dell'arte
   * A phrase meaning "Go below," used to indicate a character is to fall into a trap door

10. Passerelle
    * A walkway leading beyond the proscenium arch around the audience side of the orchestra pit
    * A bouqet presented to the leading lady
    * A corridor adjacent to the stage door that leads nowhere, into which bothersome autograph-seekers are directed
    * An actor who is noted for learning the lines of all the other actors

WELCOME TO THE THEATRE!

ANSWERS

Name That Theatre!

1. Richard Rodgers—46th Street. (Opened in 1925 as Chanin's 46th St. and from 1932 to 1990 simply the 46th St. Theatre, it was renamed in 1990 for composer Rodgers.)
2. Bernard B. Jacobs—Royale. (Opened in 1927 as the Royale and renamed the John Golden from 1934 to 1940, it was the Royale again until it was named for Jacobs, former president of the Shubert Organization, in 2005.)
3. Gerald Schoenfeld—Plymouth. (Named in 2005 for the chairman of the Shubert Organization; it was the Plymouth from 1917.)
4. Neil Simon—Alvin. (Named for the playwright in 1983, it was the Alvin from 1927.)
5. August Wilson—Virginia. (Named for the playwright in 2005, it went through a series of names since it opened in 1925 as the Guild. Thereafter it was the WOR Mutual Radio Theatre in 1943, the ANTA Playhouse in 1950, and the Virginia in 1981.)
6. The Al Hirschfeld—Martin Beck (from 1924 until 2003, when it was named for the legendary theatre caricaturist.)
7. Stephen Sondheim—Henry Miller's. (Named for the composer-lyricist in 2010, it was Henry Miller's from 1918, as well as a movie theatre and night club under other names in between.)
8. Walter Kerr—Ritz (from 1921 to 1990, when it was named to honor the longtime theatre critic of the *New York Herald Tribune* and later of the *New York Times*.)
9. Samuel J. Friedman—Biltmore (from 1925 to 2008. Friedman was a theatre publicist.)
10. Gershwin—Uris. (Named for both composer George and lyricist Ira, it was the Uris from 1972 until 1983.)

At a Theatre Near You

1. Colonial Theatre, Boston—*Curtains*
2. Ford's Theatre, Baltimore—*Kiss Me, Kate*

Continued on next page

3. Zangler Theatre, New York—*Crazy for You*
4. Arch Street Theatre, Philadelphia—*42nd Street*
5. Minsky's Burlesque, New York—*Gypsy*
6. Niblo's Garden, New York—*The Girl in Pink Tights*
7. Apollo Theatre, Harlem—*Dreamgirls*
8. Weismann Theatre, New York—*Follies*
9. Columbia Theatre, Cedar Rapids—*George M!*
10. Shubert Theatre, New Haven—*Mame*

In Residence

1. Guthrie Theatre, Minneapolis (named for its initial artistic director, Tyrone Guthrie)
2. Alley Theatre, Houston
3. Goodman Theatre, Chicago (named for Chicago playwright Kenneth Sawyer Goodman, who had dreamed of creating a resident theatre, but died in the influenza epidemic of 1918)
4. Asolo Repertory Theatre, Sarasota (initially housed in an 18th-century theatre from Asolo in northern Italy, which was dismantled in 1931, acquired by the Ringling Museum in 1949, and reconstructed in Sarasota)
5. Barter Theatre, Abingdon (originally accepted produce from the farms and gardens of cash-strapped Depression-era farmers in lieu of the 35-cent ticket price. Its motto was, "With vegetables you cannot sell, you can buy a good laugh.")
6. Wilma Theatre, Philadelphia (took its name from a feminist collective called the Wilma Project, alluding to an invented talented sister of Shakespeare)
7. Clarence Brown Theatre, Knoxville (named for Brown, a University of Tennessee alumnus, who contributed funding for a new building on the university campus)
8. Long Wharf Theatre, New Haven
9. Old Globe Theatre, San Diego (so named because it was first housed in a building patterned after Shakespeare's Globe Theatre in London and used for Shakespearean performances at the California Pacific International Exposition in 1935 to 1936)
10. Trinity Repertory, Providence (got its name from the Trinity United Methodist Church in Trinity Square, where the first performances were held)

Who Was That Theatre I Saw You With?

1. Fox (named for William Fox, who founded Fox pictures, later merged into Twentieth Century Fox)

2. Saenger (established by brothers Abe and Julian Saenger. The New Orleans Saenger, badly damaged by Hurricane Katrina, has been restored.)
3. Fisher (financed with proceeds of the sale of Fisher Body Company to General Motors in 1919)
4. Pantages (established by theatrical impresario Alexander Pantages)
5. Curran (founded by Homer Curran)
6. Roxy (nickname of Samuel Lionel Rothafel, who later opened Radio City Music Hall featuring the "Roxyettes"—later known as the Rockettes)
7. Mechanic (named for entrepreneur Morris A. Mechanic)
8. Forrest (named for Edwin Forrest, the nineteenth-century Shakespearean actor, whose feud with British actor William Charles Macready caused the Astor Place Riot in New York in 1849)
9. The Shubert Theatre in New Haven was named for Sam S. Shubert by his brothers Lee and J. J.
10. Ford's Theatre in Washington, DC, named for its manager John T. Ford, closed after John Wilkes Booth shot President Abraham Lincoln and did not reopen for more than one hundred years.

You Gotta Know the Lingo

1. French scene—section of a play between the entrance or exit of any character
2. Tormentor—a hard, vertical piece attached to a horizontal piece known as a teaser (often used to create a reduced size or "false" proscenium)
3. The gods—the highest balcony of a theatre (or, sometimes, a raised section at the back of the theatre on which patrons may stand to watch a performance)
4. Ghost light—a light bulb that is left burning onstage during periods when the stage is not in use, for safety reasons
5. Italian—a rehearsal at which the lines are said rapidly (thought to be an aid in memorization and in picking up cues promptly)
6. Sitzprobe—in musical theatre, a rehearsal with singers and orchestra, at which all the actors are usually seated
7. Swing—a chorus member who covers many, or sometimes all, of the chorus parts and who performs only when the primary performer of that part is unable to go on
8. Vomitorium—a passage from the stage that goes below a tier of seats
9. Gobo—a stencil or template placed in front of a lighting source to control the shape of the light emitted
10. Passerelle—a walkway leading beyond the proscenium arch around the audience side of the orchestra pit

XIV

HOME, SWEET HOME

Be it ever so humble, home is where the heart is. It's also where lots of plays and musicals find their inspiration. Kick off your shoes and make yourself at home while you answer these quizzes.

No Place Like Home

Fill in the titles of these Broadway plays and musicals with the missing words—all dwelling places— found in the second column.

1. _____ *in the Sky*, musical by Vernon Duke, Lynn Root, and John La Touche   *Hut*

2. _____ *of Flowers*, musical by Harold Arlen and Truman Capote   *Cottage*

3. _____ *in the Air*, musical by Percy Weinrich and Raymond W. Peck   *Mansions*

4. *Judy Garland "At Home at the _____"*, variety revue   *Hotel*

5. *The Enchanted _____*, play by Arthur Wing Pinero   *Cabin*

6. *The Little _____*, play by Andre Roussin   *Apartment*

7. *Zoya's _____*, play by Mikhail Bulgakov   *Room*

8. _____ *Service*, play by Allen Boretz and John Murray   *House*

9. *More Stately _____*, play by Eugene O'Neill   *Castles*

10. *Grand _____*, play by William A. Drake and musical by George Forrest, Robert Wright, and Luther Davis   *Palace*

All Around the House

Match the playwrights with the play titles—all of which contain the name of an area in a house.

1.	Harold Pinter	*Toys in the Attic*
2.	Graham Greene	*Staircase*
3.	A. R. Gurney	*The Basement*
4.	Arnold Wesker	*Bedroom Farce*
5.	Charles Dyer	*Cat on a Hot Tin Roof*
6.	Alan Ayckbourn	*The Living Room*
7.	Spike Milligan and John Antrobus	*The Kitchen*
8.	Arthur Wilmurt	*The Dining Room*
9.	Lillian Hellman	*The Guest Room*
10.	Tennessee Williams	*The Bed-Sitting Room*

House Party

Match the descriptions with the plays and musicals, each of which has the word "House" in its title—and fill in the missing words.

1.	By Henrik Ibsen, it was the world's most performed play in 2006.	*My _____ in This House*	*Grandmother*
2.	John Guare's 1966 play is about a zoo worker who wants to be a songwriter.	*_____ House*	*Beautiful*
3.	Edith Wharton and Clyde Fitch based this 1906 play on Wharton's novel about Lily Bart.	*The House _____*	*Doll*
4.	This 1931 play by Paul Green is set on a Southern plantation in 1905.	*The _____ House*	*Sister*
5.	A 1980 play by Wendy Kesselman, it is based on a true murder case in France.	*The House of Bernarda _____*	*Leaves*

6. George Bernard Shaw subtitled this 1919 play "A Fantasia in the Russian Manner on English Themes." — *A _____'s House* — Connelly

7. Dorothy Parker famously reviewed this 1931 play by Channing Pollock as "the play lousy." — *To _____'s House We Go* — Mirth

8. Federico García Lorca's last play, it was written in 1936. — *The House of Blue _____* — Heartbreak

9. A 1909 comedy by Granville Barker, it's about a London dressmaker who wants to sell his business. — *The House of _____* — Alba

10. This 1980 play by Joanna M. Glass starred Eva Le Gallienne and Kim Hunter on Broadway. — *The House of _____* — Madras

HOME, SWEET HOME

ANSWERS

No Place Like Home

1. *Cabin in the Sky*
2. *House of Flowers*
3. *Castles in the Air*
4. *Judy Garland "At Home at the Palace"*
5. *The Enchanted Cottage*
6. *The Little Hut*
7. *Zoya's Apartment*
8. *Room Service*
9. *More Stately Mansions*
10. *Grand Hotel*

All Around the House

1. Harold Pinter—*The Basement*
2. Graham Greene—*The Living Room*
3. A. R. Gurney—*The Dining Room*
4. Arnold Wesker—*The Kitchen*
5. Charles Dyer—*Staircase*
6. Alan Ayckbourn—*Bedroom Farce*
7. Spike Millligan and John Antrobus—*The Bed-Sitting Room*
8. Arthur Wilmurt—*The Guest Room*
9. Lillian Hellman—*Toys in the Attic*
10. Tennessee Williams—*Cat on a Hot Tin Roof*

House Party

1. *A Doll's House*
2. *The House of Blue Leaves*
3. *The House of Mirth*
4. *The House of Connelly*
5. *My Sister in This House*
6. *Heartbreak House*
7. *The House Beautiful*
8. *The House of Bernarda Alba*
9. *The Madras House*
10. *To Grandmother's House We Go*

XV

PLACES WE'LL GO!

The theatre can take you all over the world without having to leave the comfort of your seat. Here are some quizzes based on places you can visit with just a flick of your pencil.

City Slickers

Match the descriptions with the plays—and fill in the missing words, each of which is the name of an American city.

1.	Brian Friel's play about an Irishman who moves to America	_____'s Calling Me . . . But I'm Not Going	Laramie
2.	Horton Foote's play about the later life of Will and Lily Dale Kidder	_____ Bound!	Dubuque
3.	John Orlock's play about two spinster sisters who order suitors from a mail order catalog	_____, Here I Come!	Baltimore
4.	Musical by Sally Benson, Don Walker, and Albert Wineman Barker about a group of performers marooned when their ship hits a sandbar	The Lady from _____	Philadelphia
5.	Musical by Harold Arlen and Johnny Mercer about a jockey named Little Augie	Indulgences in the _____ Harem	Atlanta

Continued on next page

6. Edward Albee's play about a visit from an angel of death   *The Young Man from* _____   *Louisville*

7. Musical by Bill Heyer, Hank Beebe, and Sam Dann about the vicissitudes of life in New York   *Hot l* _____   *Buffalo*

8. Ken Ludwig's comedy about a pair of traveling actors   _____ *Woman*   *Memphis*

9. Lanford Wilson's play about a group of people faced with eviction   *The* _____ *Project*   *Tuscaloosa*

10. Play by Moisés Kaufman and the Tectonic Theater Project based on the murder of a college student   *Moon Over* _____   *St. Louis*

State of the Art

Match one musical from the first column and one from the second column with a state in the third column in which both musicals take place.

1. *The Most Happy Fella*	*Rent*	Louisiana
2. *The Music Man*	*Urban Cowboy*	New Jersey
3. *The Cocoanuts*	*Plain and Fancy*	Arizona
4. *High Button Shoes*	*Thou Shalt Not*	New York
5. *1776*	*Funny Face*	Iowa
6. *Annie*	*The Pajama Game*	California
7. *Pal Joey*	*The Yearling*	Texas
8. *Girl Crazy*	*City of Angels*	Florida
9. *The New Moon*	*Clybourne Park*	Pennsylvania
10. *Something for the Boys*	*Whoopee*	Illinois

States of the Union
Fill in the correct name of the state in these titles of plays and musicals.

1. _____ *Purchase*, musical by Morrie Ryskind and Irving Berlin
2. *The Marriage of Mr. _____*, play by Friedrich Dürrenmatt
3. *The Girl from _____*, musical by James T. Tanner, Sydney Jones, Paul A. Rubens, Percy Greenback, Adrian Ross, and Jerome D. Kern
4. *The _____ Idea*, play by Langdon Mitchell
5. *The _____ Cycle*, play by Robert Schenkkan
6. *_____, Li'l Darlin'* musical by Sam Moore, John Whedon, Robert Emmett Dolan, and Johnny Mercer
7. *Abe Lincoln in _____*, play by Robert E. Sherwood
8. *_____ Suite*, play by Neil Simon
9. *Winesburg, _____*, play by Christopher Sergel
10. *A _____ Yankee*, musical by Herbert Fields, Richard Rodgers, and Lorenz Hart

Hometown Folks
Match these characters in plays or musicals with their home towns.

1. Ruth and Eileen Sherwood — Dallas, TX
2. Peggy Sawyer—and Rose Grant — Hannibal, MO
3. Nellie Forbush—and Lorelei Lee — Pittsburgh, PA
4. Joe Hardy—and Molly Brown—and Huckleberry Finn — Salt Lake City, UT
5. Elder Kevin Price—and Una Trance — Chicago, IL
6. Lt. Joseph Cable—and Rocky Balboa — Little Rock, AR
7. Taylor Collins—and Eddie Carbone — Columbus, OH
8. Cleo and Herman — Allentown, PA
9. Big Jule—and King Marchan — Brooklyn, NY
10. Vera Charles—and Troy Maxson — Philadelphia, PA

World Capitals

Match these world capitals with the plays or musicals for which they are settings.

1.	Berlin	*Kismet*
2.	Paris and Moscow	*The King and I*
3.	Vienna	*The Diary of Anne Frank*
4.	Washington, DC	*She Loves Me*
5.	Athens	*The Happiest Girl in the World*
6.	Buenos Aires	*Blossom Time*
7.	Baghdad	*I Am a Camera*
8.	Amsterdam	*Evita*
9.	Bangkok	*First Monday in October*
10.	Budapest	*Silk Stockings*

Vive la France!

Match these characters, all of whom are French—or purport to be—with the musicals and plays in which they appear.

1.	Charlemagne	*No Strings*
2.	Paul Berthalet	*The Merry Wives of Windsor*
3.	Edouard Dindon	*Irma la Douce*
4.	Solange LaFitte	*South Pacific*
5.	Doctor Caius	*Big River*
6.	Luc Delbert	*Can-Can*
7.	"The King," self-proclaimed heir to the French throne	*Follies*
8.	Nestor-le-Fripé	*La Cage aux Folles*
9.	La Môme Pistache	*Pippin*
10.	Emile de Becque	*Carnival!*

Where It's At

Match these settings with the proper plays.

1. Chinquapin, Louisiana. Truvy's beauty salon.	*The Playboy of the Western World*
2. Red Hook, on the Bay seaward from the Brooklyn Bridge.	*Miss Julie*
3. Just outside Silver Creek, Colorado.	*Waiting for Godot*
4. Mme. Ranevskayas's estate.	*The Little Foxes*
5. The large kitchen of a Swedish manor house.	*A View from the Bridge*
6. In and immediately outside of the Cabot farmhouse in New England.	*The Bald Soprano*
7. A country road. A tree.	*Misery*
8. A middle-class English interior, with English armchairs, on an English evening.	*Steel Magnolias*
9. Near a village on a wild coast of Mayo.	*Desire Under the Elms*
10. The living room of the Giddens house in a small town in the South.	*The Cherry Orchard*

French 101

Match these French playwrights with their works and with their customary English translations. (Not all the translations are literal.)

	Playwright	Work	Translation
1.	Jean Cocteau	*Huis Clos*	*The Game of Love and Chance*
2.	Molière	*Les Paravents*	*Tiger at the Gates*
3.	Jean Anouilh	*Les Pattes de Mouche*	*No Exit*
4.	Jean Giraudoux	*Partage de midi*	*The School for Wives*
5.	Pierre de Marivaux	*La Puce à l'oreille*	*Intimate Relations*
6.	Victorien Sardou	*Le Bal des Voleurs*	*A Flea in Her Ear*
7.	Paul Claudel	*La Guerre de Troie n'aura pas lieu*	*The Screens*
8.	Jean-Paul Sartre	*Les Parents terribles*	*Thieves' Carnival*
9.	Georges Feydeau	*Le Jeu de l'amour et du hasard*	*A Scrap of Paper*
10.	Jean Genet	*L'école des Femmes*	*Break of Noon*

Great Day for the Irish!
Name these Irish playwrights:

1. Born in Dublin in 1751, he was the author of *A Trip to Scarborough*, the longtime owner of London's Drury Lane Theatre, and a member of the House of Commons.

   Brian Friel

2. Born in Dublin in 1854, he wrote *A Woman of No Importance* and once toured the United States to help Richard D'Oyly Carte promote Gilbert and Sullivan's operetta *Patience*.

   John Millington Synge

3. Born in Ballymahon, County Longford, in 1730, he wrote *The Good-Natur'd Man* and is thought to have coined the phrase "goody two-shoes" in a children's book.

   Brendan Behan

4. Born in Sandymount, County Dublin, in 1865, he was the author of *The Herne's Egg*, a founder of the Abbey Theatre, and the first Irishman to win a Nobel Prize for literature.

   Conor McPherson

5. Born in Dublin in 1971, he is the author of *The Weir*, which won the 1999 Olivier Award for Best New Play.

   Oliver Goldsmith

6. Born in Rathfarnham, County Dublin, in 1871, he died of Hodgkin's disease at the age of thirty-eight, while working on *Deirdre of the Sorrows*.

   Samuel Beckett

7. Born in Dublin in 1880, his play *The Silver Tassie* was rejected by the Abbey Theatre in 1928 but performed in London eighteen months later, directed by Raymond Massey and starring Charles Laughton.

   William Butler Yeats

8. Born in Omagh, County Tyrone, in 1929, he is the author of *Faith Healer* and *Dancing at Lughnasa*.

   Sean O'Casey

9. Born in Dublin in 1923, he was a member of the IRA at the age of sixteen and served time in a British "borstal" youth prison, about which he wrote *Borstal Boy*.

   Richard Brinsley Sheridan

10. Born in Dublin in 1906, he wrote plays in both French and English, including *That Time*.

    Oscar Wilde

V Marks the Spot

Match these descriptions of plays and musicals with their titles—and fill in the missing word, each of which is the name of a place that begins with the letter "V."

1.	A 1964 play by Arthur Miller that takes place during World War II	*The Merchant of _____*	*Vichy*
2.	A 1931 play by Robert E. Sherwood that starred Alfred Lunt and Lynn Fontanne	*_____ Forge*	*Venus*
3.	A play by William Shakespeare that has been produced fifty times on Broadway, recently starring Al Pacino	*Incident at _____*	*Verona*
4.	A Shakespeare play adapted into a 1971 musical by John Guare, Mel Shapiro, and Galt MacDermot	*Miracle at _____*	*Venice*
5.	A 1931 satire by Hans Chlumberg set twenty-five years after World War I	*Reunion in _____*	*Vermont*
6.	A 1907 play by William C. De Mille set during the Civil War, featuring Mary Pickford and Cecil B. De Mille (William's brother) in the cast	*Two Gentlemen of _____*	*Venice*
7.	A 1929 play by A. E. Thomas produced by George M. Cohan	*Men Are from Mars, Women Are from _____*	*Vienna*

8. Either a 1929 musical revue with   _____   *Valley*
choreography by Busby Berkeley
or a 1900 musical by Johann
Strauss

9. A 1939 play by Maxwell   *The Warrens of*   *Verdun*
Anderson in which George   _____
Washington is a character

10. A 1997 solo performance by John   *A Night in* _____   *Virginia*
Gray

Up from Down Under

Identify these noted actors, all of whom were born in Australia, and match their first and last names.

1. She played Lady Macbeth opposite Laurence Olivier, won a Tony Award for her Medea opposite John Gielgud, and was made a Dame in 1960.

   Cate   Humphries

2. He won an Emmy as host of the Tony Awards—and also hosted the Academy Awards.

   Leo   Kidman

3. Her only Broadway appearance was in *The Blue Room* in 1998.

   Zoe   Rush

4. He created the role of the Common Man in *A Man for All Seasons*, but played Thomas Cromwell in that play on Broadway and in the film version.

   Barry   Anderson

5. From 2008 to 2013 she and her husband were Artistic Directors of the Sydney Theatre Company.

   Diane   McKern

6. He played in *Irma la Douce*, *Man of La Mancha*, and *La Cage aux Folles* on Broadway, but is more widely known for TV work as Henry VIII and Heathcliff.

   Geoffrey   Caldwell

7. She won four Tony Awards for *Slapstick Tragedy*, *The Prime of Miss Jean Brodie*, *Medea*, and *Master Class*.

   Judith   Blanchett

8. He created the character of Dame
   Edna Everage.   Hugh   Cilento

9. A Tony Award nominee for *Tiger at   Nicole   Michell
   the Gates*, she was at one time married
   to actor Sean Connery and later to
   playwright Anthony Shaffer.

10. He has won a Tony Award (*Exit the   Keith   Jackman
    King*), an Oscar (*Shine*), and an Emmy
    (*The Life and Death of Peter Sellers*).

PLACES WE'LL GO!

ANSWERS

City Slickers
1. *Philadelphia, Here I Come!*
2. *The Young Man from Atlanta*
3. *Indulgences in the Louisville Harem*
4. *Memphis Bound!*
5. *St. Louis Woman*
6. *The Lady from Dubuque*
7. *Tuscaloosa's Calling Me . . . But I'm Not Going*
8. *Moon Over Buffalo*
9. *Hot l Baltimore*
10. *The Laramie Project*

State of the Art
1. *The Most Happy Fella* and *City of Angels*—California
2. *The Music Man* and *The Pajama Game*—Iowa
3. *The Cocoanuts* and *The Yearling*—Florida
4. *High Button Shoes* and *Funny Face*—New Jersey
5. *1776* and *Plain and Fancy*—Pennsylvania
6. *Annie* and *Rent*—New York
7. *Pal Joey* and *Clybourne Park*—Illinois
8. *Girl Crazy* and *Whoopee*—Arizona
9. *The New Moon* and *Thou Shalt Not*—Louisiana
10. *Something for the Boys* and *Urban Cowboy*—Texas

States of the Union
1. *Louisiana Purchase*
2. *The Marriage of Mr. Mississippi*
3. *The Girl from Utah*
4. *The New York Idea*
5. *The Kentucky Cycle*
6. *Texas, Li'l Darlin'*
7. *Abe Lincoln in Illinois*
8. *California Suite*
9. *Winesburg, Ohio*
10. *A Connecticut Yankee*

Hometown Folks

1. Ruth and Eileen Sherwood are sisters from Columbus, OH, in *Wonderful Town*.
2. Peggy Sawyer in *42nd Street* and Rose Grant in *Bye Bye Birdie* are both from Allentown, PA.
3. Nellie Forbush in *South Pacific* and Lorelei Lee in *Gentlemen Prefer Blondes* are both from Little Rock, AR.
4. Joe Hardy in *Damn Yankees*, Molly Brown in *The Unsinkable Molly Brown*, and Huckleberry Finn in *Big River* are all from Hannibal, MO.
5. Elder Kevin Price in *The Book of Mormon* and Una Trance in *The Girl from Utah* are from Salt Lake City, UT.
6. Lt. Joseph Cable in *South Pacific* and Rocky Balboa in *Rocky* are from Philadelphia, PA.
7. Taylor Collins in *Brooklyn* and Eddie Carbone in *A View from the Bridge* are from Brooklyn, NY.
8. Cleo and Herman in *The Most Happy Fella* are from Dallas, TX.
9. Big Jule in *Guys and Dolls* and King Marchan in *Victor/Victoria* are from Chicago, IL.
10. Vera Charles in *Mame* or *Auntie Mame* and Troy Maxson in *Fences* are from Pittsburgh, PA.

World Capitals

1. Berlin—*I Am a Camera*
2. Paris and Moscow—*Silk Stockings*
3. Vienna—*Blossom Time*
4. Washington, DC—*First Monday in October*
5. Athens—*The Happiest Girl in the World*
6. Buenos Aires—*Evita*
7. Baghdad—*Kismet*
8. Amsterdam—*The Diary of Anne Frank*
9. Bangkok—*The King and I*
10. Budapest—*She Loves Me*

Vive la France!

1. Charlemagne (known as Charles) is Pippin's father in *Pippin*.
2. Paul Berthalet is the crippled puppeteer in *Carnival!*
3. Edouard Dindon is the head of the Tradition, Family, and Morality Party in *La Cage aux Folles*.
4. Solange LaFitte is a former "Weismann Girl" in *Follies*.
5. Doctor Caius is one of Anne Page's wooers in *The Merry Wives of Windsor*.
6. Luc Delbert is a fashion photographer in *No Strings*.
7. "The King" is the self-proclaimed heir to the French throne, who along with his pal, "The Duke," meets up with Huck and Jim in *Big River*.
8. Nestor-le-Fripé is the law student who loves Irma in *Irma la Douce*.
9. La Môme Pistache owns the Bal du Paradis dance hall in *Can-Can*.
10. Emile de Becque is the French planter on the Pacific island in *South Pacific*.

Where It's At

1. *Steel Magnolias*
2. *A View from the Bridge*
3. *Misery*
4. *The Cherry Orchard*
5. *Miss Julie*
6. *Desire Under the Elms*
7. *Waiting for Godot*
8. *The Bald Soprano*
9. *The Playboy of the Western World*
10. *The Little Foxes*

French 101

1. Jean Cocteau—*Les Parents terribles*—*Intimate Relations*
2. Molière—*L'école des Femmes*—*The School for Wives*
3. Jean Anouilh—*Le Bal des Voleurs*—*Thieves' Carnival*
4. Jean Giraudoux—*La Guerre de Troie n'aura pas lieu*—*Tiger at the Gates*
5. Pierre de Marivaux—*Le Jeu de l'amour et du hasard*—*The Game of Love and Chance*
6. Victorien Sardou—*Les Pattes de Mouche*—*A Scrap of Paper*
7. Paul Claudel—*Partage de midi*—*Break of Noon*
8. Jean-Paul Sartre—*Huis Clos*—*No Exit*
9. Georges Feydeau—*La Puce à l'oreille*—*A Flea in Her Ear*
10. Jean Genet—*Les Paravents*—*The Screens*

Great Day for the Irish!

1. Richard Brinsley Sheridan
2. Oscar Wilde
3. Oliver Goldsmith
4. William Butler Yeats
5. Conor McPherson
6. John Millington Synge
7. Sean O'Casey
8. Brian Friel
9. Brendan Behan
10. Samuel Beckett

V Marks the Spot
1. *Incident at Vichy*
2. *Reunion in Vienna*
3. *The Merchant of Venice*
4. *The Two Gentlemen of Verona*
5. *Miracle at Verdun*
6. *The Warrens of Virginia*
7. *Vermont*
8. *A Night in Venice*
9. *Valley Forge*
10. *Men Are from Mars, Women Are from Venus*

Up from Down Under
1. Judith Anderson
2. Hugh Jackman
3. Nicole Kidman
4. Leo McKern
5. Cate Blanchett
6. Keith Michell
7. Zoe Caldwell
8. Barry Humphries
9. Diane Cilento
10. Geoffrey Rush

XVI

HAPPY HOLIDAYS!

Everybody loves a holiday, and the people who write for the theatre are no exception. Here are some quizzes about various holidays throughout the year. And it's okay if you don't show up for work while you're answering them.

'Tis the Season

Match the Christmas songs in the left column with the correct musicals in the right column:

1. "It's Beginning to Look a Lot Like Christmas"	*Rent*
2. "We Need a Little Christmas"	*She Loves Me*
3. "Christmas Child"	*Billy Elliot: The Musical*
4. "Hard Candy Christmas"	*Irma la Douce*
5. "Christmas Bells"	*Annie*
6. "A New Deal for Christmas"	*Catch Me If You Can*
7. "Merry Christmas, Maggie Thatcher"	*A Christmas Story: The Musical*
8. "Christmas Is My Favorite Time of Year"	*Mame*
9. "Twelve Days to Christmas"	*Here's Love*
10. "It All Comes Down to Christmas"	*The Best Little Whorehouse in Texas*

Holiday Greetings

Match the situations described in the first column with the correct holidays and the musicals in which they are featured.

1. This holiday is celebrated in the 5th Avenue townhouse of Edward Seton in 1933 to 1934, in a musical based on Philip Barry's play *Holiday*.

   May Day   *Banjo Eyes*

2. Eulalie Mackecknie Shinn leads the singing of "Columbia, the Gem of the Ocean," then joins the Wa Tan Ye girls in an Indian dance.

   Thanksgiving Day   *Promises, Promises*

3. Babe and Sid lead fellow factory workers in "Once a Year Day."

   Christmas   *As Thousands Cheer*

4. Unemployed musicians Jerry and Joe witness a Chicago gangland killing, then flee from Spats Palazzo and his henchmen.

   Easter Sunday   *Thou Shalt Not*

5. This show-stopping number by Irving Berlin featured elaborate hats in a 1933 musical revue.

   New Year's Eve   *The Music Man*

6. Guenevere meets Lancelot on this occasion.

   Fourth of July   *Here's Love*

7. Set in the Carver Greeting Card Company, a 1941 musical with a score by Vernon Duke and John La Touche features songs about Valentine's Day, Easter, Christmas—and one other holiday.

   Annual Company Picnic   *Happy New Year*

8. In this musical by David Thompson and Harry Connick Jr., based on a novel by Émile Zola, Thérèse, her husband Camille, and her lover Laurent sing about this holiday event.   Mother's Day   *Sugar*

9. Three secretaries dance and sing about "Turkey Lurkey Time."   St. Valentine's Day   *Camelot*

10. Doris Walker is organizing a parade in New York, culminating in the number "Big Clown Balloons."   Mardi Gras   *The Pajama Game*

April Foolery
In honor of April Fool's Day:

1. Actor-comedian Ed Wynn wrote and appeared in a Broadway revue, the title of which became his nickname. It was
   * ★ *The Crazy Fool*
   * ★ *The Perfect Fool*
   * ★ *The Foolish Fop*
   * ★ *The Great Profile*

2. Playwright Sam Shepard played the leading role in the movie adaptation of his play *Fool for Love*. Who played opposite him?
   * ★ Jessica Lange
   * ★ Meryl Streep
   * ★ Kim Basinger
   * ★ Marjorie Main

Continued on next page

3. Neil Simon's *Fools* ran a disappointing forty performances on Broadway. Who directed it?
   * Mike Nichols
   * Jack O'Brien
   * Harold Prince
   * Judd Apatow

4. Alan Bates and Frank Langella starred in the Broadway premiere of *Fortune's Fool*, a Russian play written in 1848 by . . .
   * Anton Chekhov
   * Boris Trigorin
   * Ivan Turgenev
   * Tsar Nicholas

5. Shakespeare used the character of a fool or jester in many of his plays. Which of these is not a fool?
   * Touchstone
   * Horatio
   * Feste
   * Trinculo

6. "That, of course, is the great secret of the successful fool—that he is no fool at all." This is a comment on Shakespeare's fools by . . .
   * William Shakespeare
   * Isaac Asimov
   * Charles Dickens
   * Buster Keaton

7. Theresa Rebeck's play *Fool*, which premiered in 2014 at the Alley Theatre, is about . . .
   * A competition between the fools of two medieval kings
   * An unnamed president of the United States
   * Ed Wynn
   * A well-known network news anchor

8. The Fool in *King Lear* tells Lear he will make "two crowns" out of
   * One crown
   * An egg
   * A piece of gold
   * Lear's head

9. *Fool Moon* is a Broadway show devised by Bill Irwin and David Shiner that featured
   * No spoken lines
   * A chorus line of tap-dancing kangaroos
   * Costumes by Andy Warhol
   * A surprise guest appearance by Donald Trump

10. In *As You Like It*, what kind of fool does Jaques report he met in the forest?
    * A foolish fool
    * A wise fool
    * A motley fool
    * A silly fool

Which Witch?

In the spirit of Halloween, match these witches with the plays or musicals in which they appear.

1. Elphaba Thropp	*Dark of the Moon*
2. Tituba	*The Milk Train Doesn't Stop Here Anymore*
3. John, a "witch boy"	*The Witch of Edmonton*
4. The White Witch	*The Lady's Not for Burning*
5. Gillian Holroyd	*Wicked*
6. Alexandra Spofford, Jane Smart, and Sukie Rougemont	*The Crucible*
7. Congo Witch Doctor	*The Lion, the Witch, and the Wardrobe*
8. Jennet Jourdemayne	*The Emperor Jones*
9. Vera Ridgeway Condotti	*Bell, Book and Candle*
10. Mother Sawyer	*The Witches of Eastwick*

Happy Haunting

And in the same vein of ghosties and ghoulies and things that go bump in the night, identify the plays and musicals in which these ghosts figure.

1. A deceased wife is inadvertently summoned by an eccentric medium and then tries to break up her former husband's second marriage.

   Carousel

2. A carnival barker killed in a robbery is allowed to return to earth to do one good deed.

   A Christmas Carol

3. A king's ghost urges his son to avenge his death and his widow's remarriage to his brother.

   The Innocents

4. A deceased husband gives his widow a sign that it's all right for her to remarry.

   Sunday in the Park with George

5. After he's murdered, a banker contacts his girlfriend via a fraudulent psychic.

   Fiddler on the Roof

6. Ghosts of a governess and a valet possess two children.

   Hamlet

7. A sculptor is encouraged to "just keep moving on" by his grandmother's ghost.

   Hello, Dolly!

8. A ghost appears at a banquet to haunt the man who ordered his murder.

   Ghost the Musical

9. The grandmother of a bride-to-be and the late wife of her intended return from the grave to stop the marriage.

   Macbeth

10. A businessman who is as "dead as a doornail" tries to save his former partner from his fate.

    Blithe Spirit

Thank You Very Much!

As a Thanksgiving tribute, see if you know who is thanking whom or for what in these plays and musicals.

1. In *Annie,* whom do the Hooverville-ites "thank" for their plight in "We'd Like to Thank You"?
    * Franklin D. Roosevelt
    * Herbert Hoover
    * Miss Hannigan
    * their lucky stars

2. In the original *Gigi,* the aging roué Honoré sings "Thank Heaven" for something, but in the 2015 revival, it is Mamita and Aunt Alicia who are thankful—for what?
    * Champagne
    * Little girls
    * Being old
    * Being French

3. What song, which begins "Thank God . . . ," popularized by John Denver, is sung to open Act II of the musical *Priscilla, Queen of the Desert?*
    * "Thank God It's Friday"
    * "Thank God I'm a Country Boy"
    * "Thank God for the Next Oasis"
    * "Thank God for the Rockies"

4. What does Joice Heth thank God for in a song from *Barnum?*
    * I'm old
    * I'm rich
    * I'm beautiful
    * I'm working

5. In *The Chocolate Soldier*, Major Spiridoff, Colonel Popoff, Mascha, and Aurelia Popoff lead the ensemble in singing "Thank the Lord . . ."
   ★ For chocolate
   ★ The war is over
   ★ It's five o'clock
   ★ We're in the army

6. In *Mamma Mia*, Sophie, Sam, Harry, and Bill sing what song that is sometimes regarded as ABBA's farewell song?
   ★ "Thank You for the Music"
   ★ "Thank You for Listening"
   ★ "Thank You for Buying Our Records"
   ★ "Thank You and Good Night"

7. In *She Loves Me*, Ladislav, Georg, Steven, and Ilona sing "Thank You, Madam" to . . .
   ★ Their boss
   ★ Their customers
   ★ A madam in a brothel
   ★ Madame Tussaud

8. What Academy Award–winning song sung by Bob Hope and Shirley Ross in *The Big Broadcast of 1938* later popped up in *A Day in Hollywood/A Night in the Ukraine*?
   ★ "Thanks for Everything"
   ★ "Thanks for Nothing"
   ★ "Thanks, but No Thanks"
   ★ "Thanks for the Memory"

Continued on next page

9. In *Cabaret*, Fräulein Schneider expresses her gratitude to Herr Schultz for a gift by singing "It Couldn't Please Me More." What is the gift?
   * A diamond ring
   * A bottle of French champagne
   * A fake passport
   * A pineapple

10. In the song that opens Act II of *Wicked*, the lyrics "thank goodness" for . . .
    * Yesterday
    * Today
    * Tomorrow
    * Next year

Merry Christmas!

Here are some questions about plays and musicals whose theme is the Yuletide season.

1. Several dramatic adaptations have been made of *A Christmas Memory*, about Buddy and his elderly cousin Sook and the making of a Christmas fruitcake. It was originally a short story by . . .
   * Truman Capote
   * Charles Dickens
   * Harper Lee
   * Stephen King

2. In *A Christmas Story: The Musical,* nine-year-old Ralphie is warned, "You'll shoot your eye out," if he gets what Christmas gift that he covets?
   * A slingshot
   * An air rifle
   * A blowgun
   * A dartboard

3. Two Broadway musicals—*Irving Berlin's White Christmas* and *Holiday Inn, the New Irving Berlin Musical*—both include Berlin's "White Christmas" and which other song?
   * "I've Got My Love to Keep Me Warm"
   * "Easter Parade"
   * "Blue Skies"
   * "Heat Wave"

4. In *A Christmas Carol,* the main course of the Cratchits' Christmas dinner before Scrooge brings them the "prize turkey" is . . .
   * Roast goose
   * Fish and chips
   * Pork pie
   * Gruel

5. Broadway's *Dr. Seuss' How the Grinch Stole Christmas!* was commissioned and first produced by the Children's Theatre Company in . . .
   * Seattle
   * San Diego
   * Washington, DC
   * Minneapolis

Continued on next page

6. In *Here's Love*, Doris Walker is an executive at . . .
   * ★ Tiffany's
   * ★ Macy's
   * ★ Saks Fifth Avenue
   * ★ F.A.O. Schwarz

7. *SantaLand Diaries* is about David Sedaris's Christmas season job as one of Santa's elves in . . .
   * ★ Bloomingdale's
   * ★ Lord & Taylor
   * ★ Whole Foods
   * ★ Macy's

8. In the musical *Elf*, Buddy, the oversized elf, gets into a fight with Santa Claus at . . .
   * ★ Macy's
   * ★ Marshall Field
   * ★ Gimbel's
   * ★ Walmart

9. Thornton Wilder's *The Long Christmas Dinner* takes place over a period of . . .
   * ★ Four hours
   * ★ Three days
   * ★ One week
   * ★ Ninety years

10. Two numbers have been part of the *Radio City Christmas Spectacular* every year since the first production in 1932. One is "The Living Nativity," and the other is . . .
    ★ "Parade of the Wooden Soldiers"
    ★ "Frosty the Snowman"
    ★ "Rudolph the Red-Nosed Reindeer"
    ★ "Winter Wonderland"

Happy New Year!

These questions are all about plays or musicals dealing with the New Year.

1. "Going Home on New Year's Morning" is a song in the 1925 opera *Song of the Flame*, which takes place during the Russian Revolution. Which of the following was not among the composers and lyricists of this work?
   ★ George Gershwin
   ★ Oscar Hammerstein II
   ★ Irving Berlin
   ★ Otto Harbach

2. *Happy New Year* is a musical based on Philip Barry's play *Holiday* featuring a score by . . .
   ★ Cole Porter
   ★ Sigmund Romberg
   ★ Rodgers and Hart
   ★ Tom Lehrer

Continued on next page

3. At the end of "Happy New Year" in *Rent,* The Man enters and hands Mimi a small plastic bag containing . . .
   * Hershey's Chocolate Kisses
   * A white powder
   * Half of a ham-on-rye sandwich
   * Mimi's false eyelashes

4. *Dance a Little Closer,* a musical by Alan Jay Lerner and Charles Strouse, set on New Year's Eve "in the avoidable future," is based on Robert E. Sherwood's antiwar comedy . . .
   * *The Petrified Forest*
   * *Idiot's Delight*
   * *Reunion in Vienna*
   * *Waterloo Bridge*

5. "I Feel Like New Year's Eve" is a song from the 1964 musical *Something More* that was sung by a performer who had starred the previous year in *She Loves Me* . . .
   * Barbara Cook
   * Barbara Baxley
   * Barbara Lang
   * Barbra Streisand

6. The original 1997 production of the musical *Side Show* had a song called "New Year's Day." In the 2014 revival, the song was changed to
   * "Christmas Day"
   * "Halloween"
   * "Easter Parade"
   * "New Year's Eve"

7. The lyrics for "New Year's Eve," a song from the musical *A Doll's Life*, were written by
   ★ Alan and Marilyn Bergman
   ★ Alan Jay Lerner
   ★ Betty Comden and Adolph Green
   ★ Harold Prince

8. *Chance and Chemistry* was a 2009 tribute to what composer, who wrote "What Are You Doing New Year's Eve?"
   ★ Jimmy McHugh
   ★ Jule Styne
   ★ Frank Loesser
   ★ Irving Berlin

9. In *Show Boat*, on New Year's Eve Cap'n Andy goes to hear his daughter, Magnolia, sing at the Trocadero club in . . .
   ★ New Orleans
   ★ New York
   ★ Chicago
   ★ Natchez

10. In *Sunset Boulevard*, two movie directors are mentioned in the New Year's Eve party song "This Time Next Year." They are . . .
    ★ Martin Scorsese and Francis Ford Coppola
    ★ Stephen Spielberg and Alfred Hitchcock
    ★ Cecil B. DeMille and Billy Wilder
    ★ Ingmar Bergman and Orson Welles

HAPPY HOLIDAYS!

ANSWERS

'Tis the Season
1. "It's Beginning to Look a Lot Like Christmas" from *Here's Love* (Written by Meredith Willson twelve years before *Here's Love*, this song appears in the musical under the title "Pine Cones and Holly Berries.")
2. "We Need a Little Christmas" from *Mame*
3. "Christmas Child" from *Irma la Douce*
4. "Hard Candy Christmas" from *The Best Little Whorehouse in Texas*
5. "Christmas Bells" from *Rent*
6. "A New Deal for Christmas" from *Annie*
7. "Merry Christmas, Maggie Thatcher" from *Billy Elliot: The Musical*
8. "Christmas Is My Favorite Time of Year" from *Catch Me If You Can*
9. "Twelve Days to Christmas" from *She Loves Me*
10. "It All Comes Down to Christmas" from *A Christmas Story: The Musical*

Holiday Greetings
1. New Year's Eve is celebrated in *Happy New Year*, a 1980 musical by Burt Shevelove.
2. Eulalie Mackecknie Shinn is observing the Fourth of July in *The Music Man*.
3. "Once a Year Day" refers to the Sleep-Tite Pajama Company's Annual Picnic in *The Pajama Game*.
4. Jerry and Joe witness the St. Valentine's Day Massacre in *Sugar*.
5. Irving Berlin's show-stopping number is "Her Easter Bonnet" (later known as "Easter Parade") in *As Thousands Cheer*.
6. King Arthur introduces Guenevere and Lancelot at a May Day celebration in *Camelot*.

Continued on next page

7. "Mother's Day," as well as "Valentine's Day Card," "Easter Greetings," "Merry Christmas," are all musical numbers in *Banjo Eyes*.

8. Thérèse Raquin, her husband Camille, and her lover Laurent sing "Take Her to the Mardi Gras" in *Thou Shalt Not*, based on Émile Zola's *Thérèse Raquin*, reset from Paris to New Orleans.

9. "Turkey Lurkey Time" is a number at an office Christmas party in *Promises, Promises*.

10. Doris Walker is planning Macy's Thanksgiving Day parade in *Here's Love*.

April Foolery

1. *The Perfect Fool*
2. Kim Basinger
3. Mike Nichols
4. Ivan Turgenev
5. Horatio (He is Hamlet's school friend and confidant and not a fool. Touchstone is the fool in *As You Like It*; Feste is the fool in *Twelfth Night*, and Trinculo is a fool in *The Tempest*.)
6. Isaac Asimov (in his *Guide to Shakespeare*)
7. Two medieval kings bet which of their fools is funnier and the winner of the competition gets to keep his head.
8. The Fool in *King Lear* tells Lear: "Give me an egg, and I'll give thee two crowns . . . after I have cut the egg i' the middle and eat up the meat, the two crowns of the egg."
9. No spoken lines
10. Jaques says, "A fool, a fool! I met a fool i' the forest, / A motley fool . . ."

Which Witch?

1. Elphaba Thropp, the illegitimate daughter of Melena Thropp and the Wizard of Oz, is the young woman who later becomes "The Wicked Witch of the West" in *Wicked*.

2. Tituba is the slave who is accused of witchcraft in *The Crucible*.

3. John is a witch boy who is given human form when he falls in love with Barbara Allen in *Dark of the Moon*.

4. The White Witch is the queen of Narnia in *The Lion, the Witch, and the Wardrobe*.

5. Gillian Holroyd is the witch in *Bell, Book and Candle*.

6. Alexandra Spofford, Jane Smart, and Sukie Rougemont are the three witches in *The Witches of Eastwick.*
7. The Congo Witch Doctor is a dancer in *The Emperor Jones.*
8. Jennet Jourdemayne is accused of being a witch in *The Lady's Not for Burning.*
9. Vera Ridgeway Condotti, original name of the character known as "The Witch of Capri," is a gossipy neighbor of Sissy Goforth's in Tennessee Williams's *The Milk Train Doesn't Stop Here Anymore.* Although written for a woman (and originated by Mildred Dunnock), the role is often played by a man (including Noël Coward in the film version called *Boom!*).
10. Mother Sawyer is an elderly woman who sells her soul to the Devil in order to wreak revenge on her neighbors in *The Witch of Edmonton,* a 1621 play by William Rowley, Thomas Dekker, and John Ford.

Happy Haunting

1. Elvira Condomine tries to break up the second marriage of her former husband, Charles, in *Blithe Spirit.*
2. Carnival barker Billy Bigelow is allowed to return to earth in *Carousel.*
3. King Hamlet urges his son, Prince Hamlet, to avenge his death and his widow's marriage to his brother in *Hamlet.*
4. Ephraim Levi gives his widow, Dolly Levi, permission to remarry in *Hello, Dolly!* (and in *The Matchmaker,* on which it is based).
5. The banker Sam Wheat contacts his fiancée, Molly Jensen, via the psychic Oda Mae Brown in *Ghost the Musical.*
6. Ghosts of the governess, Miss Jessel, and the valet, Peter Quint, haunt the children, Miles and Flora, in *The Innocents* (based on Henry James's *The Turn of the Screw*).
7. George, the sculptor, is encouraged by the ghost of his grandmother Marie in *Sunday in the Park with George.*
8. Banquo appears at a banquet to haunt Macbeth in *Macbeth.*
9. Grandmother Tzeitel and Lazar Wolf's late wife, Fruma-Sarah, appear as ghosts to stop young Tzeitel from marrying Lazar in *Fiddler on the Roof.*
10. Jacob Marley tries to save his former partner, Ebenezer Scrooge, in *A Christmas Carol.*

Thank You Very Much!

1. Herbert Hoover
2. Little girls (In the revival, the sentiments were thought to be more proper coming from Mamita and Aunt Alicia.)
3. "Thank God I'm a Country Boy" by John Martin Sommers was in John Denver's album "Back Home Again" and was at the top of the Billboard Hot 100 in 1975.
4. "I'm old" (Joice Heth was billed by Barnum as "the oldest woman alive.")
5. "Thank the Lord the war is over"
6. "Thank You for the Music"
7. Their customers (in Maraczek's Parfumerie)
8. "Thanks for the Memory" (by Ralph Rainger and Leo Robin, which also became Bob Hope's theme song)
9. A pineapple
10. "Thank goodness for today"

Merry Christmas!

1. Truman Capote
2. Air rifle (a Red Ryder Carbine Action 200-Shot Range Model)
3. "Blue Skies" is in both musicals.
4. Roast goose
5. Minneapolis (Commissioned in 1994, it opened on Broadway for the first time in 2006.)
6. Macy's
7. Macy's
8. Macy's
9. Ninety years
10. "Parade of the Wooden Soldiers"

Happy New Year!

1. Irving Berlin (Gershwin and Herbert J. Stothart composed the music, and the lyrics were by Hammerstein and Harbach.)
2. Cole Porter (standards)
3. A white powder
4. *Idiot's Delight*
5. Barbara Cook
6. "New Year's Eve"
7. Betty Comden and Adolph Green
8. Frank Loesser
9. Chicago
10. Cecil B. DeMille and Billy Wilder

XVII

CREATIVE TYPES

Who wrote the play, or the book and the lyrics? Who composed the music? Who directed the show? Who choreographed it? These quizzes will provide those answers. Can you?

Teamwork

Match the musicals with their composer-lyricist teams—all of whom are better known for more famous works.

1. *Dearest Enemy, Peggy-Ann, Simple Simon*   George Gershwin and Ira Gershwin

2. *Life of the Party, The Day Before Spring, What's Up?*   John Kander and Fred Ebb

3. *Sweet Adeline, Music in the Air, Very Warm for May*   Alan Jay Lerner and Frederick Loewe

4. *Flora the Red Menace, The Rink, All About Us*   Charles Strouse and Lee Adams

5. *The Apple Tree, Tenderloin, The Body Beautiful*   Jerome Kern and Oscar Hammerstein II

6. *Hold Everything, Flying High, Manhattan Mary*   Sheldon Harnick and Jerry Bock

7. *All American, I and Albert, A Broadway Musical*   Jerome Kern, Guy Bolton, and P. G. Wodehouse

8. *Two on the Aisle, Subways Are for Sleeping, Fade Out-Fade In*   B. G. DeSylva, Lew Brown, and Ray Henderson

9. *Tip-Toes, Treasure Girl, Let 'Em Eat Cake*   Betty Comden, Adolph Green, and Jule Styne

10. *Have A Heart, Oh, Lady! Lady!, Sitting Pretty*   Richard Rodgers and Lorenz Hart

With a Little Help from My Friends

Match the playwrights in the first column with their collaborators in the second column—and then with the plays they wrote together.

1.	Tennessee Williams	Robert E. Lee	*The Royal Family*
2.	William Shakespeare	Jerome Chodorov	*The Duchess of Malfi*
3.	George S. Kaufman	Robert Chapman	*Inherit the Wind*
4.	Howard Lindsay	John Ford	*Pravda*
5.	Joseph A. Fields	Donald Windham	*Billy Budd*
6.	Jerome Lawrence	John Fletcher	*You Touched Me*
7.	John Webster	Edna Ferber	*What Price Glory?*
8.	Louis O. Coxe	Russel Crouse	*My Sister Eileen*
9.	Maxwell Anderson	David Hare	*Life with Father*
10.	Howard Brenton	Laurence Stallings	*The Two Noble Kinsmen*

Author! Author!

These questions are all about noted playwrights.

1. Who is the only playwright who has won Pulitzer Prizes in both fiction (1928) and in drama (1938 and 1943)?
   * ✶ Thornton Wilder
   * ✶ Carson McCullers
   * ✶ Maxwell Anderson
   * ✶ David Mamet

2. Alfred Tennyson, T. S. Eliot, and Jean Anouilh all wrote plays about the same martyred saint. Who was it?
   * ✶ Joan of Arc
   * ✶ Thomas Becket
   * ✶ Galileo
   * ✶ Thomas More

3. Of what playwright did critic Clive Barnes say: "He is destined to remain rich, successful, and under-rated"?
   * Edward Albee
   * Tennessee Williams
   * Sam Shepard
   * Neil Simon

4. Who coined the word "nincompoop" in a play?
   * William Wycherley
   * William Shakespeare
   * Lillian Hellman
   * Christopher Durang

5. Who is the only playwright to win both an Oscar and a Nobel Prize?
   * Tennessee Williams
   * Harold Pinter
   * George Bernard Shaw
   * Edward Albee

6. Friedrich Schiller, George Bernard Shaw, Maxwell Anderson, Jean Anouilh, and Bertolt Brecht all wrote plays about the same martyred saint. Who was it?
   * Joan of Arc
   * Thomas Becket
   * Galileo
   * Thomas More

Continued on next page

7. Who is the only American playwright to have won Pulitzer
   Prizes in both drama and poetry?
   ★ William Saroyan
   ★ Robert Penn Warren
   ★ Archibald MacLeish
   ★ William Inge

8. Shakespeare's play *The Tempest* was suggested by accounts of an
   actual shipwreck in 1609 on what island?
   ★ Hispaniola
   ★ Jamaica
   ★ Bermuda
   ★ The Isle of Wight

9. Which playwright's daughter married the film comedian
   Charlie Chaplin?
   ★ Eugene O'Neill
   ★ Thornton Wilder
   ★ George Bernard Shaw
   ★ Georges Feydeau

10. Who was the first woman playwright to win a Tony Award for
    Best Play?
    ★ Lorraine Hansberry
    ★ Jean Kerr
    ★ Wendy Wasserstein
    ★ Marsha Norman

That's Absurd!

Match the playwright with the Absurdist play and fill in the missing word.

1.	Eugene Ionesco	*The _____ Party*	*Automobile*
2.	N. F. Simpson	*Rosencrantz and Guildenstern Are _____*	*Sing*
3.	James Saunders	*_____ Graveyard*	*Birthday*
4.	Edward Albee	*The _____ Soprano*	*Dead*
5.	Jack Richardson	*_____ Days*	*Balcony*
6.	Samuel Beckett	*_____ Humor*	*Dream*
7.	Fernando Arrabal	*The _____*	*Pendulum*
8.	Jean Genet	*Next Time I'll _____ to You*	*Bald*
9.	Harold Pinter	*The American _____*	*Gallows*
10.	Tom Stoppard	*One Way _____*	*Happy*

Playwrights on Parade

More questions about playwrights, this time about their private lives.

1. What American playwright's sister, named Joan, is an actress who has appeared in her brother's plays?
   * ★ Lin-Manuel Miranda
   * ★ Tracy Letts
   * ★ Clifford Odets
   * ★ Arthur Miller

2. What playwright engaged in espionage for his government?
   * ★ Christopher Marlowe
   * ★ Noël Coward
   * ★ Graham Greene
   * ★ W. Somerset Maugham

Continued on next page

3. What playwright was expelled from Princeton for throwing a beer bottle through the office window of future US President Woodrow Wilson?
   ★ Eugene O'Neill
   ★ Thornton Wilder
   ★ George S. Kaufman
   ★ Moss Hart

4. What playwright excelled at cricket in college and earned a listing in *Wisden's Cricketers Almanack*?
   ★ Oscar Wilde
   ★ Samuel Beckett
   ★ T. S. Eliot
   ★ Terence Rattigan

5. When this playwright fell into debt, the United States Congress offered him the equivalent of more than $1 million as a token of its gratitude.
   ★ George M. Cohan
   ★ Richard Brinsley Sheridan
   ★ Neil Simon
   ★ David Belasco

6. Which playwright's exchange of vows was the first same-sex commitment ceremony featured in the *New York Times* Vows section?
   ★ Tennessee Williams
   ★ Larry Kramer
   ★ Tony Kushner
   ★ Paula Vogel

7. What playwright liked to borrow books from the public library and make outlandish alterations to their illustrations before returning them?
   * Joe Orton
   * Thornton Wilder
   * William Inge
   * Wendy Wasserstein

8. What playwright, who was also a physician, said "Medicine is my lawful wife, and literature is my mistress"?
   * Clifford Odets
   * Anton Chekhov
   * Henrik Ibsen
   * Luigi Pirandello

9. After serving a prison term, what playwright lived in Paris and began calling himself Sebastian Melmoth?
   * Brendan Behan
   * Eugene Ionesco
   * Ben Jonson
   * Oscar Wilde

10. Ronald Harwood, author of the play *The Dresser*, about the relationship between a noted actor and his theatrical dresser, actually served in that capacity for what noted English actor?
    * Sir Cedric Harwicke
    * Sir Donald Wolfit
    * Sir Michael Redgrave
    * Dame Maggie Smith

Cole Porter: You're the Top!

1. Cole Porter's father, Samuel Porter, was a . . .
   * ☆ Railroad engineer
   * ☆ Druggist
   * ☆ Vaudeville star
   * ☆ Symphony conductor

2. Cole was born in . . .
   * ☆ Cairo, Illinois
   * ☆ A trunk in Pocatello, Idaho
   * ☆ Peru, Indiana
   * ☆ Paris, France

3. By age six, Cole had learned to play the piano and the . . .
   * ☆ Ocarina
   * ☆ Accordion
   * ☆ Tuba
   * ☆ Violin

4. At the age of ten, Cole wrote a song, which his mother published one hundred copies of. It was called . . .
   * ☆ "Anything Goes"
   * ☆ "The Song of the Birds"
   * ☆ "School Days"
   * ☆ "Happy Birthday"

5. Cole's first Broadway show, a flop produced in 1916 when he was twenty-five years old, was . . .
   * ☆ *Silk Stockings*
   * ☆ *Leave It to Jane*
   * ☆ *See America First*
   * ☆ *The Jazz Singer*

6. During World War I, Porter . . .
   * Was a conscientious objector
   * Enlisted in the French Foreign Legion
   * Lived in a Tibetan monastery
   * Moved to Canada

7. Porter's first success on Broadway was *Paris* in 1928, with the hit song "Let's Do It." Porter was not the first choice of the producer or of the star to write the score. Who was?
   * Sigmund Romberg
   * Aaron Copland
   * The star herself, Irene Bordoni
   * Rodgers and Hart

8. When Porter's Broadway show *The Gay Divorce* was made into a movie, the title was changed to *The Gay Divorcee* because . . .
   * The Hays Office objected to the idea of a happy divorce, but conceded the divorcee herself might be cheerful.
   * The studio was afraid people would think it was about an unhappy same-sex marriage.
   * The producer was angry at Porter and wanted to annoy him.
   * It was a typographical error in the initial publicity that wasn't noticed until too late.

9. In 1937 Porter lost the use of his legs in an accident . . .
   * On a roller coaster
   * While horseback riding
   * During an onstage rehearsal
   * In a helicopter

Continued on next page

10. Porter's Steinway piano is displayed in what hotel, where he lived from 1939 to 1964?
   ★ The Hollywood Roosevelt in Los Angeles
   ★ The George V in Paris
   ★ The Waldorf Astoria in New York
   ★ Motel 6 in Indianapolis

Getting to Know Rodgers & Hammerstein

Probably the most famous partnership in musical theatre history, Richard Rodgers and Oscar Hammerstein II wrote almost a dozen musicals together, many of which have become classics of the "golden age" of musicals.

1. With whom did Rodgers & Hammerstein share their Pulitzer Prize for *South Pacific?*
   ★ Joshua Logan
   ★ James Michener
   ★ Lorenz Hart
   ★ No one

2. Which Rodgers & Hammerstein musical had the longest initial run on Broadway?
   ★ *South Pacific*
   ★ *The Sound of Music*
   ★ *Oklahoma!*
   ★ *The King and I*

3. What was the last musical that Rodgers & Hammerstein wrote together?
   ★ *South Pacific*
   ★ *The Sound of Music*
   ★ *Flower Drum Song*
   ★ *Me and Juliet*

4. Who was the lyricist for *No Strings*, which Rodgers composed after Hammerstein's death?
   * Stephen Sondheim
   * Irving Berlin
   * Frank Loesser
   * Richard Rodgers

5. Who orchestrated the music for most of the original Broadway productions of Rodgers and Hammerstein shows?
   * Robert Russell Bennett
   * Don Walker
   * Philip J. Lang
   * Richard Rodgers

6. Hammerstein wrote lyrics for many composers before he teamed with Rodgers. With which of the following did he *not* collaborate?
   * Vincent Youmans
   * Rudolf Friml
   * Irving Berlin
   * Sigmund Romberg

7. Who costarred in both the 1955 movie of *Oklahoma!* and the 1956 movie of *Carousel*?
   * Doris Day and Frank Sinatra
   * Shirley Jones and Gordon MacRae
   * Mitzi Gaynor and Howard Keel
   * Kathryn Grayson and John Raitt

Continued on next page

8. Rodgers & Hammerstein's *Pipe Dream* is based on a work by what Nobel Prize–winning author?
   ★ Pearl S. Buck
   ★ T. S. Eliot
   ★ Eugene O'Neill
   ★ John Steinbeck

9. What actor, who had played the role of the king in the movie *Anna and the King of Siam*, was initially sought for the same role in the Broadway musical version, *The King and I?*
   ★ Alfred Drake
   ★ Rex Harrison
   ★ Noël Coward
   ★ Clark Gable

10. Which Rodgers & Hammerstein musical did Richard Rodgers say was his favorite?
    ★ *Carousel*
    ★ *Pipe Dream*
    ★ *Allegro*
    ★ None of the above; he hated them all

It's the Little Things . . . About Sondheim

Stephen Sondheim, winner of eight Tony Awards, more than any other composer, has written the scores for more than fifteen major musicals and the lyrics for three others. These questions are all about shows he has written.

1. In *Follies,* what is Buddy Plummer's mistress's name?
   * Margie
   * Sally
   * Phyllis
   * Trixie

2. Whom did Dean Jones replace in the opening night cast of *Company?*
   * Robert Preston
   * Anthony Perkins
   * Larry Kert
   * Zero Mostel

3. What is Sweeney Todd's real name?
   * Tobias Ragg
   * Adolfo Pirelli
   * Benjamin Barker
   * Mr. Lovett

4. What kind of hat does Kayama sing about as a symbol of Westernization in *Pacific Overtures?*
   * Bowler
   * Stetson
   * Fedora
   * Beanie

Continued on next page

5. In "Liaisons" in *A Little Night Music*, Madame Armfeldt recalls that in the palace of the Duke of Ferrara she acquired "some position" and what?
   * ★ Great ambition
   * ★ A tiny Titian
   * ★ A first edition
   * ★ A thyroid condition

6. In *Passion*, what is the name of the woman who is obsessed by love for the young soldier Giorgio?
   * ★ Fresca
   * ★ Georgina
   * ★ Lucrezia
   * ★ Fosca

7. Who turned down the role of Fay Apple that was played by Lee Remick in *Anyone Can Whistle?*
   * ★ Pearl Bailey
   * ★ Angela Lansbury
   * ★ Bernadette Peters
   * ★ Barbra Streisand

8. In *Assassins,* two women who tried to assassinate President Gerald Ford are portrayed. One is Sara Jane Moore. Who is the other?
   * ★ Carrie Nation
   * ★ Lynette Fromme
   * ★ Bonnie Parker
   * ★ Patricia Krenwinkel

9. In the opening number of *Into the Woods*, what is Jack's wish?
  * Some beans to plant
  * To attend the King's ball
  * That his cow would give milk
  * To meet a giant

10. On the plays of what classical author is *A Funny Thing Happened on the Way to the Forum* based?
  * Aristophanes
  * Sophocles
  * Seneca
  * Plautus

Sing Noël!

Playwright, actor, director, and songwriter Noël Coward always insisted on those two little dots—known as a diaeresis—over the "e" in his name to indicate that the syllable should be voiced. Otherwise, he said, people would call him "Nool." Whatever you wish to call him, see you if you can answer these bits of trivia about him and his work.

1. Coward was often known to his friends and colleagues as . . .
  * Uncle Noël
  * The Blithe Spirit
  * Bubba
  * The Master

2. Coward's first stage appearance at age eleven was as . . .
  * Prince Mussel in *The Goldfish*
  * A Lost Boy in *Peter Pan*
  * Macbeth in *Macbeth*
  * Elyot in *Private Lives*

Continued on next page

3. As a lyricist, Coward had his first song published in 1919. It was called . . .
   * "Someday I'll Find You"
   * "The Baseball Rag"
   * "Alexander's Ragtime Band"
   * "God Save the King"

4. *The Vortex*, Coward's first major West End hit, which he wrote and starred in, is about a nymphomaniac mother and her son, who is addicted to . . .
   * Womanizing
   * Cocaine
   * Gambling
   * Sherry

5. After the opening of his play *Sirocco* in 1927, Coward . . .
   * Was knighted by the King
   * Became the director of the Old Vic
   * Broke his leg during curtain calls
   * Was booed and spat upon

6. During the Second World War, Coward . . .
   * Worked for the British Secret Service
   * Spent the duration in Hollywood
   * Fought on the front lines
   * Was a nurse in field hospitals

7. Coward was the model for the character Beverly Carlton in . . .
   * *The Producers*
   * *The Man Who Came to Dinner*
   * *Blithe Spirit*
   * *Tobacco Road*

8. Coward's Jamaica home was called
   * Junebug
   * Firefly
   * Goldeneye
   * Reggae Hill

9. When Coward was finally knighted at age seventy, which
   fellow knight said, "We have been like a row of teeth with the
   front tooth missing"?
   * Sir Laurence Olivier
   * Sir Alec Guinness
   * Sir John Gielgud
   * Sir Paul McCartney

10. At Coward's last public appearance at a performance of the
    revue *Oh, Coward!* in New York on January 14, 1973, he was
    accompanied by . . .
    * Gertrude Lawrence
    * Mary Martin
    * Marlene Dietrich
    * President Richard Nixon

By Richard Rodgers and . . .

Rodgers and Hart, Rodgers & Hammerstein, and Rodgers and . . .? Richard Rodgers collaborated with several lyricists besides his two most famous partners, Lorenz Hart and Oscar Hammerstein II. Match these Richard Rodgers songs with their lyricists and the musicals in which they appeared. (Note: some matches are used more than once.)

1.	"No Song More Pleasing"	Martin Charnin	*No Strings*
2.	"I Do Not Know a Day I Did Not Love You"	Stephen Sondheim	*Allegro*
3.	"Here We Are Again"	Lorenz Hart	*Rex*
4.	"Easy Come, Easy Go"	Richard Rodgers	*Too Many Girls*
5.	"You Could Not Please Me More"	Oscar Hammerstein II	*Victory at Sea* (TV documentary)
6.	"The Sweetest Sounds"	Sheldon Harnick	*I Remember Mama*
7.	"The Gentleman Is a Dope"	Raymond Jessel	*Two by Two*
8.	"I Didn't Know What Time It Was"		*Do I Hear a Waltz?*
9.	"Don't Be Afraid of an Animal"		*Androcles and the Lion* (TV musical)
10.	"Hard Work and Horseplay"		

Red, White, and Cohan

George M. Cohan, composer, lyricist, playwright, and actor, was associated with American patriotism throughout his theatrical career. With such star-spangled songs as "The Yankee Doodle Boy," "You're a Grand Old Flag," and "Over There," he remains unsurpassed for his expressions of love of country.

1. Cohan always claimed to have been "born on the Fourth of July." His baptismal certificate states that the actual date was . . .
   * July 4
   * July 3
   * August 15
   * December 25

2. In the original title of Cohan's "You're a Grand Old Flag" from *George Washington, Jr.*, the word "flag" was . . .
   * Standard
   * Banner
   * Thing
   * Rag

3. When producer A. L. Erlanger asked Cohan if he could write a show without a flag in it, Cohan replied he could write a show without anything—except a . . .
   * Pencil
   * Leading lady
   * Juicy part for himself
   * Hit song

Continued on next page

4. In Cohan's *Little Johnny Jones*, the brash American hero quips, "A French pastry ain't worth thirty cents compared to American . . .
   ★ Apple pie
   ★ Doughnuts
   ★ Twinkies
   ★ Hot dogs

5. The first recording of Cohan's World War I song "Over There" was made by . . .
   ★ Al Jolson
   ★ Nora Bayes
   ★ Bing Crosby
   ★ Enrico Caruso

6. In *Yankee Doodle Dandy*, the biographical film starring James Cagney as Cohan, the character of President Franklin D. Roosevelt appears only . . .
   ★ From a distance
   ★ From the back
   ★ As an off-camera voice
   ★ In a dream sequence

7. Cohan himself played President Franklin D. Roosevelt in the musical . . .
   ★ *Mr. President*
   ★ *Miss Liberty*
   ★ *I'd Rather Be Right*
   ★ *Annie*

8. In the lyrics to "If Washington Should Come to Life," from *George Washington, Jr.,* Cohan wonders if Washington would laugh at . . .
   ⋆ Will Rogers
   ⋆ Eddie Foy
   ⋆ George M. Cohan
   ⋆ Teddy Roosevelt

9. Cohan spent his childhood summers in a Massachusetts town that he later made famous by joking about its name:
   ⋆ Boondock
   ⋆ Podunk
   ⋆ Jerkwater
   ⋆ Onehorse

10. Cohan said he would quit the theatre and run an elevator before joining . . .
   ⋆ ASCAP
   ⋆ Catholic Actors League
   ⋆ Actors' Equity Association
   ⋆ The Army

All About Albee

"A trenchant playwright for a desperate era," in the words of the *New York Times*, Edward Albee was one of the giants of American drama. How much do you know about him and his work?

1. Albee's adoptive grandfather was a founder of a chain of vaudeville theatres known as the Keith-Albee-_____ Circuit.
    ★ Roxy
    ★ Shubert
    ★ Orpheum
    ★ Broadway

2. Albee's first play, *The Zoo Story*, received its premiere performance:
    ★ In a high school gym in Poughkeepsie
    ★ In Berlin
    ★ On a cruise ship
    ★ In Chicago

3. In *The American Dream*, Mommy buys a new beige hat, but someone tells her it's not beige but . . .
    ★ Tan
    ★ Wheat
    ★ Magenta
    ★ Ecru

4. During the initial Broadway production of *Who's Afraid of Virginia Woolf?* from 1962 to 1964, which of the following was NOT a replacement for Uta Hagen in the role of Martha?
    ★ Tallulah Bankhead
    ★ Mercedes McCambridge
    ★ Elaine Stritch
    ★ Nancy Kelly

5. Albee wrote the book for a musical adaptation of *Breakfast at Tiffany's*—which played previews on Broadway but never officially opened. Who wrote the score?
   ★ Stephen Sondheim
   ★ Jerry Herman
   ★ Irving Berlin
   ★ Bob Merrill

6. From 1989 until 2003 Albee taught playwriting as a Distinguished Professor of Theatre at . . .
   ★ Harvard University
   ★ Oxford University
   ★ New York University
   ★ The University of Houston

7. Noël Coward wrote in his diary that the New York production of Albee's *Tiny Alice* was "beautifully directed and acted"— except for the actor who played Julian. Who was he?
   ★ Michael Redgrave
   ★ Christopher Plummer
   ★ John Gielgud
   ★ Lee J. Cobb

8. Martin is a character in one of Albee's plays who is in love with Sylvia, who is a . . .
   ★ Burlesque performer
   ★ Tattoo artist
   ★ Snake charmer
   ★ Goat

Continued on next page

9. In *Three Tall Women*, the character of A says that life's happiest moment comes "When we can _____."
    ★ Make love
    ★ Help others
    ★ Bake an apple pie
    ★ Stop

10. For which of the following plays did Albee NOT win a Pulitzer Prize?
    ★ *Seascape*
    ★ *A Delicate Balance*
    ★ *Three Tall Women*
    ★ *Who's Afraid of Virginia Woolf?*

Directorial Debuts

Match these Broadway directors with the shows in which they made their Broadway debuts as directors.

1. Jerry Zaks	*Cock-A-Doodle Dandy* (1969 revival)
2. Casey Nicholaw	*The House of Blue Leaves* (1986)
3. Jack O'Brien	*The Drowsy Chaperone* (2006)
4. Mike Nichols	*The Life and Adventures of Nicholas Nickleby* (1981)
5. Harold Prince	*Jelly's Last Jam* (1992)
6. Trevor Nunn	*Hair* (2009 revival)
7. José Quintero	*A Raisin in the Sun* (1959)
8. Lloyd Richards	*In the Summer House* (1953)
9. George C. Wolfe	*Barefoot in the Park* (1963)
10. Diane Paulus	*A Family Affair* (1962)

Shall We Dance?

Match these dances from Broadway musicals with the choreographers who originally created them and the musicals in which they appeared.

1.	Bottle Dance	Bob Fosse	*Can-Can*
2.	Ascot Gavotte	George Balanchine	*Brigadoon*
3.	Sword Dance	Tommy Tune	*Bye Bye Birdie*
4.	Shriners Ballet	Michael Bennett	*The Will Rogers Follies*
5.	Cell Block Tango	Onna White	*My Fair Lady*
6.	Garden of Eden Ballet	Jerome Robbins	*Chicago*
7.	Shipoopi	Hanya Holm	*Fiddler on the Roof*
8.	Princess Zenobia Ballet	Agnes de Mille	*Follies*
9.	Will-A-Mania	Gower Champion	*The Music Man*
10.	Bolero d'Amour	Michael Kidd	*On Your Toes*

First Steps

Match these choreographers with the musicals in which they had their first Broadway credits as principal choreographers.

1.	Michael Bennett	*Swinging on a Star* (1995)
2.	Tommy Tune	*Spring Awakening* (2006)
3.	Twyla Tharp	*You're a Good Man, Charlie Brown* (1999 revival)
4.	Jerome Robbins	*A Joyful Noise* (1966)
5.	Gower Champion	*On the Town* (1944)
6.	Jerry Mitchell	*The Pajama Game* (1954)
7.	Kathleen Marshall	*A Day in Hollywood /A Night in the Ukraine* (1980)
8.	Susan Stroman	*Singin' in the Rain* (1985)
9.	Bill T. Jones	*Small Wonder* (1948)
10.	Bob Fosse	*Crazy for You* (1992)

Curtains

Identify the playwrights who met their deaths as follows:

1. He died at the age of seventy-five, eleven days after marrying a
   sixteen-year-old girl.
   ★ Sophocles   ★ William Wycherley
   ★ Sean O'Casey   ★ Arthur Miller

2. He was fatally stabbed through an eye during a brawl in a
   tavern.
   ★ Jean Racine   ★ Euripides
   ★ Christopher Marlowe   ★ Thornton Wilder

3. Mistaking his shiny bald head for a rock, an eagle dropped a
   turtle on him, killing him instantly.
   ★ Oliver Goldsmith   ★ Noël Coward
   ★ Aeschylus   ★ Terence Rattigan

4. He was bludgeoned to death by his lover, who administered
   nine blows to his head with a hammer.
   ★ Ben Jonson   ★ Eugene Ionesco
   ★ Joe Orton   ★ Eugene O'Neill

5. Putting in some eyedrops, he apparently choked to death
   on the bottle cap, which he was holding between his
   teeth—although his brother maintained he was mysteriously
   murdered.
   ★ Tennessee Williams   ★ George S. Kaufman
   ★ Brendan Behan   ★ Cllifford Odets

6. While playing the part of a hypochondriac in one of his own comedies, he suffered a tubercular seizure on stage and died several hours later.
   - ★ Aristophanes
   - ★ Moss Hart
   - ★ William Shakespeare
   - ★ Molière

7. Gunned down by a fascist death squad during a civil war, he was assassinated for his left-wing views; his body has never been found.
   - ★ Henrik Ibsen
   - ★ Jean Anouilh
   - ★ Federico García Lorca
   - ★ Samuel Beckett

8. A physician himself, he died of tuberculosis right after drinking a glass of champagne.
   - ★ Anton Chekhov
   - ★ Luigi Pirandello
   - ★ Bertolt Brecht
   - ★ Sean O'Casey

9. He died of an infection at the age of ninety-four, after falling from a ladder while pruning a tree.
   - ★ Sophocles
   - ★ Seneca
   - ★ George Bernard Shaw
   - ★ Maxwell Anderson

10. He died in a Paris hotel room, of which he said, "My *wallpaper* and I are fighting a duel to the death. One or the other of us has to go."
    - ★ Jean Giraudoux
    - ★ Oscar Wilde
    - ★ Georges Feydeau
    - ★ John Osborne

CREATIVE TYPES

ANSWERS

Teamwork

1. *Dearest Enemy, Peggy-Ann, Simple Simon*—Richard Rodgers and Lorenz Hart
2. *Life of the Party, The Day Before Spring, What's Up?*—Alan Jay Lerner and Frederick Loewe
3. *Sweet Adeline, Music in the Air, Very Warm for May*—Jerome Kern and Oscar Hammerstein II
4. *Flora the Red Menace, The Rink, All About Us*—John Kander and Fred Ebb
5. *The Apple Tree, Tenderloin, The Body Beautiful*—Sheldon Harnick and Jerry Bock
6. *Hold Everything, Flying High, Manhattan Mary*—B. G. DeSylva, Lew Brown, and Ray Henderson
7. *All American, I and Albert, A Broadway Musical*—Charles Strouse and Lee Adams
8. *Two on the Aisle, Subways Are for Sleeping, Fade Out-Fade In*—Betty Comden, Adolph Green, and Jule Styne
9. *Tip-Toes, Treasure Girl, Let 'Em Eat Cake*—George Gershwin and Ira Gershwin
10. *Have A Heart, Oh, Lady! Lady!, Sitting Pretty*—Jerome Kern, Guy Bolton, and P. G. Wodehouse

With A Little Help from My Friends

1. Tennessee Williams and Donald Windham collaborated on *You Touched Me*.
2. Shakespeare and John Fletcher are generally thought to have collaborated on *The Two Noble Kinsmen* (as well as *Henry VIII*).
3. George S. Kaufman and Edna Ferber are the coauthors of *The Royal Family*. They also wrote *Dinner at Eight* and *Stage Door* together. Known as "The Great Collaborator," Kaufman is also famous for plays cowritten with Moss Hart, Morrie Ryskind, and Ring Lardner. The only full-length work Kaufman wrote alone was *The Butter and Egg Man*.
4. Howard Lindsay and Russel Crouse wrote *Life With Father* (as well as *The Great Sebastians*, other plays, and the books for several musicals, including *The Sound of Music, Call Me Madam,* and *Anything Goes*).
5. Joseph A. Fields and Jerome Chodorov are coauthors of *My Sister Eileen* (and several other plays and musicals).
6. Jerome Lawrence and Robert E. Lee are noted for *Inherit the Wind* (and other plays and musicals, including *Auntie Mame, The First Monday in October, Mame,* and *Dear World*).
7. John Webster and John Ford were the coauthors of *The Duchess of Malfi* (plus *The White Devil, 'Tis Pity She's a Whore,* and other plays).
8. Louis O. Coxe and Robert Chapman are remembered for the play *Billy Budd*.
9. Maxwell Anderson and Laurence Stallings coauthored *What Price Glory?*
10. Howard Brenton and David Hare wrote *Pravda*.

Author! Author!

1. Thornton Wilder won the Pulitzer Prize for fiction in 1923 for *The Bridge of San Luis Rey,* and for drama in 1938 for *Our Town* and in 1943 for *The Skin of Our Teeth*.
2. Thomas Becket. Tennyson and Anouilh each wrote a play called *Becket,* and Becket is the protagonist of T. S. Eliot's *Murder in the Cathedral*.
3. Neil Simon
4. William Wycherley first used the word "nincompoop" in *The Plain Dealer,* his 1676 play.
5. George Bernard Shaw is the only playwright to win both an Oscar (for *Pygmalion* in 1939) and the Nobel Prize for Literature (in 1925).
6. Joan of Arc. Schiller's *Maid of Orléans,* Shaw's *Saint Joan,* Anderson's *Joan of Lorraine,* Anouilh's *The Lark,* and Brecht's *Saint Joan of the Stockyards* are all based on her life.

7. Archibald MacLeish won Pulitzers for poetry in 1933 and 1953 and for the play *J. B.* in 1959.
8. Bermuda
9. Eugene O'Neill's daughter, Oona, married Chaplin when he was fifty-three and she was eighteen; they had eight children and remained married for thirty years until Chaplin's death.
10. Wendy Wasserstein, for *The Heidi Chronicles* in 1989.

That's Absurd!

1. Eugene Ionesco—*The Bald Soprano*
2. N. F. Simpson—*One Way Pendulum*
3. James Saunders—*Next Time I'll Sing to You*
4. Edward Albee—*The American Dream*
5. Jack Richardson—*Gallows Humor*
6. Samuel Beckett—*Happy Days*
7. Fernando Arrabal—*Automobile Graveyard*
8. Jean Genet—*The Balcony*
9. Harold Pinter—*The Birthday Party*
10. Tom Stoppard—*Rosencrantz and Guildenstern Are Dead*

Playwrights on Parade

1. Arthur Miller's sister, Joan Copeland, lists her brother's plays *The Price* and *The American Clock* among her many theatrical credits.
2. Christopher Marlowe, Noël Coward, Graham Greene, and W. Somerset Maugham all served their governments in espionage; Marlowe for Queen Elizabeth I, Coward with the British secret service in Paris and New York during World War II, and Greene and Maugham for Britain's MI6 during World War II.
3. Eugene O'Neill allegedly threw a beer bottle through the office window of Woodrow Wilson, then president of Princeton.
4. Samuel Beckett was an accomplished cricketer at Dublin University and is listed as a First-Class Cricket player in *Wisden's Cricketers Almanack*.
5. Richard Brinsley Sheridan, who had supported the American colonists when he was a member of the British Parliament, was offered £20,000, the equivalent of more than $1 million today, by the US Congress in 1780. Although he was deeply in debt, he proudly refused the assistance.

Continued on next page

6. Tony Kushner's exchange of vows with Mark Harris was featured in the *New York Times* on May 3, 2003.
7. Joe Orton amused himself by borrowing library books and defacing them with outlandish additions. He and his partner, Kenneth Halliwell, were eventually charged with malicious damage, fined £262, and sentenced to six months in prison.
8. Anton Chekhov was a physician-playwright, who was given a glass of champagne on his deathbed.
9. After serving a two-year term in a British prison for "gross indecency," Oscar Wilde moved to Paris under the name Sebastian Melmoth.
10. Sir Donald Wolfit

Cole Porter: You're the Top!

1. Druggist (His mother, Kate Cole, was the daughter of J. O. Cole, one of the richest men in Indiana.)
2. Peru, Indiana, on June 9, 1891
3. Violin (but he thought the violin sound was harsh and gave it up to concentrate on the piano, which he practiced two hours a day).
4. "The Song of the Birds" was dedicated to his mother, who had a hundred copies printed and distributed.
5. *See America First* was the first show for which Cole Porter was credited for all the music and lyrics. It was a flop that opened at Maxine Elliott's Theatre on March 28, 1916, and ran for fifteen performances.
6. Enlisted in the French Foreign Legion. Some biographers have disputed this fact, but the French Foreign Legion has officially confirmed his service.
7. Rodgers and Hart were the first choice of producer E. Ray Goetz and his wife, Irene Bordoni, the star of *Paris,* but the songwriting team was unavailable, and Porter's agent was successful in pushing his client for the show.
8. The Hays Office, which enforced the Motion Picture Production Code from 1934 to 1968, objected to the idea of a gay (that is, light-hearted) divorce as an immoral concept, although it was acknowledged the divorcee herself might be cheerful enough.
9. A horse rolled on top of him during a horseback ride, and Porter lost the use of both legs. Although in constant pain, he resisted amputation until 1958, when one leg was removed and replaced with a prosthesis.

10. Waldorf Astoria Towers in New York, where Porter was a resident for twenty-five years. His piano, known as "High Society," is displayed in the lobby and has occasionally been used by entertainers in the Cocktail Terrace.

Getting to Know Rodgers & Hammerstein

1. Joshua Logan, the director of *South Pacific*, shared in the 1950 Pulitzer Prize for drama as the coauthor with Hammerstein of the book. James Michener had previously won the Pulitzer for fiction in 1948 for the stories on which the musical was based.

2. *Oklahoma!* ran for 2,212 performances in its initial Broadway run from March 31, 1943, until May 29, 1948. It was the longest-running Broadway musical until its record was broken by *My Fair Lady*. *South Pacific* had an initial run of 1,925 performances, *The Sound of Music*, 1,443, and *The King and I*, 1,246.

3. *The Sound of Music*, which opened November 16, 1959, was Hammerstein's last show. He died on August 23, 1960.

4. Richard Rodgers wrote his own lyrics for *No Strings*, the only Broadway score for which he did so; Samuel A. Taylor wrote the book. Other lyricists whom Rodgers worked with after Hammerstein's death were Stephen Sondheim (*Do I Hear a Waltz?*), Martin Charnin (*Two By Two, I Remember Mama*), and Sheldon Harnick (*Rex*).

5. Robert Russell Bennett was the orchestrator for *Oklahoma!*, *Allegro*, *South Pacific*, *The King and I*, *Pipe Dream*, *Flower Drum Song*, and *The Sound of Music*. Don Walker orchestrated *Carousel* and *Me and Juliet*.

6. Irving Berlin always wrote both music and lyrics, and Hammerstein did not collaborate with him.

7. Shirley Jones and Gordon MacRae were the stars of both movies. Joanne Woodward was first offered the role of Laurey in *Oklahoma!*; James Dean and Paul Newman both auditioned for Curly before MacRae won the part. Frank Sinatra was originally cast as Billy Bigelow in *Carousel* and actually prerecorded the score, but withdrew from the production before filming began.

8. John Steinbeck was the author of the novel *Sweet Thursday* (a sequel to *Cannery Row*), on which *Pipe Dream*'s book was based.

Continued on next page

9. Rex Harrison, who played the King in the movie *Anna and the King of Siam*, was first choice for the part, but he was unavailable. Noël Coward and Alfred Drake were also considered before Yul Brynner was cast.

10. *Carousel* was the favorite musical of Rodgers, who wrote in his autobiography, "It affects me deeply every time I see it performed."

It's the Little Things . . . About Sondheim

1. Margie is Buddy Plummer's mistress, about whom he sings in "The Right Girl." Sally Durant Plummer is his wife.

2. Dean Jones replaced Anthony Perkins, who left the *Company* cast in order to direct a play. Jones, in turn, was replaced shortly after opening night by Larry Kert.

3. Benjamin Barker

4. "A Bowler Hat" is Kayama's number.

5. "A tiny Titian"

6. Fosca

7. Barbra Streisand turned down the role of Fay in order to do *Funny Girl* instead.

8. Lynette "Squeaky" Fromme

9. That his cow would give milk

10. Plautus's farces *Pseudolus, Miles Gloriosus,* and *Mostellaria* are the basis of *A Funny Thing Happened on the Way to the Forum.*

Sing Noel!

1. The Master. Enumerating his multiple talents, Lord Mountbatten said on Coward's seventieth birthday, *"Only one man combined all fourteen different labels—The Master."*

2. Prince Mussel in *The Goldfish,* a fantasy play by Lila Field, "with a star cast of wonder children," at the Little Theatre in London on January 27, 1911. Coward played Slightly in *Peter Pan* when he was thirteen.

3. "The Baseball Rag," with music by Doris Joel, was Coward's first published song. His lyrics included the lines "It's a cinch, / It's a go, / It's a Jazz, / Tally-ho / For that Baseball Rag."

4. Cocaine

5. Coward was booed and spat upon by audience members on the opening night of *Sirocco,* which is a play about free love among the upper classes.

6. Worked for the British Secret Service, to gather information during his overseas travels. Coward also headed the British wartime propaganda office in Paris.
7. *The Man Who Came to Dinner* by George S. Kaufman and Moss Hart
8. Firefly. Goldeneye was the name of his neighbor Ian Fleming's estate.
9. Sir Alec Guinness made the comment after Coward received his knighthood, adding, "Now we can smile again."
10. Marlene Dietrich was on Coward's arm at a performance of *Oh, Coward!* He returned to his home in Jamaica the next day and died there two months later.

By Richard Rodgers and . . .
1. "No Song More Pleasing," lyrics by Sheldon Harnick, from *Rex*
2. "I Do Not Know a Day I Did Not Love You," lyrics by Martin Charnin, from *Two by Two*
3. "Here We Are Again," lyrics by Stephen Sondheim, from *Do I Hear a Waltz?*
4. "Easy Come, Easy Go," lyrics by Raymond Jessel, from *I Remember Mama*
5. "You Could Not Please Me More," lyrics by Martin Charnin, from *I Remember Mama*
6. "The Sweetest Sounds," lyrics by Richard Rodgers, from *No Strings*
7. "The Gentleman Is a Dope," lyrics by Oscar Hammerstein II, from *Allegro*
8. "I Didn't Know What Time It Was," lyrics by Lorenz Hart, from *Too Many Girls*
9. "Don't Be Afraid of an Animal," lyrics by Richard Rodgers, from *Androcles and the Lion*
10. "Hard Work and Horseplay" is a theme from the TV documentary *Victory at Sea*, and it has no lyrics.

Red, White, and Cohan

1. July 3, 1878, is the date on Cohan's baptismal certificate, the only official record of his birth.
2. Rag. "You're a Grand Old Flag" was originally titled "You're a Grand Old Rag"—a phrase Cohan heard used by a Civil War veteran about a tattered Union flag. But too many people objected to calling the flag a "rag," so he changed it.
3. A pencil
4. Apple pie
5. Nora Bayes, a vaudeville star
6. From the back, in a conversation with Cohan. Roosevelt was portrayed by a lookalike named Jack Young, and his voice was dubbed in by Art Gilmore.
7. *I'd Rather Be Right*, the 1937 musical by Moss Hart, George S. Kaufman, Richard Rodgers, and Lorenz Hart
8. Eddie Foy. The song "If Washington Should Come to Life" has the lyric "He'd soon discover we're no second-raters, / I know he'd sing the 'Yankee Doodle Boy', / I wonder if he'd visit our theaters, / I wonder if he'd laugh at Eddie Foy."
9. Podunk (an Algonquin word denoting a marshy location, and also the name of towns in Connecticut, Vermont, New York, and other states)
10. Actors' Equity Association, which Cohan refused to join as an actor or deal with as a producer, forming instead a rival organization known as the Actors' Fidelity League

All About Albee

1. Orpheum. Edward Albee's grandfather, whose name was Edward Franklin Albee II, was a founder of the Keith-Albee-Orpheum Circuit. At its height, the chain consisted of more than 700 theatres. In 1928, it was sold to Joseph P. Kennedy, who in turn sold it to the Radio Corporation of America (RCA), which then formed a motion picture studio known as Radio-Keith-Orpheum (RKO).
2. Berlin. Having been rejected by several New York producers, *The Zoo Story* had its first performance at the Schiller Theatre in Berlin in September of 1959, on a double bill with the German premiere of Beckett's *Krapp's Last Tape*.
3. Wheat
4. Tallulah Bankhead
5. Bob Merrill
6. The University of Houston
7. John Gielgud
8. A goat, in Albee's *The Goat: or Who Is Sylvia?*
9. Stop. The character A says, "That's the happiest moment. When it's all done. When we stop. When we can stop."
10. *Who's Afraid of Virginia Woolf?* The drama jury selected it for the Pulitzer Prize in 1963, but the advisory committee vetoed that choice and declined to give a drama award that year.

Directorial Debuts

1. Jerry Zaks—*The House of Blue Leaves*
2. Casey Nicholaw—*The Drowsy Chaperone*
3. Jack O'Brien—*Cock-A-Doodle Dandy*
4. Mike Nichols—*Barefoot in the Park*
5. Harold Prince—*A Family Affair*
6. Trevor Nunn—*The Life and Adventures of Nicholas Nickleby*
7. José Quintero—*In the Summer House*
8. Lloyd Richards—*A Raisin in the Sun*
9. George C. Wolfe—*Jelly's Last Jam*
10. Diane Paulus—*Hair*

Shall We Dance?
1. Bottle Dance, by Jerome Robbins, from *Fiddler on the Roof*
2. Ascot Gavotte, by Hanya Holm, from *My Fair Lady*
3. Sword Dance, by Agnes de Mille, from *Brigadoon*
4. Shriners Ballet, by Gower Champion, from *Bye Bye Birdie*
5. Cell Block Tango, by Bob Fosse, from *Chicago*
6. Garden of Eden Ballet, by Michael Kidd, from *Can-Can*
7. Shipoopi, by Onna White, from *The Music Man*
8. Princess Zenobia Ballet, by George Balanchine, from *On Your Toes*
9. Will-A-Mania, by Tommy Tune, from *The Will Rogers Follies*
10. Bolero d'Amour, by Michael Bennett, from *Follies*

First Steps
1. Michael Bennett—*A Joyful Noise*
2. Tommy Tune—*A Day in Hollywood/A Night in the Ukraine*. (Tune previously choreographed and codirected *The Best Little Whorehouse in Texas* in 1978, but the Playbill credit was "Musical Numbers Staged by," rather than "Choreographed by.")
3. Twyla Tharp—*Singin' in the Rain*. (Tharp was credited as choreographer in two earlier Broadway productions, but these were ballets, not musicals.)
4. Jerome Robbins—*On the Town*
5. Gower Champion—*Small Wonder*
6. Jerry Mitchell—*You're a Good Man, Charlie Brown* (revival)
7. Kathleen Marshall—*Swinging on a Star*
8. Susan Stroman—*Crazy for You*
9. Bill T. Jones—*Spring Awakening*
10. Bob Fosse—*The Pajama Game*

Curtains

1. William Wycherley
2. Christopher Marlowe
3. Aeschylus
4. Joe Orton
5. Tennessee Williams
6. Molière
7. Federico García Lorca
8. Anton Chekhov
9. George Bernard Shaw
10. Oscar Wilde

XVIII

GRAND FINALE

It's time for your final bows—provided you get through these last quizzes.

Stop and Smell the Flowers

Identify these plays or musicals in which flowers are featured:

1. An actress receives a bouquet of snowdrops, pansies, and rosemary from her leading man and sings "So In Love." Then she finds out the flowers were intended for someone else.

2. A Mexican street vendor cries, "Flores, flores para los muertos."

3. A young man collides with a flower girl, knocking her basket of violets into the mud.

4. A Venus flytrap–like plant in a florist shop demands blood.

5. A son purchases a bouquet and suggests his father gives it to his mother.

6. At the climax of a discussion between two couples about an altercation between their sons, a vase of tulips is violently scattered around a living room.

7. A young woman who has gone mad carries an armful of flowers that includes rosemary, pansies, fennel, columbines, rue, and a daisy—but no violets, because they withered.

8. A quartet of young men in the Gay '90s sing "We All Wear a Green Carnation."

9. Its original title was *I Picked a Daisy*.

10. A group of nuns quotes scripture to an itinerant worker to persuade him to help them build a chapel.

God of Carnage

Look to the Lilies

Bitter Sweet

The Subject Was Roses

A Streetcar Named Desire

Kiss Me, Kate

On A Clear Day You Can See Forever

Pygmalion

Little Shop of Horrors

Hamlet

Meow Mix

Match these felines with the plays and musicals in which they appear or are referred to.

1. mehitabel	*Seussical*
2. Pyewacket	*Breakfast at Tiffany's*
3. Graymalkin	*Bell, Book and Candle*
4. Wee Thomas	*The Lieutenant of Inishmore*
5. Sarafina	*Cats*
6. Skimbleshanks	*Pinocchio*
7. The Cat in the Hat	*Alice in Wonderland*
8. The Cheshire Cat	*Shinbone Alley*
9. Cat	*Macbeth*
10. Gepetto's Cat	*The Lion King*

Do You Know the Way?

These plays and musicals all contain a word that means a thorough-fare or passageway. Match the description with the show and fill in the missing word.

1. A 1935 play by James Warwick, about a gangster who takes refuge in the home of a psychology professor.

   Tobacco _____   *Path*

2. A 2014 play by Lisa D'Amour about a funeral for a burlesque queen who is still alive.

   Angel _____   *Trail*

3. A melodrama of 1906 by Edward Peple about a young female ranch-owner's fight against a powerful railroad.

   Lover's _____   *Highway*

4. Andrew Lloyd Webber's musical based on a film by Billy Wilder.

   Airline _____   *Road*

5. Thriller by Patrick Hamilton, known in the United Kingdom as *Gas Light*.

   Blind _____   *Boulevard*

6. Controversial 1933 play by Jack Kirkland, based on an Erskine Caldwell novel and set on a Georgia farm.

   _____ *Q*   *Route*

7. Clyde Fitch's 1901 play about a New England woman who resists marrying a New England country doctor.

   Sunset _____   *Lane*

8. A 2003 musical by Jeff Marx, Robert Lopez, and Jeff Whitty, in which the stars are puppets.

   The Love _____   *Alley*

9. Taken from a phrase from *Hamlet*, this is the title of two different plays, one in 1907 by Bayard Veiller, and one in 1939 by Robert Buckner and Walter Hart.

   The _____ *of the Lonesome Pine*   *Avenue*

10. A 1912 play by Eugene Walter, it is based on John Fox Jr.'s novel about a feud between two Appalachian families.

    The Primrose _____   *Street*

Firsts

1. What musical won the first Tony Award for Best Musical?
   * ★ *Oklahoma!*
   * ★ *Kiss Me, Kate*
   * ★ *Annie Get Your Gun*
   * ★ *Show Boat*

2. Who was the first actor to be knighted for his services to the theatre?
   * ★ Sir Henry Irving
   * ★ Sir David Garrick
   * ★ Sir Cedric Hardwicke
   * ★ Sir Squire Bancroft

3. Who was the first American playwright to win the Nobel Prize for literature?
   * ★ Tennessee Williams
   * ★ Maxwell Anderson
   * ★ Eugene O'Neill
   * ★ Edward Albee

4. How many plays attributed to Shakespeare were published in the First Folio in 1623?
   * ★ 1
   * ★ 6
   * ★ 23
   * ★ 36

5. Margaret Hughes, who was born in 1630, is generally credited with being the first English actress to do what?

  ★ Play a nude scene

  ★ Appear professionally onstage in England

  ★ Fly on wires suspended from a stage loft

  ★ Be made a dame of the British Empire

6. What ancient Greek is generally regarded as the first professional European actor?

  ★ Aristotle

  ★ Sophocles

  ★ Thespis

  ★ Homer

7. Who was the first African-American woman to write a play produced on Broadway?

  ★ Ntozake Shange

  ★ Lorraine Hansberry

  ★ Zora Neale Hurston

  ★ Suzan-Lori Parks

8. What was the first play to win a Pulitzer Prize in drama?

  ★ *Beyond the Horizon* by Eugene O'Neill

  ★ *Why Marry?* by Jesse Lynch Williams

  ★ *They Knew What They Wanted* by Sidney Howard

  ★ *Barefoot in the Park* by Neil Simon

Continued on next page

9. What was the first Broadway musical with an all-female creative team: bookwriter, composer and lyricist, director, and choreographer?
   - ★ *70, Girls, 70*
   - ★ *Ladies First*
   - ★ *Girl Crazy*
   - ★ *Waitress*

10. What was the first professionally produced play written by an American citizen?
    - ★ *The Contrast* by Royall Tyler
    - ★ *The Girl of the Golden West* by David Belasco
    - ★ *Captain Jinks of the Horse Marines* by Clyde Fitch
    - ★ *The Black Crook* by Charles M. Barras

Show-Within-A-Show Time

Each of the following titles in the first column is a "show-within-a-show." Identify the play or musical in the second column in which it appears.

1.	*Pretty Lady*	*Hamlet*
2.	*Robbin' Hood of the Old West*	*Kiss Me, Kate*
3.	*The Small House of Uncle Thomas*	*Annie Get Your Gun*
4.	*Feldzieg's Follies*	*Crazy for You*
5.	*The Murder of Gonzago*	*On Your Toes*
6.	*Pawnee Bill's Far East Show*	*Babes in Arms*
7.	*The Zangler Follies*	*Curtains*
8.	*The Taming of the Shrew*	*42nd Street*
9.	*The Deep North*	*The King and I*
10.	*La Princesse Zenobia*	*The Drowsy Chaperone*

It's a Drag

Match the characters named in column one—all of whom dress in drag—with the play or musical in column two and with the actor who originated the role in column three.

1.	Roger De Bris	*Sugar*	Billy Porter
2.	Jerry (and his pal Joe)	*La Cage aux Folles*	Wilson Jermaine Heredia
3.	Dr. Frank 'N' Furter	*Casa Valentina*	Will Swenson
4.	Charley Wykeham	*The Producers*	Robert Morse
5.	Albin	*The Rocky Horror Show*	Gary Beach
6.	Angel Schunard	*Kinky Boots*	Patrick Page
7.	Lola (Simon)	*Where's Charley?*	Tim Curry
8.	Tick Belrose (Mitzi Mitosis)	*Victor/Victoria*	Ray Bolger
9.	George/Valentina	*Rent*	Julie Andrews
10.	Victoria Grant	*Priscilla, Queen of the Desert*	George Hearn

On the Go

Name the means of transportation used by the following characters—and the musicals in which they appear.

1. By what means does Elphaba flee the palace guards in the Emerald City?
   * ★ Pogo stick
   * ★ Magic carpet
   * ★ Camelback
   * ★ Enchanted broomstick

Continued on next page

2. How does Eliza Doolittle travel on her first visit to 27-A Wimpole St.?
   * Taxi
   * Bus
   * Flower cart
   * Limousine

3. How do Reno Sweeney, Billy Crocker, and Moonface Martin cross the Atlantic?
   * Concorde
   * Ocean liner
   * Dirigible
   * Lifeboat

4. How do Sky Masterson and Sarah Brown get from New York to Havana?
   * Hot-air balloon
   * Airplane
   * Sailboat
   * Tugboat

5. By what means does Porgy get around Catfish Row?
   * Roller skates
   * Goat cart
   * Wheelchair
   * Crutches

6. How does Chris Scott leave Saigon in a nightmare flashback?
   * Humvee
   * Refugee boat
   * Helicopter
   * Tunnel to Cambodia

7. How do Huck and Jim go from Hannibal, Missouri, to Hillsboro, Arkansas?
    * Hitchhiking
    * River raft
    * Steamboat
    * Horseback

8. How do Oscar Jaffee and Lily Garland travel from Chicago to New York?
    * Piper Cub
    * Limousine
    * Train
    * Stagecoach

9. What does Annie Oakley ride in her shooting exhibition at the Minneapolis Fair Grounds?
    * Motorcycle
    * Bicycle
    * Shetland pony
    * Roller skates

10. How does Mrs. J. J. Brown set out from Europe to New York?
    * The *Spirit of St. Louis*
    * The *Lusitania*
    * The *Titanic*
    * British Airways

Final Exits

How does each of the following characters in musicals die?

1. Jud Fry in *Oklahoma!*...
   * ★ Is caught in a stampede
   * ★ Falls on his own knife
   * ★ Is poisoned by a box supper
   * ★ Burns to death in a fire

2. Beauregard Jackson Pickett Burnside in *Mame*...
   * ★ Overindulges in mint juleps
   * ★ Is thrown by his horse during a fox hunt
   * ★ Has a heart attack
   * ★ Falls off an Alp

3. Harry Beaton in *Brigadoon*...
   * ★ Cuts a deep gash in his leg during a sword dance
   * ★ Hits his head on a rock when he is tripped
   * ★ Drowns in a river
   * ★ Eats a bad haggis

4. Tony in *West Side Story*...
   * ★ Is shot to death by a rival gang member
   * ★ Is stabbed by a girl he has jilted
   * ★ Dies in the electric chair
   * ★ Takes a drug overdose

5. Billy Bigelow in *Carousel*...
   * ★ Falls off the carousel and is fatally injured
   * ★ Has a ruptured appendix
   * ★ Is hit by a train
   * ★ Stabs himself during a robbery attempt

6. Lt. Joseph Cable in *South Pacific* . . .
   * Is lost at sea
   * Is killed by enemy fighter plane strafing
   * Dies from ptomaine poisoning after eating a meal prepared by Bloody Mary
   * Is murdered by a rival suitor of Liat's

7. Little Joe Jackson in *Cabin in the Sky* . . .
   * Is killed when his parachute fails to open
   * Is fatally shot in a brawl
   * Is poisoned by his girlfriend
   * Is run down by a runaway horse

8. Orin Scrivello in *Little Shop of Horrors* . . .
   * Asphyxiates on nitrous oxide
   * Strangles on a jungle vine
   * Is run over by a bulldozer
   * Is eaten by a carnivorous plant

9. Danny O'Higgins in *Sweeney Todd* . . .
   * Contracts bubonic plague
   * Is strangled and then has his throat slit
   * Falls into a hot oven
   * Is hanged for murder

10. Private Fred Poitrine in *Little Me* . . .
    * Is shot by a firing squad for desertion
    * Is run over by a Sherman tank
    * Bleeds to death after peeling potatoes on KP duty
    * Gets his little finger caught in a typewriter

Broadway Intramurals

Here are some imaginary match-ups for a Broadway sports league. Match all twenty "teams" with the musicals that they are in—which are listed below in alphabetical order.

1. River City Boys Band   vs.   Save-A-Soul Mission Band

2. Orphan Boys of the Workhouse   vs.   Orphan Girls of the Municipal Orphanage

3. Texas Rangers   vs.   Forest Rangers

4. Kit Kat Girls   vs.   Chicken Ranch Girls

5. Fan-Dango Taxi Dancers   vs.   Sweet Sue and Her Society Syncopaters

6. Consolidated Life   vs.   World Wide Wicket Company

7. Nuns of Nonnberg Abbey   vs.   Little Sisters of Hoboken

8. Tait College Football Team   vs.   Southern Baptist Institute of Technology Football Team

9. Siamese Children   vs.   Lost Boys

10. Riff and the Jets   vs.   Red Shadow and the Riffs

All American; Annie; The Best Little Whorehouse in Texas; Cabaret; The Desert Song; Good News!; Guys and Dolls; How to Succeed in Business without Really Trying; The King and I; Little Mary Sunshine; The Music Man; Nunsense, Oliver!; Peter Pan; Promises, Promises; Rio Rita; The Sound of Music; Sugar; Sweet Charity; West Side Story

Under Arrest

Match the criminal activities in the first column with the characters who engage in them and the plays or musicals in which they appear.

1.	Creating a public disturbance in the Harmonia Gardens	Claudio	*My Three Angels*
2.	Corruption of a minor and Marxist revolutionary activities	Mame and Patrick	*Irma la Douce*
3.	Dancing a tango in a speakeasy during Prohibition	Luis and Valentin	*Chicago*
4.	Conceiving a child with his beloved Juliet	Jean Val Jean	*Kiss of the Spider Woman*
5.	Murdering her lover, Fred Casely	Dolly Levi et al	*Richard III*
6.	Foreclosing on a monastery for nonpayment of taxes	Nestor-le-Fripé	*Les Misérables*
7.	Murdering the imaginary "Oscar"	Jules, Alfred, Joseph	*Hello, Dolly!*
8.	Having a name beginning with the letter "G"	Alonso Quijano	*Mame*
9.	Stealing bread for his sister's son, then trying to escape	Roxie Hart	*Measure for Measure*
10.	Murdering his wife, murdering his stepfather, forgery, and swindling	Duke of Clarence	*Man of La Mancha*

School Days

Match the musical with the school or college featured in it.

1. *Leave It to Jane*	Rydell High School
2. *Best Foot Forward*	University of Heidelberg
3. *Grease*	Atwater College
4. *Bring It On*	Knickerbocker University
5. *High School Musical*	Oxford University
6. *Legally Blonde*	Truman High School
7. *Where's Charley?*	East High School
8. *Good News!*	Tait College
9. *The Student Prince*	Winsocki Prep School
10. *On Your Toes*	UCLA and Harvard Law School

Best Buddies

Match the character in the first column with the character with whom he is paired.

1. S. L. Jacobowsky	Proteus
2. Vladimir	Henry II
3. William Brown	Dion Anthony
4. Thomas Becket	Andrew Wyke
5. Valentine	Willie Clark
6. Spooner	Hirst
7. Harry C. Leeds	Tadeusz Boleslav Stjerbinsky
8. Al Lewis	Oscar Madison
9. Felix Unger	Charles Dyer
10. Milo Tindle	Estragon

That Is the Question

Can you match these descriptions with the correct plays or musicals, each of which has a title ending with a question mark—and provide the missing words?

1. Brian Clark's play about a quadriplegic sculptor played in different productions by Tom Conti and Mary Tyler Moore.

   What Makes Sammy _____?

2. Edward Albee's play about the breakdown of a marriage after a boozy faculty party.

   Shall We Join the _____?

3. A musical by Frank Loesser and George Abbott about an Oxford undergraduate masquerading as his aunt.

   Aren't We _____?

4. A musical by John R. Powers, James Quinn and Alaric Jans about eight children in a Catholic school in Chicago.

   Whose _____ Is It Anyway?

5. A one-act play by James M. Barrie about a dinner party with thirteen guests.

   Who Was That _____ I Saw You With?

6. A musical by Arthur Laurents, Richard Rodgers, and Stephen Sondheim, based on Laurents's play *The Time of the Cuckoo*.

   Where's _____?

7. A musical by Ervin Drake, Budd Schulberg, and Stuart Schulberg, about a young man from New York's Lower East Side who lets nothing stand in the way of success.

   Who's Afraid of _____?

8. William Inge's play about a young couple expecting a child they intend to put up for adoption.

   Do Black _____ Leather Shoes Really Reflect Up?

9. Frederick Lonsdale's comedy about hanky-panky among the upper class in Mayfair.

   _____ Daddy?

10. Norman Krasna's comedy about a chemistry professor whose wife catches him kissing another woman.

    Do I Hear A _____?

Tag Lines

Match these advertising tag lines with the correct Broadway shows.

1.	The hardest part of falling in love is taking the first step.	*Charlie and the Chocolate Factory*
2.	Wear your heart on your heels.	*Once*
3.	Seriously	*The Little Mermaid*
4.	Some lives are meant to be extraordinary.	*Aladdin*
5.	Every ticket is golden.	*Side Show*
6.	Discover a whole new world in a whole new way.	*Kinky Boots*
7.	It will never leave you.	*Starlight Express*
8.	His music needed one thing—her.	*Xanadu*
9.	The race is on.	*Aida*
10.	We all lead such elaborate lives.	*Pippin*

Playing Tag (Again)

If you got the first set of tag lines correct, these should be a breeze.
If you didn't—well, try, try again!

1. Best damn musical I've seen in years!	*Rent*
2. Life's an adventure. Dress accordingly.	*Phantom of the Opera*
3. Now and forever	*Amazing Grace*
4. To change the world it takes a little genius.	*Bloody Bloody Andrew Jackson*
5. Drop everything.	*Gypsy*
6. You already know you're gonna love it!	*The Full Monty*
7. The song the world knows. The story it doesn't.	*Priscilla, Queen of the Desert*
8. History just got all sexypants.	*Matilda the Musical*
9. Remember your first time.	*Mamma Mia*
10. No day but today	*Cats*

Up a Tree

Match these descriptions of plays and musicals that have do with trees with the correct titles and fill in the missing words.

1. Musical by Betty Smith, George Abbott, Arthur Schwartz, and Dorothy Fields — *The _____ Trees* — Oak

2. Play by Anton Chekhov — *Wind in the _____* — Halfway

3. Musical by Jerry Bock and Sheldon Harnick — *Under the _____ Tree* — Elms

4. Comedy by Peter Ustinov — *Fumed _____* — Bay

5. Drama by Mordaunt Shairp — *Desire Under the _____* — Brooklyn

6. Drama by Joshua Logan — *A Tree Grows in _____* — Cherry

7. Play by Lawrence Roman — *The _____ Tree* — Wisteria

8. Musical by Jane Iredale, William Perry, and Roger McGough; adapted from a classic by Kenneth Grahame — *_____ Up the Tree* — Apple

9. Play by Eugene O'Neill — *The _____ Orchard* — Willows

10. One-act comedy by Noël Coward — *The Green _____ Tree* — Yum Yum

How's That Again?

These circumlocutions are paraphrases of the titles of well-known plays.

1. So Factual That It Has No Virtue
2. The Significance of Possessing Serious Sincerity
3. It Is Not Possible to Be Accompanied by One's Material Possessions in the Afterlife
4. Considerable Commotion Concerning Zilch
5. Felis Catus Atop a Thermal Stannic Building Cover
6. A Vendor's Demise
7. Recall the Past Irately
8. How One Prefers Things to Be
9. The Feral Mallard
10. The Male Homo Sapiens That Arrived for a Principal Prandial Activity

GRAND FINALE

ANSWERS

Stop and Smell the Flowers

1. *Kiss Me, Kate*
2. *A Streetcar Named Desire*
3. *Pygmalion* (and *My Fair Lady)*
4. *Little Shop of Horrors*
5. *The Subject Was Roses*
6. *God of Carnage*
7. *Hamlet*
8. *Bitter Sweet*
9. *On a Clear Day You Can See Forever*
10. *Look to the Lilies*

Meow Mix

1. mehitabel—*Shinbone Alley* (archy and mehitabel's names generally appear in lower case because archy, a cockroach who is the typist, cannot operate the shift key.)
2. Pyewacket—*Bell, Book and Candle*
3. Graymalkin—*Macbeth*
4. Wee Thomas—*The Lieutenant of Inishmore*
5. Sarafina—*The Lion King*
6. Skimbleshanks—*Cats*
7. The Cat in the Hat—*Seussical*
8. The Cheshire Cat—*Alice in Wonderland*
9. Cat—*Breakfast at Tiffany's*
10. Gepetto's Cat—*Pinocchio* (In the Disney movie, the cat was named Figaro.)

Do You Know the Way?

1. *Blind Alley*
2. *Airline Highway*
3. *The Love Route*
4. *Sunset Boulevard*
5. *Angel Street*
6. *Tobacco Road*
7. *Lover's Lane*
8. *Avenue Q*
9. *The Primrose Path*
10. *The Trail of the Lonesome Pine*

Firsts

1. *Kiss Me, Kate*, with book by Samuel and Bella Spewack and music and lyrics by Cole Porter, won the Tony in 1949; it was the third year of the Tonys, but also the first year in which a Best Musical award was given.
2. Sir Henry Irving, honored by Queen Victoria in 1895
3. Eugene O'Neill received the Nobel Prize for Literature in 1936.
4. The *First Folio* contained thirty-six plays by Shakespeare, which are all that are generally attributed to him, except *Pericles, Prince of Tyre*, and *The Two Noble Kinsmen*.
5. Margaret Hughes is generally regarded as the first woman ever to appear professionally on the English stage, as Desdemona in *Othello*, on December 8, 1660, following the Restoration of the monarchy. Prior to that time, women's roles were played by young men or boys. Some historians differ and believe the honor of being first goes to Katherine Corey or Anne Marshall.
6. Thespis, who lived in Athens in the fifth century BC, was regarded by Aristotle as the first person ever to appear on stage as an actor playing a character other than himself.
7. Lorraine Hansberry, whose play *A Raisin in the Sun* was produced on Broadway in 1959
8. *Why Marry?* by Jesse Lynch Williams was the first play to win a Pulitzer Prize, in 1918. O'Neill's *Beyond the Horizon* won the prize in 1920 and Howard's *They Knew What They Wanted* in 1925.

9. *Waitress*, the 2016 musical with book by Jessie Nelson, music and lyrics by Sara Bareilles, direction by Diane Paulus, and choreography by Lorin Latarro

10. *The Contrast* by Royall Tyler, produced in New York in 1787

Show-Within-A-Show Time

1. *Pretty Lady* is the musical in which Peggy Sawyer replaces Dorothy Brock in *42nd Street*.

2. *Robbin' Hood of the Old West*, the musical in *Curtains*, is trying out in Boston when the leading lady is murdered during the curtain call.

3. *The Small House of Uncle Thomas* is a ballet version of *Uncle Tom's Cabin* that is staged by Tuptim in *The King and I*.

4. *Feldzieg's Follies* is in *The Drowsy Chaperone*.

5. *The Murder of Gonzago* is the "dumb show" in *Hamlet* that the players perform at Hamlet's request as an eerie echo of his father's murder.

6. *Pawnee Bill's Far East Show*, the rival of *Buffalo Bill's Wild West Show*, is the show Annie Oakley joins in *Annie Get Your Gun*.

7. The *Zangler Follies* is the revue produced by Bela Zangler, for which Bobby Child wants to audition in *Crazy for You*.

8. *The Taming of the Shrew* is the Shakespearean play being produced in *Kiss Me, Kate*.

9. *The Deep North* is the play in rehearsal at the Surf and Sand Playhouse in *Babes in Arms*.

10. *La Princesse Zenobia* is the ballet in which Junior Dolan unexpectedly substitutes for an absent dancer in *On Your Toes*.

It's a Drag

1. Roger De Bris is the cross-dressing director in *The Producers*, originally played by Gary Beach.
2. Jerry (along with his pal Joe) dress as women members of Sweet Sue's Society Syncopaters to flee gangsters in *Sugar*. Robert Morse was Jerry (and Tony Roberts was Joe) in the Broadway production.
3. Dr. Frank 'N' Furter in *The Rocky Horror Show* is the cross-dressing scientist played by Tim Curry.
4. Charley Wykeham pretends to be his aunt, Donna Lucia D'Alvadorez, in *Where's Charley?* Ray Bolger was the original Charley.
5. Albin is the drag star in *La Cage aux Folles* originally played by George Hearn.
6. Angel Schunard is a drag queen in *Rent*, first played by Wilson Jermaine Heredia.
7. Lola, whose birth name was Simon, is a drag performer in *Kinky Boots*. Billy Porter created the role on Broadway.
8. Tick Belrose, otherwise known as Mitzi Mitosis, is a drag performer in *Priscilla, Queen of the Desert*. Will Swenson originated the role on Broadway.
9. George/Valentina is the proprietor of the transvestite retreat in *Casa Valentina*, played by Patrick Page.
10. Victoria Grant, who impersonates a man who is a female impersonator in *Victor/Victoria*, was played by Julie Andrews.

On the Go

1. Enchanted broomstick, in *Wicked*
2. Taxi, in *My Fair Lady*
3. Ocean liner, the *S. S. American*, in *Anything Goes*
4. Airplane, in *Guys and Dolls*

5. Goat cart, in the original version of *Porgy and Bess,* but sometimes crutches or a cane in later productions
6. Helicopter, in *Miss Saigon*
7. River raft, in *Big River*
8. Train, the luxurious "Twentieth Century Limited," in *On the Twentieth Century*
9. Motorcycle, in *Annie Get Your Gun*
10. *R. M. S. Titanic,* in *The Unsinkable Molly Brown*

Final Exits

1. "Pore" Jud Fry accidentally falls on his own knife after attacking Curly.
2. Beauregard Burnside falls off an Alp while trying to take a snapshot of Mame.
3. Harry Beaton hits his head on a rock after Jeff Douglas trips him.
4. Tony, ex-leader of the Jets gang, is shot to death by Chino, a member of the rival Sharks.
5. Billy Bigelow stabs himself to death during a foiled robbery attempt in order to avoid prison.
6. Lt. Joseph Cable is killed by strafing from a fighter plane during a reconnaissance mission to a Japanese-held island.
7. Little Joe Jackson is fatally shot in a brawl over his gambling debts.
8. Orin Scrivello, a dentist, asphyxiates on an overdose of nitrous oxide, and is then devoured by the carnivorous plant Audrey II.
9. Danny O'Higgins is strangled by Sweeney Todd, who then slits his throat. Mrs. Lovett then has the idea of baking him and other Todd victims in meat pies.
10. Private Fred Poitrine, serving at the front during World War I, injures his pinky finger by getting it stuck in the keyboard of a field typewriter and dies "from a serious digit wound."

Broadway Intramural

1. River City Boys Band (*The Music Man*) vs. Save-A-Soul Mission Band (*Guys and Dolls*)
2. Orphan Boys of the Workhouse (*Oliver!*) vs. Orphan Girls of the Municipal Orphanage (*Annie*)
3. Texas Rangers (*Rio Rita*) vs. Forest Rangers (*Little Mary Sunshine*)
4. Kit Kat Girls (*Cabaret*) vs. Chicken Ranch Girls (*The Best Little Whorehouse in Texas*)
5. Fan-Dango Taxi Dancers (*Sweet Charity*) vs. Sweet Sue and Her Society Syncopaters (*Sugar*)
6. Consolidated Life (*Promises, Promises*) vs. World Wide Wicket Company (*How to Succeed in Business without Really Trying*)
7. Nuns of Nonnberg Abey (*The Sound of Music*) vs. Little Sisters of Hoboken (*Nunsense*)
8. Tait College Football Team (*Good News!*) vs. Southern Baptist Institute of Technology Football Team (*All American*)
9. Siamese Children (*The King and I*) vs. Lost Boys (*Peter Pan*)
10. Riff and the Jets (*West Side Story*) vs. Red Shadow and the Riffs (*The Desert Song*)

Under Arrest

1. In *Hello, Dolly!* Dolly Levi and virtually all the principal characters are arrested for creating a disturbance in the Harmonia Gardens. They are found innocent, except for Horace Vandergelder, who is ordered to pay for the damages.

2. In *Kiss of the Spider Woman*, Luis Alberto Molina, in prison for corruption of a minor, is joined by his cellmate, Valentin Arregui Paz, a Marxist revolutionary activist.

3. Mame Dennis and her nephew Patrick, along with other patrons, are arrested while dancing a tango in a raid of a speakeasy in *Mame*.

4. Claudio is imprisoned for conceiving a child with his beloved Juliet in *Measure for Measure*.

5. Roxie Hart is jailed for the murder of Fred Casely in *Chicago*.

6. In *Man of La Mancha*, author and tax collector Miguel de Cervantes, a.k.a. Alonso Quijano, is imprisoned with his servant Sancho Panza for having foreclosed on a monastery for nonpayment of taxes.

7. Nestor le Fripé is arrested and imprisoned for murdering an imaginary character of his own invention named "Oscar" in *Irma la Douce*.

8. The Duke of Clarence in *Richard III*, whose given name is George, is imprisoned in the Tower because his brother, King Edward IV, was told by a wizard that someone whose name started with the letter "G" would seize the throne from his heirs.

9. Jean Valjean is imprisoned for stealing bread in *Les Misérables*, then has his sentence extended for trying to escape.

10. In *My Three Angels*, three convicts are released from Devil's Island, where Jules has been imprisoned for murdering his wife, Alfred for murdering his stepfather, and Joseph for forgery and swindling.

School Days

1. *Leave It to Jane*—Atwater College
2. *Best Foot Forward*—Winsocki Prep School
3. *Grease*—Rydell High School
4. *Bring It On*—Truman High School
5. *High School Musical*—East High School
6. *Legally Blonde*—UCLA and Harvard Law School
7. *Where's Charley?*—Oxford University
8. *Good News!*—Tait College
9. *The Student Prince*—University of Heidelberg
10. *On Your Toes*—Knickerbocker University

Best Buddies

1. S. L. Jacobowsky and (Col.) Tadeusz Boleslav Stjerbinsky in *Jacobowsky and the Colonel*
2. Vladimir and Estragon in *Waiting for Godot*
3. William Brown and Dion Anthony in *The Great God Brown*
4. Thomas Becket and Henry II in *Becket*
5. Valentine and Proteus in *The Two Gentlemen of Verona*
6. Spooner and Hirst in *No Man's Land*
7. Harry C. Leeds and Charles Dyer in *Staircase*
8. Al Lewis and Willie Clark in *The Sunshine Boys*
9. Felix Unger and Oscar Madison in *The Odd Couple*
10. Milo Tindle and Andrew Wyke in *Sleuth*

That Is the Question
1. *Whose Life Is It Anyway?*
2. *Who's Afraid of Virginia Woolf?*
3. *Where's Charley?*
4. *Do Black Patent Leather Shoes Really Reflect Up?*
5. *Shall We Join the Ladies?*
6. *Do I Hear a Waltz?*
7. *What Makes Sammy Run?*
8. *Where's Daddy?*
9. *Aren't We All?*
10. *Who Was That Lady I Saw You With?*

Tag Lines
1. The hardest part of falling in love is taking the first step.—*The Little Mermaid*
2. Wear your heart on your heels.—*Kinky Boots*
3. Seriously—*Xanadu*
4. Some lives are meant to be extraordinary.—*Pippin*
5. Every ticket is golden.—*Charlie and the Chocolate Factory*
6. Discover a whole new world in a whole new way.—*Aladdin*
7. It will never leave you.—*Side Show*
8. His music needed one thing—her.—*Once*
9. The race is on.—*Starlight Express*
10. We all lead such elaborate lives.—*Aida*

Playing Tag (Again)

1. Best damn musical I've seen in years!—*Gypsy*. The phrase is a quote from Walter Kerr's rave review in the *New York Herald Tribune*.
2. Life's an adventure. Dress accordingly.—*Priscilla, Queen of the Desert*
3. Now and forever—*Cats*
4. To change the world it takes a little genius.—*Matilda the Musical*
5. Drop everything.—*The Full Monty*
6. You already know you're gonna love it!—*Mamma Mia*
7. The song the world knows. The story it doesn't.—*Amazing Grace*
8. History just got all sexypants.—*Bloody Bloody Andrew Jackson*
9. Remember your first time.—*Phantom of the Opera*
10. No day but today.—*Rent*

Up a Tree

1. *A Tree Grows in Brooklyn*
2. *The Cherry Orchard*
3. *The Apple Tree*
4. *Halfway Up the Tree*
5. *The Green Bay Tree*
6. *The Wisteria Trees*
7. *Under the Yum Yum Tree*
8. *Wind in the Willows*
9. *Desire Under the Elms*
10. *Fumed Oak*

How's That Again?

1. *So Factual That It Has No Virtue—Too True to Be Good*
2. *The Significance of Possessing Serious Sincerity—The Importance of Being Earnest*
3. *It Is Not Possible to Be Accompanied by One's Material Possessions in the Afterlife—You Can't Take It with You*
4. *Considerable Commotion Concerning Zilch—Much Ado About Nothing*
5. *Felis Catus Atop a Thermal Stannic Building Cover—Cat on a Hot Tin Roof*
6. *A Vendor's Demise—Death of a Salesman*
7. *Recall the Past Irately—Look Back in Anger*
8. *How One Prefers Things to Be—As You Like It*
9. *The Feral Mallard—The Wild Duck*
10. *The Male Homo Sapiens That Arrived for a Principal Prandial Activity—The Man Who Came to Dinner*